The Jew Returns
to Israel

The Jew Returns to Israel

by
ANTON DARMS

ZONDERVAN PUBLISHING HOUSE
GRAND RAPIDS, MICHIGAN

Library of Congress Catalog Card Number 65-19495

Printed in the United States of America

This volume is dedicated to the memory of
THEODOR HERZL, 1860–1904,
the founder of the "The State of Israel"
and to
DAVID BEN GURION, born 1886,
the greatest champion of "The State of Israel"

INTRODUCTION

REVEREND DARMS' most recent literary venture, *The Jew Returns to Israel,* belies his ninety-six years.

In this book he vigorously carries the reader through the ages, with an insight into the Jewish mind and heart which proclaims for Jew and Gentile alike his understanding, admiration, and love for the "Chosen People," his very real sadness and concern for those Gentiles who do not love their brother as themselves.

The Jew Returns to Israel, a difficult and provocative subject, is masterfully handled. It is a powerful treatise decrying the intolerance, ignorance and concious or unconscious fear, jealousy, and disdain for the Jew which sooner or later becomes an integral part of the makeup of the non-Jew. Clasping the hand of the Jew in brotherhood, Reverend Darms reveals, clarifies, and forthrightly rents the veil of disbelief in Jesus as the Messiah which covers the mind's eye of the Jew.

Authoritative in its entirety — *The Jew Returns to Israel* is a masterpiece of logic. Reverend Darms has done with the pen what many have attempted with the sword. His objectivity will be hailed and cherished by any and all who are privileged to read his book as the writer has — any and all who are concerned with or interested in or even unaware of the place of the Jew in history, the place of the Jew in God's plan. . . . the reason why, in spite of the bloody pages, there has always been spared a remnant of the Jews. The author carries the reader along on a tide of clarity and vitality which is seldom, if ever, found in a book of this nature.

The Jew Returns to Israel traces the Jew historically from Abraham — to the magnificent Theodor Herzl. From the inception of the idea of a State of Israel, through the boy Herzl's dream — to the great Ben Gurion, head of the infant State of Israel. He looks inside the heads and hearts of such men as Tolstoy, Luther, and others, sparing neither the Church nor the Jew — admitting that it is not just the Jewish problem — but perhaps it is also the Gentile problem.

The dedication of heart and mind; the background of years of study; the zealous longing to dissuade and persuade the Jew to set aside his non-belief — coupled with the discomforting knowledge that the "Church" has indeed not been guiltless in the creation of what is one of the most shameful pages of history — sets this book apart.

Reverend Darms has proven himself a pioneer — a learned humanitarian — a dedicated Rabbi, if you will.

Introduction

Whether his book is read by the layman, the clergyman, the Jew, or the Gentile, each reader will be profoundly aware of its triune significance, for it is at once a logical answer to the gnostic — a hopeful revelation and beacon to guide the Jew — a strong and inspired reprimand to the Church, whether outright anti-Semites or ambivalent tolerants of the Jew.

LINDA DARMS HINDEN

GREETINGS TO THE NEW-BORN STATE OF ISRAEL

To the Sons of Israel, Greetings!
Multitudes of followers of our Lord Jesus Christ join with me in sending our sincere congratulations to you who have at last achieved Israel's National Rebirth in the establishment of the Jewish Free State in Palestine — the Land of your Fathers, promised to Abraham, Isaac, and Jacob by Jehovah forty centuries ago.

This is indeed a momentous event in world history. Zionism, founded by Theodor Herzl more than fifty years ago, is responsible for this great achievement. Zionism was born with a far-reaching vision, inspired by the prophet of Israel. Zionism has not toiled in vain to translate the vision of a renewed and restored Palestine into a practical reality. It has given many of its noblest sons as laborers to till the soil, to organize hundreds of colonies, establish many varied industries, and build cities, by the faith of their ancient fathers in Israel, in the Land of Palestine.

The Prophet Isaiah in the long ago spoke of a nation's being "born" in a day (Isaiah 66:8). The Word of God also declares that when the Fig Tree shoots forth its new buds in a newly-awakened Jewish nationalism, then the "Kingdom of God is nigh at hand" (Luke 21: 29-31).

The rebirth of Israel as a nation is positive proof of the Jewish Fig Tree's putting forth new life. This momentous event will have its repercussions throughout the whole world, inspiring millions of oppressed and downtrodden with new hope for liberty and freedom.

The rebirth of Israel is prophetic of the Messianic Kingdom promised to David, which shall "endure forever," a government based on righteousness and justice. The earth is yet to "be full of the knowledge of the Lord, as the waters cover the sea" (Isaiah 11:9).

It is indeed lamentable that the weapons of warfare must be used in fighting Israel's battles for freedom, but the day is not far distant when, with Israel's National Rebirth and with Israel's individual New Birth, "they shall beat their swords into plowshares, and their spears into pruninghooks: nation shall not lift up a sword against nation, neither shall they learn war any more" (Micah 4:3). Under the reign of Israel's Messiah "over all the earth," every man "shall sit under his own fig tree," and ignorance and poverty shall be banished from the earth.

Greetings to the New-Born State of Israel

Rejoice, ye Sons of Israel — rejoice for your God-given national rebirth and freedom; and again I say, Rejoice, ye Sons of Israel!

In the bonds of Abraham's faith in the coming Messiah, I remain

Sincerely yours,

ANTON DARMS

JOSEPHUS' ESTIMATE OF THE MESSIAH

THE GREAT Jewish historian, Flavius Josephus, wrote, "Now it was about this time, Jesus a wise man, if it be lawful to call Him a Man, for He was a doer of wonderful works, a Teacher of such men as receive truth with pleasure. He drew over to Him both many of the Jews and many of the Gentiles. He was the Christ, and when Pilate at the suggestion of the principal men among us had condemned Him to the cross, those that loved Him at the first did not forsake Him: for He appeared to them alive again the third day, as the divine prophets had foretold this and ten thousand other things concerning Him. And the tribe of Christians, so named from Him, are not extinct to this day."

(Whiston's translation, bk. 20, chapter 3)

WHAT IS A JEW?
by

LEO TOLSTOY
1828–1910

THIS QUESTION is not at all so odd as it seems. Let us see what peculiar kind of creature the Jew is, which all the rulers and all the nations have together and separately abused and molested, oppressed and persecuted. trampled and butchered, burned and hanged, and, in spite of all this, is yet alive. What is a Jew who has never allowed himself to be led astray by all the earthly possessions which his oppressors and persecutors have constantly offered him in order that he should change his religion?

The Jew is that sacred being who has brought down from Heaven the Everlasting Fire and has lightened with it the entire world. *He is the religious source, spring, and fountain* out of which all the rest of the peoples have drawn their beliefs and their religions.

The Jew is a pioneer of liberty. Even in olden days, when the people were divided into but two distinct classes — slaves and masters, even so long ago, the law of Moses prohibited the keeping in bondage for more than six years any person who willingly came to accept the Jewish practice.

The Jew is a pioneer of civilization. Ignorance was condemned in olden Palestine even more than it is today in civilized Europe. Moreover, in those wild and barbarous days when neither life nor death of anyone was counted for anything at all, Rabbi Akiba did not refrain from expressing himself as being against capital punishment — a practice which is recognized today as a highly civilized way of punishment.

The Jew is an emblem of civil and religious tolerance. "Love the stranger and the sojourner," Moses commanded, "because you have been strangers in the Land of Egypt." And this in those remote days — those savage days when the principal ambition of the races and nations consisted in crushing and enslaving one another. As concerns religious tolerance, the Jewish faith is not only not far from the missionary spirit of converting people of denominations but, on the contrary, the Talmud commands the Rabbis to inform and explain to every one who willingly comes to accept the Jewish religion all the difficulties involved in its acceptance, and to point out to the would-be proselyte that the righteous of all nations have a share in immortality. Of such a lofty and ideal religious tolerance not even the moralist of our present day can boast.

What Is a Jew?

The Jew is the emblem of eternity. He whom neither slaughter nor torture of himself for years could destroy; he whom neither fire nor sword, nor inquisition was able to wipe from off the face of the earth; he who was the first to produce the *oracles of God;* he who has been for so long a time the guardian of prophecy, and who has transmitted it to the rest of the world — such a nation cannot be destroyed. The Jew is everlasting as eternity itself.

PONTIUS PILATE TO TIBERIUS CAESAR*

To Tiberius Caesar:

A young man appeared in Galilee preaching with humble unction, a new law in the Name of the God that had sent Him. At first I was apprehensive that His design was to stir up the people against the Romans, but my fears were soon dispelled. Jesus of Nazareth spoke rather as a friend of the Romans than of the Jews. One day I observed in the midst of a group of people a young man who was leaning against a tree, calmly addressing the multitude. I was told it was Jesus. This I could easily have suspected so great was the difference between Him and those who were listening to Him. His golden colored hair and beard gave to His appearance a celestial aspect. He appeared to be about 30 years of age. Never have I seen a sweeter or more serene countenance. What a contrast between Him and His hearers with their black beards and tawny complexions! Unwilling to interrupt Him by my presence, I continued my walk but signified to my secretary to join the group and listen. Later, my secretary reported that never had he read in the works of all the philosophers anything that compared to the teachings of Jesus. He told me that Jesus was neither seditious nor rebellious, so we extended to Him our protection. He was at liberty to act, to speak, to assemble and to address the people. This unlimited freedom provoked the Jews — not the poor but the rich and powerful.

Later I wrote to Jesus requesting an interview with Him at the Praetorium. He came. When the Nazarene made His appearance I was having my morning walk and as I faced Him my feet seemed fastened with an iron band to the marble pavement and I trembled in every limb as a guilty culprit, though He was calm. For some time I stood admiring this extraordinary Man. There was nothing in Him that was repelling, nor in His character, yet I felt awed in His presence. I told Him that there was a magnetic simplicity about Him and His person-ality that elevated Him far above the philosophers and teachers of His day. All in all He made a deep impression upon me and everyone be-cause of His kindness, simplicity, humility and love.

Now, Noble Sovereign, these are the facts concerning Jesus of Nazareth and I have taken the time to write you in detail concerning these matters. I say that such a man who could convert water into wine, change death into life, disease into health; calm the stormy seas,

Pontius Pilate to Tiberius Caesar

is not guilty of any criminal offense and as others have said, we must agree — truly this is the Son of God.

Your most obedient servant,
PONTIUS PILATE

* We reprint a letter from Pontius Pilate to Tiberius Caesar describing the physical appearance of Jesus. The original of this letter is in the Library at Rome. Copies are in the Congressional Library in Washington.

THE SOLITARY LIFE OF JESUS

HERE IS A YOUNG MAN who was born in an obscure village, the child of a peasant woman. He grew up in another village. He worked in a carpenter shop until He was thirty, and then for three years He was an itinerant preacher. He never wrote a book. He never held an office. He never owned a home. He never had a family. He never went to a college. He never put His foot inside a big city. He never traveled two hundred miles from the place where He was born. He never did one of the things that usually accompany greatness. He had no credentials but Himself.

While He was still a young man, the tide of public opinion turned against Him. His friends ran away. He was turned over to His enemies. He went through the mockery of a trial. He was nailed to a cross, between two thieves. While He was dying, His executioners gambled for the only piece of property He had on earth, and that was His coat. When He was dead, He was laid in a borrowed grave through the pity of a friend. Nineteen centuries wide have come and gone, and today He is the central figure of the human race, and the leader of the column of progress.

I am far within the mark when I say that all the armies that ever marched, and all the navies that ever sailed, and all the parliaments that ever sat, and all the kings that ever reigned, put together, have not affected the life of man upon this earth as has that

ONE SOLITARY LIFE!

CONTENTS

✡ *1* ✡

THE PREPARATION FOR THE STATE OF ISRAEL

THE SCRIPTURES, THE CHANNEL FOR THE MESSIAH

OF ALL NATIONS of earth, it can be said that Israel is the most unique and important. Israel already has served the great purpose of being the channel through which the Oracles of God were made known in the Sacred Scriptures. It has served a still greater purpose in giving to a sinful world a Redeemer, who is able to solve every problem that vexes the human race.

Israel is the only nation which is called the "Chosen People of God." The nation was inaugurated with the call of Abraham, to whom was promised a Seed which was to bless all the families of earth, so that the prayer taught by Jesus can be answered, "Thy will be done on earth as it is in Heaven."

Its history covers a span of four thousand years during which great world empires such as Babylon, Medo-Persia, Greece, Rome, and many others have swayed the world with their power and glory but at last have decayed.

The Bible is the only Book that has foretold the rise and fall of these world empires. The Bible is the only Book that tells of a kingdom of righteousness and justice to be established on the earth. This kingdom is to be a universal kingdom over which our Lord Jesus Christ will exercise dominion over all the earth as King of kings and Lord of lords.

This kingdom is to be brought about through the channel of Israel. The entire Old Testament sets forth God's dealings with Israel: He delivered them from the bondage of Egypt and led them through a forty-year wilderness journey to the land promised to Abraham and his seed.

Instead of Israel's being faithful to God's calling, we read of her rebellion against God, and waywardness into idolatry and many other

19

gross evils. God had to punish the nation by subjecting her to the Assyrian and Babylonian captivities.

A small remnant returned to their homeland in Palestine to rebuild the Temple and the walls of Jerusalem in preparation for the long-promised Messiah. The nation of Israel in time takes on the name of *Jews,* a nation made up of all the twelve tribes of Israel.

When Jesus was born, He was called the "King of the Jews." The message proclaimed by John the Baptist, the forerunner of Jesus, was, "The Kingdom of Heaven is at hand." Jesus began His ministry at thirty years of age. It was said of Him that "He came unto his own and his own received him not." No sooner had Jesus begun His ministry in giving His first address in the synagogue of Nazareth, than we find Satan plotting to bring about His death. On many occasions of His teaching, preaching, and healing, the ruling Pharisees, Sadducees, and Herodians sought to kill Him. At last they succeeded in their council, called at night by Caiaphas, the High Priest, to bring about His crucifixion and death.

Jesus knew from the beginning of His ministry that His mission was to die on the cross. He said in His first cleansing of the Temple, "Destroy this temple, and in three days I will build it again." On a number of occasions He foretold that He would be rejected and crucified but that He would rise again on the third day. Our Lord confined His ministry to the "lost sheep of the house of Israel."

THE CHURCH THE STUMBLING BLOCK FOR THE JEWS

On three occasions He referred to the Jews when He spake the parable of the Fig Tree. The first reference to the Fig Tree is the parable of the Barren Fig Tree, taught by Jesus near the close of His ministry (Luke 13:6-9). There was no fruit on the tree, but the plea is made to Jesus to spare it for another year, and then if no fruit is found, to cut it down. The second reference to the Fig Tree is found in Mark 11:12-14, when Jesus left Bethany during the last week of His ministry. With His disciples He left the morning after the second, or last, cleansing of the Temple and coming to the fig tree He found thereon "nothing but leaves" and thereupon pronounced a curse that it should not bring forth fruit forever (for the age). This referred to the Jews' being set aside. He foretold that Jerusalem would be destroyed and the nation of Israel scattered among all nations. This took place in A.D. 70 with the destruction of Jerusalem by the Roman army.

In His infinite wisdom and foresight in the face of pious unbelief, Jesus announced the building of His church, saying, *"I will build My church* on this rock [of His deity]; and the gates of hell shall not prevail against it." The Jewish nation in their dispersion has not given forth any saving message for mankind. They have sought to be faithful in upholding the teaching of Moses and in keeping the Ten Commandments, but never once have they affirmed that salvation can only be obtained through the life and death, the shedding of the blood of our Lord Jesus Christ. The Great Commission was not given to the unbelieving Jewish leaders, but to humble fishermen, tax-gatherers, and believers to go to all nations and preach the Gospel.

Notwithstanding that the Gospel has been preached as set forth in the teachings of the New Testament, the unbelieving Jews have carelessly remained in their state as a barren fig tree with only leaves.

During the long period of their dispersion among the nations of the earth, the Jews have gone through untold suffering, persecution, and oppression. Much of this oppression of the Jews was meted out by people claiming to be followers of our Lord Jesus Christ under the name of the church. The reaction to this on the part of the Jews has been that they have no use for any message of the Gospel that heralds the name of Jesus, but their hearts have been hardened and made more bitter. In many countries of Europe the Jews were limited to live in ghettos and not allowed to engage in the industrial, economic, or educational development of the country.

The Wrong Path of Assimilation Taken by the Jews

In the providence of God a great change took place for the liberation of the common man through the period of the renaissance and revolution which swept through Europe like a prairie fire. The Jew was given liberty and freedom to engage in any pursuit that he desired.

The startling thing regarding the Jew is that he has never lost his national identity and has held firmly to his religious traditions and his love for his ancient home in Palestine.

The Early Training of Theodor Herzl

The most prominent champion of the cause of the Jews was a man named Theodor Herzl. His name is already emblazoned on the pages of history as one of Israel's greatest leaders. He devoted all his time and talent, his entire life, to the cause of Jewish emancipation and liberation. Only a brief sketch is necessary to prove that he was a providential character raised up of God for his day and hour to give forth a definite plan of the return of the Jews to Palestine, there to establish their independence and full statehood of Israel.

Theodor Herzl was born in Austria, May 2, 1860. He lived but a brief span of forty-four years, and yet in that brief time he accomplished the Herculean task of awakening Jewish consciousness to the need of becoming unified and welded together into an independent nation in Palestine.

He was given a liberal education in the schools of Austria. The seed of God's Word for his future work was sown in the heart of this youth by a startling story of the Old Testament regarding one of the most spectacular of all events in Israel's history. It was the story related in the book of Exodus regarding Israel's deliverance from the bondage of Egypt. While he was attending school at the age of seven, this story was read to the class by the teacher. This teacher ruled the boys of his class with stern discipline. After a few days the teacher asked Theodor to repeat the story to the members of the class. The lad did so in a rather perfunctory way without realizing anything of its importance. This aroused the ire of the teacher who showed his disapproval by giving the boy a good thrashing. He reprimanded him for his utter lack of interest in the great event he had told. This in later years became the key to his life's destiny to bring about the emancipation of the Jews and effecting their actual return to Palestine to form an independent statehood.

Another still more fascinating and effective story of how God reached the heart of this lad when he reached the age of twelve was in a dream in which he saw a vision of the Messiah giving him definite directions for his future life's work.

Theodor Herzl chose the pursuit of law for his profession. He graduated with the high honor of being a Doctor of Law. He opened his office in the courthouse of Vienna to the public and acquired a lucrative income from it. The one obstacle he had to face in his law profession was that of discrimination. The government of Austria withheld the practice of law in the Supreme Courts from Jewish lawyers. When he was forbidden to practice in the Supreme Courts, he determined to discontinue his law practice and enter another field which would give him greater liberty. He therefore chose to become a news commentator for the large newspapers and magazines of Austria.

The Bible reveals many ways in which God made known His plans to people at different times: the appearance of Jehovah to Abraham under the oak of Mamre; the vision of the burning bush; the vision of Jehovah to Isaiah; the appearance of Jesus to Saul of Tarsus on the way to Damascus; but more interesting are the visions given in dreams such as Jacob had with the ladder reaching from earth to heaven; the dreams of the butler and the baker which Joseph interpreted; the dreams of Samuel, Solomon, Nebuchadnezzar, and others; the dream given to Joseph, the husband of Mary.

Theodor Herzl's Dream of the Messiah

The vision given to Theodor Herzl at the age of twelve was too sacred for him to tell to anyone. He kept pondering over it many times through the short span of his life. It was not until six months prior to his death that he revealed his dream to a trusted friend.

Shortly after Theodor Herzl had reached the age of twelve, he was visited by a dream.* "The King Messiah came, a glorious and majestic old man, took me in his arms and swept off with me on the wings of the wind. On one of the iridescent clouds, we encountered the figure of Moses. The features were those familiar to me of my childhood in the statue of Michelangelo. The Messiah called to Moses: It is for this child that I have prayed. But to me he said: Go, and declare to the Jews that I shall come soon and perform great wonders and great deeds for my people and for the whole world."

Strange to say, this dream did not incite the lad to become a rabbi and carry on a religious career among the Jews. Although all through his life Theodor Herzl was a faithful attendant at the synagogue, he did not manifest any religious inclinations. He gave himself to secular work and became a news commentator, an editor of a large paper, a playwright, and a writer of novels. As a Jew, he was satisfied with the fact that he could assert his independence as a citizen of his country. His efforts were to change the status of the Jews and assimilate them into the national life to which he belonged.

The Dreyfus Case, the Cause for Theodor Herzl's Awakening

It took a drastic experience to awaken him to the fact that something radical must be done in the life of the Jews to awaken them to their danger in their national life and of losing their identity.

Theodor Herzl was commissioned by his newspaper in Vienna to be delegated to Paris in order to report to the world the changes taking place in the outcome of the French Revolution.

About that time the French government, in cooperation with others, invested millions of dollars to dig the Suez Canal. Later on the French government undertook the digging of the Panama Canal and raised vast sums from the savings of the common people, but the plan collapsed and France went bankrupt.

This bankruptcy caused a great upheaval in France, for the hard-earned savings of the people were lost. It appears that the leaders of France sought to divert the attention of the people from this scandal by conducting a public trial of a Jewish soldier in the French army,

* The above statement of Dr. Herzl's vision of the Messiah is taken by permission of the publishers of the Jewish Publication of America, Philadelphia, from the book, entitled, *Theodor Herzl*, pages 12 and 13 — the author of which is Alex Bein.

charging him with treason and betraying military secrets to Germany. The name of the French officer was Alfred Dreyfus. The press gave a great deal of attention to reporting this trial to the people of Europe.

Theodor Herzl continued to witness and report this trial. He was the only reporter convinced that the officer was innocent of the crime charged to him. He also had the conviction that this officer, being a Jew, would not betray his country, but the greatest lesson he learned from this outstanding trial was that Alfred Dreyfus was not alone to suffer from anti-Semitism: this rage and hate involved the whole Jewish population (there were several million Jews in Europe at that time).

Alfred Dreyfus was a Jew of high military rank, holding the position of a captain of the 14th Artillery in the French army. In order to divert the attention of the people of France from the national bankruptcy, the leaders of France found it convenient to resort to the rage of anti-Semitism that was prevalent throughout Europe at that time. The leaders of France sought to use Alfred Dreyfus as a scapegoat by trumping up false charges of treason against this official of high rank *because he was a Jew*.

Alfred Dreyfus was arrested on October 15, 1894, and was given a trial before a military court with charges against him for betraying high military secrets of the French army. The documents upon which these charges were based carried the fraudulent signature of Dreyfus. The trial lasted for nearly three months — from October 15, 1894, to January 5, 1895. Notwithstanding the repeated protests of absolute innocence by Dreyfus, he was sentenced to banishment from France. This scandal aroused anti-Semitism to a high degree, not only in France, but all Europe was kept in daily touch through the press correspondents who increased the flame of hatred against the Jews by imparting the details of this trial day by day.

Alfred Dreyfus had lived an upright, honorable life as the husband and father of a lovely family, and also as a loyal citizen of the French government; nevertheless he was pronounced guilty of treason by the military court. An official of the court removed the buttons and insignia on Dreyfus' coat, broke his sword, and exclaimed, "You are unworthy of bearing arms in the French militia." After being degraded in this rude manner, Dreyfus cried out, "You are degrading an innocent man."

It is important to realize that among the many press correspondents from all over Europe, Theodor Herzl *stood alone* in uttering his strong affirmation of Dreyfus' innocence and announcing that he was being made a scapegoat in this trial because he was a Jew.

Alfred Dreyfus was then banished for several years to a prison in French Guiana in South America, and later, to the French "Isle Diable."

No one can conceive the suffering and torture of mind that he suffered through four years of imprisonment. His frequent letters to his family written from prison breathe a spirit of integrity, love, and devotion for his family and for the French government, in which he continued to declare his innocence of the charges of treason brought against him.

Fortunately, through the agitation of some great leaders, a new trial was carried out in 1898. Dreyfus was vindicated from the charge of treason against the French government. It also brought about his restoration to his former position in the French army, in which he lived a noble and useful life.

Theodor Herzl was a changed man as the result of the original trial against Dreyfus and henceforth he had a new outlook as to what must be done to remedy the plight of the Jews. Dreyfus had been found guilty notwithstanding he claimed to be innocent. In a public courtroom Dreyfus had been condemned on forged documents, degraded in a shameful way, and banished. The howling mob outside the courtroom had been ready to tear him to pieces because he was a Jew. As Theodor Herzl had been obliged to report the outcome to the "free press" of France, he sounded a blast of warning that something must be done to save the Jewish people from a massacre that might break out any time.

Herzl now became the champion of the Zionist idea to arouse the Jews from their slumber to their danger of being assimilated and losing their identity as Jews. He declared that the Jew must be taken out of Europe to a place where they could have security. From this moment he considered this his life's calling: to bring liberty and freedom to his people. Now he was reminded of the great story of the Exodus of Israel from the bondage of Egypt which he had read at school in his youth. He knew he must now contact men of wealth with political and religious influence to carry out his plan of migration to Palestine.

One of the foremost financiers of his time was Baron Hirsch, who already had spent a fortune of several million dollars to make it possible for several thousand Jews to migrate to Argentina, where he had purchased large tracts of land for their new home. When Theodor Herzl presented his plan of migration to Palestine (in a document of twenty pages) he found no appreciative response. He was told that Palestine was a desolate and fruitless land that could not support a large population of Jews.

Then Theodor Herzl sought to get in contact with another great financier by the name of Lord Nathanael Rothschild. He now prepared a document of sixty-five pages in pamphlet form. This document was published with the title, *Der Juden Stadt (The Jewish State).* Herzl was thirty-five years old at this time. In this published volume he set forth the plea of self-advancement of the Jews with their own industries, commerce, and culture to be set up in Palestine. Lord Rothschild had in previous years already provided support for eighteen colonies of Zion in Palestine. He thought that Herzl's plan for a mass migration to Zion was too fantastic for practical use.

The next venture undertaken by Herzl was to send a copy of his book on the Jewish State to the Rabbinate at Vienna on June 11, 1895, but these learned men condemned his book as the product of a lunatic. Herzl's plea to the Pope was also in vain. When Herzl appealed to Pope Pius X for help to solve the Jewish problem, to assist in helping the Jews to settle in Palestine, he received the following reply as recorded in his diaries:

> The Pope answered in a stern way and categorical manner: "We are unable to favor this movement. We cannot prevent the Jews from going to Jerusalem, but we could never sanction it. The ground of Jerusalem, if it were not always sacred, has been sanctified by the life of Jesus Christ. I cannot answer you otherwise. The Jews have not recognized our Lord; therefore we cannot recognize the Jewish people."

No matter what rebuffs he encountered, Herzl knew now that the settlement of the Jews in Palestine was the only solution to the Jewish problem. He said that to be right thirty years from now one must be considered insane the first few weeks. Except for a few, Herzl received no response or encouragement from his countrymen. He was sorely tried with the opposition that he encountered from the publication of his pamphlet on *The Jewish State,* on January 15, 1896, in Vienna. He knew not which way to turn to carry out his project of founding the new State of Israel in Palestine.

THE PROVIDENTIAL HELP OF DR. WILLIAM HECKLER

In this time of utter discouragement the providence of God manifested itself. It was on March 10, 1896, that a strange man with a long gray beard appeared in Theodor Herzl's study. This stranger was none other than Dr. William Heckler, who held a high position as chaplain in the embassy of the British government in Vienna. He was in close touch with dignitaries and rulers of various countries of Europe. The strange feature of these two men meeting together for the first time was that they both were greatly concerned with the Jewish problem and both agreed that there was only one effective solution to this problem, namely, that the Jews must be enlightened and persuaded to return to their homeland of Palestine, there to have their own government, their own industries, their own edicted constitution; in other words, to be organized as a nation independent of all other nations.

These two men had arrived at the same conclusion by altogether different channels. As has already been observed, Theodor Herzl was convinced from a *strictly economic and political necessity,* not only because of large numbers of Jews living in ghettos of large cities, deprived of any economic or political rights, but also because of a still greater mass of Jews losing their racial identity in their assimilation with various nations of Europe. Both of these men realized the possibility that the Jews would be willing to yield their identity as a race eventually or become an object of race hatred and have to face extinction of their race. This became especially apparent to Herzl through the study of the famous Dreyfus case, which caused him to write his document, *Der Juden Stadt (The Jewish State),* from a strictly *political standpoint.*

On the other hand, Heckler, also a Jew greatly interested in solving this problem, had been converted to the Christian faith and had entered the Christian ministry. Yet he was not engaged either in the active ministry of the church nor in carrying on a missionary career among the Jews.

In his reading and profound study of the Scriptures, Heckler became impressed with the fact that in the Word of God, as set forth in many varied references, the Jews are the chosen people of God, and to them are given many promises in definite terms regarding their return to Palestine as the land of their forefathers, which was promised to them by God to Abraham, Isaac, and Jacob.

This stranger also had brought with him on this visit a document of his own in book form, entitled, *The Return of the Jews to Palestine in Accordance with Prophecy.* One can well imagine that when a copy of this book was offered to Theodor Herzl he gladly accepted it. In reading it he would find that his plan set forth in *The Jewish State* was sound and would learn of its full approval in the Oracles of the Scriptures.

The first visit of these two Jewish gentlemen resulted in the closest tie of friendship, which continued with fervor until the close of Theodor Herzl's life. One thing of which Herzl could be sure was that Dr. William Heckler was of a certainty to be of great assistance to him in gaining access to high officials in the various governments of Europe and even to get in touch with royalty.

In his disheartening battle to get the Jews to migrate to Palestine, and the rejection of the leading rabbis and the masses of Jews in the industrial world, he at last had found a Jewish gentleman of the *Chris-*

tian faith with whom he could counsel in the frequent visits which followed.

THE INTERVIEW OF THEODOR HERZL WITH THE GERMAN KAISER

The story of Herzl's career that was carried on from 1896 to his death on July 3, 1904, is too complicated to relate in brief form. Let it suffice that with the aid of this man of God, Dr. William Heckler, Theodor Herzl was able to get in direct contact with the German Kaiser Wilhelm. Kaiser Wilhelm had at this time planned to make a special visit to Palestine for the dedication of a German sanctuary on Mount Zion and especially to have an interview with the Sultan of Turkey to obtain his protection for German interests in Palestine.

Dr. Heckler not only was instrumental in having Herzl obtain an interview with the German Kaiser (in Constantinople on his way to Palestine) but after the Kaiser reached Palestine, Heckler was there to arrange another interview between the Kaiser and Herzl which was extremely satisfactory and of far-reaching importance in enabling Herzl to at last obtain a personal interview with the Sultan of Turkey. The Sultan was willing to give Herzl a charter to Palestine on condition of receiving a huge sum of money to prevent bankruptcy of Turkey. In the strange providence of God it became unnecessary for this vast sum of money to be raised to obtain a charter from the Sultan of Turkey, for in the outbreak of the First World War in 1914, Turkey linked herself with Germany, and after a furious war lasting for three years Germany was defeated and Turkey had to surrender to the Allied powers in 1917.

Before attention is given further regarding the conquest of Jerusalem, it is necessary to trace the result of Theodor Herzl's issuance of his document, *The Jewish State,* in the formation of the organization that has carried out his ideals with regard to the Jews' being organized to obtain possession and control of Palestine. This organization was called "Zionism," thus using the very word *Zion* used over a hundred and fifty times in the Old Testament with regard to the beauty and glory of Jerusalem as the city in which the promised seed of David, the Messianic King would set up His rule over all nations as the King of kings and Lord of lords.

Theodor Herzl set to work soon after the publication of *The Jewish State* to call for assistance to organize the Jews through the organization of a Zion Congress. His plan was for such an assembly to meet in the city of Munich in Germany. However, he was not able to get sufficient support from German Jews. He then called for the first Zion Congress to meet in Basel, Switzerland, which was held August 29, 1897. A remarkable fact should be noted, that knowing he would be met with much opposition on the part of leading Jews, Theodor Herzl invited *this Protestant minister,* this chaplain of the German embassy of Vienna, Dr. William Heckler, to deliver an address, which certainly was a Messianic influence upon this august assembly. And very remarkable it was that in connection with his challenge for a Zionist Congress to meet in London on October 3, 1897, Herzl gave opportunity for his intimate *Protestant friend,* Heckler, to address this vast assembly of ten thousand Jews.

Theodor Herzl arrived in Palestine to meet with Kaiser Wilhelm on October 28, 1898, and carried on a highly satisfactory interview with the Kaiser. When the Arabs found out about Herzl's seeking to obtain a charter from the Sultan for the purpose of establishing a Jewish State, they sought opportunity to assassinate Herzl. Thus he could remain in Palestine for only three days. In that short time he was convinced that Palestine must come to be the homeland of the Jews.

In 1901, Herzl succeeded in obtaining an interview with the Turkish Sultan in Constantinople and obtained a concession for a charter on payment of several million dollars. In 1902, Herzl organized the Zion Loan Company with a capital of five million dollars — three million being donated by Baron Rothschild, and two million subscribed by the Jews, there being seven million of them in various parts of Europe.

THE CLOSING CAREER OF THEODOR HERZL

It was most unfortunate that with the incessant travel about Europe to raise money and the holding of many meetings and interviews with Jews in many cities, Theodor Herzl's life was cut short. He had many severe heart attacks and finally contracted a fever resulting in pneumonia, so that he realized that the end of his life was drawing near. Although his wife and children and other notable friends were with him, he desired to have his special friend, Dr. William Heckler, with him. How wonderful that Heckler was with him when he expired on July 3, 1904, at the age of forty-four years!

No one ever poured out his life's blood more zealously than had Theodor Herzl. The great work to which he gave ten years of his life was not complete; it had in fact only begun to take actual shape in the last gatherings of the Zion Congress that he had held before his death. Millions lamented his early decease. He was buried in his home town of Vienna in Doebling Cemetery. After many years his coffin and those of his parents were flown to Israel in the summer of 1949, and solemnly buried on a Jerusalem hilltop, now named Herzl's Hill.

THE CAPTURE OF JERUSALEM FROM THE TURKS

The work that Theodor Herzl had begun was taken up by various of his collaborators. Herzl in his last years was carrying on important negotiations with England, but it was not until the outbreak of World War I that definite results were obtained with regard to obtaining Palestine as the permanent homeland for the Jews.

During the great world struggle between the Allied and Central powers, England began to realize that it was fast facing its greatest crisis of losing the war. However, this was all changed with an important contribution by one of the greatest chemists of Manchester University, Chaim Weizman, who discovered that a most powerful new explosive, known as TNT, could be made at a low cost. He offered it to England and England passed TNT on to its Allies, and by it the Allies won the war.

When the statesmen of England had realized that this most effective contribution was made by a Jewish scientist, they asked him what he desired as a reward. He said, "I do not want any money; just liberate Palestine and secure it for Jewish occupation." It was this Jewish chemist that saved Anglo-Saxon civilization from defeat and so the British government issued the famous Balfour Declaration. This declaration, addressed to Lord Rothschild by Arthur James Balfour, stated, "The British government looks with favor on the establishment in Palestine of a national home for the Jewish people."

This document was issued at the close of World War I, on November 2, 1917.

It is well at this juncture to stop and consider the Messianic influence in the conquest of Palestine.

A month later, Palestine was taken by the British army under the command of General Allenby. How different this seizure of Jerusalem was from that of Nebuchadnezzar in 604 B.C., or that of Titus by the Roman army in A.D. 70, or that of the Turks in the Middle Ages. This seizure was made without the shot of a gun or the loss of a single life.

General Allenby, a real Christian man, disliked the idea of destroying the city where Jesus spent the last week of His ministry, preaching in the Temple, and where He was arraigned before Caiaphas, Herod, and Pilate; where He was crucified and rose again from the dead. So General Allenby cabled to King George for his direction and the only reply he received was, "Pray." This he did, and the Turks within the walls were seized with a great terror and sent a delegation of surrender that came to the tent where General Allenby and his officers were engaged in prayer. On December 11, 1917, General Allenby marched into the city and proclaimed peace and protection to all its inhabitants. The League of Nations on July 24, 1922, gave Britain the mandate over Palestine.

THE BIRTH OF THE STATE OF ISRAEL

From this time on, large numbers of Jews came from all parts of Europe and from Asia and from Africa to enter Palestine. With their arduous labors they cleared the marshes of malaria fever. They introduced the latest agricultural methods to till the soil, making the desert to "blossom as the rose," constructed stable roads, they established new colonies and built cities with up-to-date architecture. They established schools, synagogues, and a university. They revived the Hebrew language. Chaim Weizman was appointed commissioner. He organized the large number of immigrants into a stable government so that when the British mandate had expired on May 13, 1948, he with the chosen Zionist leaders was ready at midnight of May 14th to move from its previous headquarters in Tel-Aviv to Jerusalem. He then announced to the world that the *Jewish State* had been formed with the name, *The State of Israel*. President Truman as representative of the United States was the first head of a nation to send congratulations to the newborn State of Israel. Chaim Weizman held his office as President until his death in 1952, after which Ben Gurion took over to date the government of the State of Israel.

THE MESSIANIC IMPACT UPON THE STATE OF ISRAEL

THE MIRACULOUS HISTORY OF ISRAEL

THE JEWISH NATION has had a marvelous history of ever-recurring miracles. It was miraculous in its beginning with the call of Abraham that "by thy seed all nations shall be blessed." While reference to "thy seed" has primarily in view the coming of the long-awaited Messiah, it must not be overlooked that through the redeeming work of the Messiah the to-be-redeemed descendants of Abraham became subject to the Messiah, which made them capable to govern the nations of earth and possess the Kingdom (Daniel 7:22).

The descendants of Abraham had a miraculous history as seen in their deliverance from the bondage of Egypt, the giving of the Law at Mount Sinai, their journey through the wilderness, their taking possession of the Promised Land, the judgment visited upon them in the Assyrian and Babylonian captivities, their return from exile to rebuild the temple and the walls of Jerusalem.

Those miracles all had a Messianic purpose. As the result of their preservation the Jewish nation could give to the world the long-awaited Saviour and Redeemer. Never has a nation existed with such an array of miracles. The whole life of Jesus was the greatest miracle of all history from His Virgin Birth to His Resurrection and Ascension to Heaven.

Jesus confined His ministry to "the lost sheep of the house of Israel" (Matthew 10:6, 7), yet it had to be said of His coming to His own, "they received Him not." Their leaders turned against Him and Jesus had to expose the hypocrisy of the Pharisees, Sadducees and Herodians and declare that they were false shepherds.

Of the many parables that Jesus gave to His disciples there are three that deal with the Fig Tree. These three parables compose a triad illustrating the entire course of Jewish history in its relation to the Jewish Messiah. The first of these three Fig Tree parables is that of

32

the Barren Fig Tree, which was spoken of by Jesus about six months prior to His crucifixion and death while in retirement in Ephraim; the second parable was the cursing of the Fig Tree, which was spoken of on Monday, April 2nd, during the last week of His public ministry; the third parable was that of the restored Fig Tree, given in His Olivet discourse on Tuesday, April 3rd, of the Passion week. Notice the chronological sequence of the three parables — barren — then cursed — then restored.

THREE PARABLES OF JESUS ON THE FIG TREE

The first is recorded in Luke 13:6-9, wherein the dresser (God) came and sought for fruit and found only leaves on the Fig Tree. This was true not only regarding the ministry of Jesus that the leaders gave little or no response to His teaching, but this applies for the most part to the history of Israel throughout the Old Testament that little fruit of genuine willingness was found. Although God had punished Israel in two captivities, He preserved and brought them back from their exile to prepare the nation for their coming Messiah. In examining this barren Fig Tree, Jesus pleaded for postponement of judgment upon the nation of Israel. Not only were the leaders given the opportunity to witness the trial, the crucifixion — they were assured of the resurrection of Jesus. They were given the message of repentance by the newly founded church, which was born on the Day of Pentecost, yet God's probation of forty years bore no fruit so that eventually Israel was cut down in the destruction of Jerusalem in A.D. 70 (Mark 4:9-12; Luke 21:24-29).

The second parable of the Cursed Fig Tree (Mark 11:12-20) gives expression to the tender compassion of Jesus toward the house of Israel in that Jesus never pronounced a curse upon them personally or collectively but used this opportunity a few days prior to His death to pronounce judgment on the barren Fig Tree instead of the nation — and yet it symbolizes effectively the awaiting doom upon the Jewish nation in their world-wide dispersion during which they have remained in unbelief. As a nation they have been unable to give forth the saving message of a Living Redeemer and therefore they have remained a barren, fruitless nation as far as their witnessing for God concerning Jesus their promised Messiah. A strange thing is foretold to happen to Israel during their world dispersion, that God will bring about a mighty awakening during their dispersion that will result in their national salvation (Romans 4:16), thereby becoming a nation "dwelling in the land that I have given to Jacob."

THE MEANING OF EZEKIEL'S VISION OF THE DRY BONES

This strange thing is recorded in the 37th chapter of Ezekiel in which the prophet saw the vision of "a valley of dry bones." The question was asked of the prophet as to whether these dry bones could be made to live. No — the prophet looked upon this situation as an utterly hopeless one. Man could only give a "no" for an answer. God only could give a "Yes" to this question. The command was given: "O ye dry bones, hear ye the Word of the Lord."

Ezekiel prophesied as he was commanded and "there was a noise, a shaking of bones coming together, bone to his bone." Flesh came upon the bones; "skin covered them above but there was no breath." Thus far, it represents the tremendous awakening of national and race consciousness which was caused among the dispersed Jews by the Zionist Movement organized by Theodor Herzl. Then another command follows to say to the wind, "Come from the four winds, O breath, and breathe upon these slain, that they may live." This command caused them to live and they stood on their feet, an exceeding great army (Ezekiel 37:1-10).

The solution of this vision makes certain a new race consciousness among the Jews with a passion to return to their homeland "out of the graves of nations and bringing them unto the land of Israel." It means a massive return of the Jews back to Palestine to their homeland for which they have yearned for nearly two thousand years. Here is the place that was given to Theodor Herzl to accomplish a Herculean task of awakening his nation to a realization of a great destiny for the world's welfare in their return to the land of their fathers. Theodor Herzl was given an incentive to his life's work, given as a lad only seven years old while at school, reading the story of the exodus of Israel from the bondage of Egypt to the Promised Land; and later, as a lad of twelve years, receiving the wonderful vision of "the Messiah" (Ezekiel 37:11-14).

This story was the arrow which pierced into the lad's head and later into his heart, which then led him to understand his life's work involving untold suffering because of the lack of understanding and response to his tremendous labors in behalf of Zionism. The second great awakening that happened to Theodor Herzl was the vision that was given to him of the Messiah lifting him up to the clouds when he heard the Messiah utter words too sacred for him to utter to anyone in his entire life until he confided to a close friend six months prior to his death. This dream was a vision of the Messiah, previously mentioned — yes, a vision of the Messiah revealing to this youth of twelve years that his life's work was to make known to the Jews (My people) some great deeds that Messiah will perform for His people.

Did the young lad understand the great import of the Messiah speaking to him of the mission to be given to him? What could a lad of twelve know of the Messiah who was brought up in Judaism? Yet once he had opportunity to have access to read in the New Testament how the Messiah rode upon a lowly donkey into Jerusalem, he definitely knew that Messiah had been upon earth at one time and that since then He had ascended to Heaven and that therefore He could lift this lad into the clouds of the sky far above the things of earth to tell him what part he would have in obeying the command given to him in the clouds of heaven.

THE TEACHING OF THE SCRIPTURES REGARDING THE MESSIAH IN JUDAISM

There are only two references given in one verse in the entire Old Testament where the Redeemer of mankind is referred to as "Messiah." These two references are found in Daniel 9:25, 26 in connection with the vision of the seventy weeks. In the margin of this reference is the explanation of the word Messiah, *"the anointed One."* There are many other references in the Old Testament where the word anointing is used in connection with the dedication of priests, prophets and kings to their official calling in Israel.

It is interesting to note that the teaching of Judaism accepts and uses this word "Messiah" in connection with their prayers to distinguish it from the name JESUS given to the Saviour at His birth. Judaism does not accept Jesus as the Son of God. It does not accept Jesus as the promised Messiah.

In this connection one will find that the very same term "Messiah," which is given in the above reference in the Old Testament, applies to the promised Redeemer in the New Testament. In John 1:41, it is stated that Andrew finding his brother Simon said to him, "We have found the Messiah, which being interpreted, is the Christ." The second reference to the term "Messiah" is found in John 4:25, where the woman of Samaria said to Jesus at the well, "I know that Messiah cometh, which is called Christ; when he is come, he will tell us all things." Jesus replied to her, "I that speak unto thee am he" (verse 26).

God's people in the church are equally if not more entitled to use the word Messiah given in only one verse of the Old Testament in their acceptance of Jesus as Saviour. In His first address given in the synagogue of Nazareth, Jesus quoted from the prophet Isaiah (61:1, 2) the words found in Luke 4:18, "The Spirit of the Lord is upon me, because he hath anointed me."

The Hebrew word "Messiah" translated into the Greek language is "Christ." The Greek word, "Christ," means *"The Anointed One."*

Jesus, therefore, said that the Holy Spirit had anointed "Messiah" (Himself). When Jesus asked His disciples, "What think ye of Christ?" He was really asking, "What think ye of Messiah?" "What think ye of the Anointed One?" Peter replied, "We believe that thou art the Christ [the Messiah, the Anointed One]" (Matthew 16:13-19).

The most striking proof that Jesus claimed to be the Messiah, the Anointed One, was at His trial when Caiaphas, the high priest, adjured Jesus "by the living God that thou tell us whether thou be the Christ" (the Messiah, the Anointed One, the Son of God). Jesus replied, "Thou hast said" (Matthew 26:63, 64). As proof that He was the Messiah promised, He quoted from Daniel 7:13, 14, when He said, "Coming with the clouds of heaven."

The term "Christ" used of and by Jesus in the New Testament, means exactly the same person as does "Messiah" of the Old Testament.

There are 602 references to Christ (Messiah) and 406 references to Jesus in the New Testament.

The fact above stated (of Jesus being the Messiah of the New Testament, as well as the Old Testament) is therefore well established.

An enlightening incident to prove that Jesus was accepted as Messiah, the Anointed One, is the time Jesus *appeared* to Saul of Tarsus on the way to Damascus on which occasion Saul (Paul) accepted Him as the promised Messiah. The first message he gave of his conversion from Judaism to Christianity was that "straightway he preached Christ [Messiah, the Anointed One] in the synagogues, that he is the Son of God" (Acts 9:20).

Returning to the incident of Theodor Herzl's vision of the Messiah, one can better understand the message that Messiah gave to this youth of twelve years.

This term, the Messiah, was not given at any time in the Old Testament in any theophany of appearance of the Son of God whether to Abraham, to Moses or Isaiah. It was given solely to Jesus as the Anointed One by the Holy Spirit to carry on His ministry.

To Theodor Herzl was given a commission of world-wide magnitude to perform the great things that Messiah was about to inaugurate for the emancipation of the Jews.

It need not seem strange therefore that to a young lad named Theodor Herzl at twelve years of age was given in the year 1872 a remarkable vision of the Messiah, choosing him out of all the millions of Europe to be the One entrusted with performing the great task of inaugurating an effective plan, set forth in his document of *The Jewish State*, to establish Israel as "a nation born in a day" in their homeland of Palestine.

THE WRONG INTERPRETATION OF THE MESSIAH GIVEN IN JUDAISM

The outstanding fact of the whole Bible — Old Testament as well as the New Testament — is that its contents center around the Person designated as "the Messiah," as the only channel by which sinful, fallen man can obtain redemption from God. This redemption is effected because Messiah is the only divine human being qualified to make atonement. He alone was "sent" (a word used by Jesus over twenty times) from Heaven to earth to be a substitute for man to suffer the wages of man's sinfulness by the shedding of His blood on Calvary's cross (I Peter 1:18, 19).

The first promise given to man after his fall designated clearly that Messiah should accomplish His redeeming work in two separate and distinct stages. God said of the serpent, "I will put enmity between thee and the woman, and between thy seed and her seed; it shall bruise thy head, and thou shalt bruise his heel" (Genesis 3:15).

This promise makes plain that the Seed of the woman (Messiah) will bruise the head of the serpent, thereby declaring complete triumph over Satan's dominion on the earth. This part of the first Messianic promise is willingly accepted by the teaching of Judaism in our day. Notice the first verse in the New Testament, "The book of the generation of Jesus Christ [Jesus, the Messiah], the son of David, the son of Abraham" (Matthew 1:1).

A golden Messianic thread binds together each link of the genealogy of Joseph through Solomon back to David to prove Jesus as the son of David (Matthew 1:16) and that of Mary, reaching back all the way to Adam through Nathan the son of David to prove Jesus as being the son of man (Luke 3:23-38).

In the standard prayer book of Judaism are set forth "thirteen principles of faith" which were formulated by "Moses Maimonides" in the twelfth century. In the thirteen principles great emphasis is given to the marvelous work done by the Creator. A strong declaration is made that "this law will not change and that there never will be another law."

This of itself expresses condemnation of the whole teaching of the New Testament which states that "the law was given by Moses, but grace and truth came by Jesus Christ" (John 1:17). Jesus never belittled the great work that Moses had done but He had reason to set Himself above Moses, when He declared in the Sermon on the Mount that He had something deeper, something greater, something of more importance than what had been given by Moses. Repeatedly He said, "But I say" (read Matthew 5:27-44). Jesus declared distinctly that He came not "to destroy the law . . . but to *fulfil.* For verily I say unto you, Till heaven and earth pass, one jot or one tittle shall in no wise pass from the law, till all be fulfilled" (Matthew 5:17, 18).

JESUS' CHALLENGE REGARDING 'THE MESSIAH'

Jesus is the only human being who ever put out the challenge to his adversaries, "Which of you convinceth me of sin?" (John 8:46). Pilate had to declare of Him that "I find no fault in him" (John 19:4); and, the centurion who had witnessed the entire tragedy of the cross, glorified God in declaring, "Certainly this was a righteous man" (Luke 23:47). He declared thereby His perfect humanity, but he declared also His deity and divinity in saying, "Truly this was the Son of God" (Matthew 27:54).

With this in mind, it is startling to read among the articles of faith given by "Moses Maimonides" at the seventeenth article of beliefs as follows: "I believe with perfect faith in the Coming of the Messiah and though He tarry, I will wait daily for His Coming."

This declaration is in perfect harmony with the first Messianic promise given in the Garden of Eden and with the many promises of the coming Redeemer set forth in the Old Testament.

Attention needs now to be given to the first Messianic promise given in the Garden of Eden that not only is there complete triumph of the Seed of the woman (Messiah) over the seed of the serpent (Satan), but notice also that God, already having in mind that "the Lamb [Messiah] slain from the foundation of the world" (Revelation 13:8), could reveal the sufferings and death of the Messiah at His first coming by declaring that "the seed of the serpent shall bruise his [Messiah's] heel" (piercing His hands, His feet and His side).

A SUFFERING SAVIOUR IS THE PROMISED MESSIAH

Affirmation has been made that Judaism professes to believe in "the Messiah with perfect faith and though He tarry, will wait daily for His Coming." The question now arises as to whether Judaism is expecting a suffering Saviour (a Man of Sorrows) in accordance with the first Messianic promise in Scripture, wherein it states that "the woman's Seed" (Messiah) will be bruised (pierced) in His heel (a crucified Messiah) or whether they only believe in a triumphant, conquering Messiah who will conquer Satan's power for Israel and the whole world.

As the facts now stand, there begins here a great cleavage between Judaism and Christianity, right here at the beginning of the announcement made of the Coming Messiah.

If the question is asked of the leaders of Judaism as to whether they are expecting a Messiah born of "a virgin" Israel mother, they would answer "No."

If they were asked as to whether they expect their Messiah to carry on His ministry in the State of Israel, calling sinners to repentance, healing the sick and raising the dead, their answer again would be "No."

If asked as to whether they would have Him to be rejected by the leading rabbis of Judaism and beaten and spit upon and finally nailed to the cross, crowned with "a crown of thorns" — their answer would once more be a decided "No."

And if their Messiah were laid in a tomb, would they expect Him to be raised from the dead and after forty days ascend to heaven, their only answer would be positively "No."

By this repetition of denial of such a Messiah, they brush aside not only the undeniable historical facts of the life of Jesus who affirmed on various occasions His Messiahship, but they also deny the repeated Old Testament prophecies that are made with reference to the Messiah being a suffering, despised *Man of Sorrows* (Isaiah 53:1-3), betrayed by one of His trusted disciples for thirty pieces of silver, being nailed to the cross, as Moses lifted a serpent upon a pole (John 3:14, 15); being made a curse (Galatians 3:13), and by the shedding of His blood making atonement for man in bondage to sin and Satan. The only answer that can be given with reference to Judaism, still rejecting the fulfillment of Old Testament prophecies of the promised Redeemer, made flesh to dwell on earth (only Palestine) for a brief period of thirty-three years and a half, then ending His public ministry with His death upon Calvary's cross, but raised from death after three days — the only answer that the Word of God gives to such an attitude of rejection is that "without shedding of blood is no remission [of sin]" (Hebrews 9:22). The Word of God knows nothing of a Messiah that exhibits Him *only* as a "King of kings," "crowned with many crowns," and forgetting or rejecting the Messiah's coming first, set forth in the garb of the "Man of Sorrows."

In order to clarify this issue between a partial Messiah, conquering as king, and a complete Messiah, coming as the servant of Jehovah, by incarnation thereby to effect first a sure remedy for sin by His blood atonement, a very important document will follow. This document gives excerpts from an entrancing book entitled *Theodor Herzl's Memorial* published by the *New Palestine* magazine of New York City, 1929.

The following excerpts are given with the full permission of its author, the most distinguished theologian, Dr. Abba Hillel Silver, Cleveland, Ohio:

An eager, mystic and masterful religious imperialism was at the heart of Jewish Messianism at the outset. This is the essence of the visions of Micah and Isaiah. Zion must become the spiritual Capitol of a regenerated humanity. The peoples of the earth will flow unto it to receive instruction in the higher laws of justice, and of world peace. There is superb daring and pride and exultant confidence in this Messianic concept of the race.

. . . Among the choice spirits, the inexpugnable Messianic prophetism of the race continued unabated. The untoward conditions of the times and threatened desolation of the nation lent fuel even to the great tradition. Hitherto it was assumed in a rather vague and undefined way, that Israel would serve as the instrument of mankind's spiritual salvation. At the hands of the great Prophet of the Dispersion, the second Isaiah, and his disciples, this belief became definite and unmistakable. It became, in fact, the new Dogma of Jewish nationalism. Prophetic Messianism was now, however, linked up with the hope of national restoration. The political motive was introduced, and thereafter this motif gained ascendancy by Jewish Messianic thought. The first set in the great drama of the world's redemption must be the national redemption of Israel.

. . . It was now also realized that the task of reconstituting society after the highest pattern of moral perfection cannot be accomplished without much suffering and sacrifice. Israel having assumed the crown, must also assume the cross to world leadership. Thus the tragic theme of the "suffering servant of Yahveh" appears. Israel is destined to be stricken and afflicted. He will bear the chastisement of the world, but by his stripes the nations of earth will be healed.

. . . A crushed and broken people, which cannot save itself, cannot think much about saving the world. A dark obsession took hold of Israel — the thought of its homelessness. Its emotional group life became centered in the impassioned wish to return home.

The political motif took on a new coloring. Despair opened the way for super-nationalism. Israel's redemption can come not by way of self-emancipation, but only through the miraculous endowed personal redeemer, scion of the house of David. The revolutionary ardor passed out of the political ideal. The people became passive in the hands of fate. They adhered to the doctrine of prophetic Messianism forgetting or ignoring the fact that it was predicated upon a Jewish national life in Palestine. Many Jews were very loyal and very learned and very proud Jews. They believed that prophetic Messianism was capable of sustaining it, without the aid of political autonomy either in Palestine or in the Diaspora. The logic of history has proved them wrong. They are to be credited, however, with having brought forward again from the perisphere to the center of Jewish thought the irrepressible prophetic tradition.

Political Messianism as such received its fullest expression in Theodor Herzl. His Zionism was at first a purely political interest. He was far removed from Jewish life and unacquainted with the classic tradition of his people. He came to Jews by way of Anti-Semitism, not by way of Judaism. At one of the Zionist Congresses, he frankly confessed that he did not know what was meant by "Jewish Culture." His maximum program at that time was the establishment of a legally secured haven of refuge for his persecuted brethren anywhere, not necessarily Palestine. His concept of Jewish nationalism was couched in the terms of the Jewish nationalist philosophy of nineteenth century Europe.

Herzl's exclusive political Messianism, so alien to the essential genius of the race, was destined to encounter resistance. Jewry, especially Eastern European Jewry, preserved an older and nobler nationalistic philosophy. It treasured a unique national tradition of twenty-five centuries which was inseparably bound up with Palestine, with the Hebrew language, with Hebrew culture, with the Torah, and with all the imperishable dreams of its seers and prophets. Even if it was prepared and even if permission was given to Israel to assume its place as a political entity in the world, he was not at all sure that this would represent the fulfillment of its destiny. Two thousand years of heroic suffering and martyrdom cannot find their compensation in the right to play the role of a pitifully small state in a world of political intrigue, a pawn in the hands of scheming international diplomats. It was neither a matter of slight moment that prophets arose in Israel who visioned "the end of days," when righteousness would be established in the world. "The salvation of Israel" will come to pass through prophets and not through diplomacy.

These protagonists of cultural Zionism avowedly were not thinking of just another secular culture but of a quite unique and extraordinary culture, which ages ago was to be ushered in with the live coal of a prophetic inspiration, whose glow has not been quenched in the long and weary centuries. They are thinking of a crusading culture, which will transform the world, a culture of imperatives, which will reach out for "new things, the things kept in store, not hitherto known . . ." The new Jewish State . . . Palestine must come to be the workshop of our people's highest ethical culture and aspirations and mankind's experimental laboratory for social reconstruction.

Nationalism is not enough. It is a minimum requirement, not a maximum program. Our national rebirth was made possible by a war, in which nationalism was thoroughly exposed, and discredited. . . . Nationalism will not suffice the eternally questing soul of our people. After its national life is secure, Israel must push on to the frontiers of the new world — the world of internationalism, of economic freedom, of brotherhood and peace. It must resume the burden of its Messianic care. "He shall not fail, nor be crushed till he have set the right in the earth; and the isles shall wait for his teaching."

It is not the purpose of the writer to in any way belittle the valuable contents of this document which is taken from a book of great learning on the many varied aspects of the life and work of Theodor Herzl in founding Zionism, based on his book entitled, *The State of Israel*. The author of this lengthy and most valuable article is one of the most learned theologians of Judaism to this day, held in great honor, not only within the ranks of Judaism, but also in political circles of our great nation. He has contributed largely to the work begun by Theodor Herzl in aiding it to ripen into the State of Israel.

This great scholar of Judaism in his article of three two-column octavo pages does not hesitate to make Messianic Ministry an issue of greatest importance for the Jews in general and for the State of Israel in particular. There are over fifty references in this article to the Messianic Ministry that is being enacted in the history of the Jewish nation.

Fom this article it can be seen that the author sincerely believes that a Messianic Ministry is being carried on in Israel today. The dream of Theodor Herzl gave him a vision of the Messiah, calling him to be the active agent in having "the house of David" *built again* whereby to benefit the whole world. This is one of the sure signs of the Rebudding Fig Tree taking on new life in preparation for the Coming of our Lord Jesus Christ.

Let it be understood that the Jews should not be blamed for seeing and understanding only the latter part of Messiah's Coming to establish an everlasting Kingdom upon the earth, for they have had many disheartening experiences in past centuries in their being persecuted with Anti-Semites in many varied forms by the nominal church.

JESUS BECAME THE SYMBOL OF ANTI-SEMITISM

The following statement is by a Zionist Jew, Joseph Dunner, published in *The Republic of Israel,* October 1950: "To Christians of all denominations — Jesus is the symbol of all that is pure, sacred and lovely. To Jews from the fourth century, Jesus became the symbol of Anti-Semitism, of libel, of cruelty, of violent death."

There is a great deal of truth in the above statement. It reveals in part why Judaism will not yield to Jesus as their Messiah for the suffering of persecution that many of His followers have caused.

Instead of accepting Jesus as their personal Messiah, their leaders ignore His right to this high divine position and in its place prefer to make the nation of Israel to be the promised Messiah that was foretold in Isaiah 53, which tells of the sufferings endured by Jehovah's Servant.

A close survey of the following twelve statements taken from the learned article of Dr. Silver on *Jewish Messianism* shows what strange deductions are made by him to prove that because of the suffering and chastisement endured by the Jews it follows that they have become the Messianic symbol of the world's redemption according to many declarations of the prophets of old. Israel is destined to world leadership as set forth in the first four declarations but none of the prophets have ever conceived such an idea of Israel as being Jehovah's Servant for the world's redemption as given in the deductions made by Dr. Silver.

This above interpretation of Isaiah 53 is much different from that handed down by *learned elders of Zion* in the early centuries, who believed that this chapter speaks of a *personal Messiah* instead of a *national one.*

That the *Messiah* of Isaiah 53 is a personal one appears plainly on the surface of the words given in chapter 52:13-15, where the statement is made of *"my servant"* that "his visage was so marred more than any man."

In the above statement there appears the personal pronoun *three times,* applying to a *Person — Jehovah's Servant, the Messiah.*

Dr. Silver in his article makes the following deductions to prove the Messianic Mission of Israel:

1. Zion must be in the spiritual capital of a regenerated humanity.
2. *Israel* is the instrument of mankind's spiritual salvation.
3. Prophetic nationalism is linked up with the hope of national restoration.

4. Israel's redemption is the first step to the world's redemption.
5. Moral perfection cannot be accomplished without much *suffering and sacrifice*.
6. *Israel to be stricken* and afflicted.
7. He will bear the chastisement of the world.
8. *Israel,* assured the crown, must also assume the cross to world leadership.
9. Thus the tragic theme of *"the suffering servant of Yahveh appears."*
10. *Israel is destined to be stricken and afflicted.*
11. He will bear the *chastisement of the world.*
12. But by his *stripes the nations of earth will be healed.*

It is proper to ask as to whether Dr. Silver's learned thesis is in harmony with Isaiah's Messiah as seen in the following statements made by the prophet concerning "the Servant of Jehovah."

A Personal Messiah Set Forth by Isaiah

In studying Isaiah 53, one will find that only two distinct persons are referred to — references to the personal pronoun *"He, His, Him"* forty-four times, belonging only to *the Messiah* and only fifteen times to "our," referring to the *people in general.* It will now be profitable to study the following ten phases of *Messiah's* mission foretelling specifically the life of Jesus during His abode upon earth.

One will see various phases of Messiah's mission in the following statements:

1. He was despised and rejected of men (v. 3).
2. He was a Man of sorrows (v. 3).
3. He has borne our griefs (v. 4).
4. He was wounded for our transgressions (v. 5).
5. He is brought as a lamb to the slaughter (v. 7).
6. He was cut off out of the land of the living (v. 8).
7. He was with the rich in His death (v. 9).
8. He was made an offering for sin (v. 10).
9. He shall be satisfied with the travail of His soul (v. 11).
10. He poured out His soul unto death (v. 12).

Of these ten declarations here given, the one outstanding characteristic of *Messiah's* work is No. 8 that declares that *"Messiah made an offering for sin."* In other words, Messiah presented Himself as "the Lamb of God which taketh away the sin of the world" (John 1:29).

Among the ordinances of sacrifice instituted by Moses was that of the daily offering of a lamb for the Tabernacle (later Temple) for morning and evening sacrifice. He designated that the lamb was to be *"without blemish"* for a blemish is an abomination to the Lord (Deuteronomy 17:1).

In the scholarly treatise of Dr. Silver on *Jewish Messianism* can it be said that the nation of Israel at any time was *blameless,* so that it could offer itself through its suffering that "by his stripes," the nations of earth will be healed?

If Israel is not blameless with regard to the subject of sin, how can it be the "Servant of Jehovah" representing *the Messiah* in Isaiah, chapter 53? There can be no question that this prophecy of Isaiah looks forward to a Son born of a Virgin (Isaiah 7:14) upon whose shoulders will be the government, sitting upon the throne of David, the Prince of peace (Isaiah 9:6, 7).

DANIEL'S VISION OF THE SEVENTY WEEKS

This divinely anointed One to be the world's only Messiah can be none other than Jesus, the Son of God, referred to in the New Testament as the *Christ* (the Messiah).

Many more references to the work of divine redemption could be given both in the Old and New Testaments but one more at least must be given, taken from the Old Testament, which positively proves that none other can be the *promised Messiah* than Jesus Christ, our blessed Lord. This one reference is given in the book of Daniel, as follows:

Seventy weeks are determined upon thy people and upon thy holy city, to finish the transgression, and to make an end of sins, and to make reconciliation for iniquity, and to bring in everlasting righteousness, and to seal up the vision and prophecy, and to anoint the most Holy. Know therefore and understand, that from the going forth of the commandment to restore and to build Jerusalem unto the Messiah the Prince shall be seven weeks, and threescore and two weeks: the street shall be built again, and the wall, even in troublous times (Daniel 9:24, 25).

This chapter deals with the great prayer Daniel offered to God for the restoration of Jerusalem at the end of seventy years of Babylonian captivity under Darius the king of the Medes and Persians. Daniel realized that the captivity had come upon Israel to Assyria and upon Judah to Babylon on account of their rebellion and disloyalty to God. Therefore, he confessed the sin of *all Israel* and pleaded for mercy that God would forgive their transgressions and bring about the restoration of Jerusalem.

God sent the angel Gabriel to reveal to Daniel how He would answer the prayer of Daniel. Gabriel then gave to Daniel the vision of what is known as "the Seventy Weeks" representing a period of 490 years, at the end of which Jerusalem would become "the Holy City" to bring in everlasting righteousness and bring reconciliation of Israel to their God.

This vision of "Seventy Weeks" is divided into *three* parts — first a period of 7 weeks of 49 years for the building of the walls of Jerusalem under Nehemiah. This was followed by a period of 62 weeks making

434 years, thus making a total with the former 49 years of 483 years at which time *Messiah* will have finished His mission in dying upon the cross. After these 69 weeks or 483 years follows the period known as the *Church Age* ending with the rapture of the saints. Then follows the last of the 70 weeks making a 7-year period in which *God resumes His program with Israel*. During this last period of 7 years God will have them purged with the judgments (Matthew 24) and tribulation and the rule of the Antichrist ending with the great battle of Armageddon.

THE JEWS, THE LOST SHEEP OF THE HOUSE OF ISRAEL

It is necessary for everyone to understand that the twice mention of the *Messiah* is the only reference to Him as Messiah in the entire Old Testament. These two references to the Messiah were given for God's chosen people *the Jews* to know at the time of His appearing that He was the long *Promised Redeemer* who was to give His life and ministry primarily to *"the lost sheep of the house of Israel"* (Matthew 10:6; 15:24), to give to them the message of God's salvation.

Now consider that when John the Baptist, the forerunner of Jesus, had announced that "the kingdom of heaven is at hand," "[Jesus] came unto his own, and his own received him not. But as many as received him, to them gave he power to become the sons of God . . ." (John 1:11, 12). The Jews at that time were under the Roman yoke and had to pay tribute to Caesar at Rome. They were waiting to have this yoke broken and to be set free. At one time after the feeding of the five thousand, the people were ready to make *Jesus King* to organize a rebellion against Rome.

Jesus utterly refused to exercise His powers as King over an unrepentant nation. The leaders of the Jews had nothing (Daniel 9:26, Revised Version) but hatred for Jesus and repeatedly sought to put Him to death. Jesus had foretold to His disciples repeatedly that He would be killed and rise again after three days (Luke 18:31-34). As the last Passover week drew nigh, Jesus gave direction to His disciples to obtain a colt for Him to use in entering Jerusalem. At this time the acclaim of multitudes was given to Jesus, "Hosanna to the Son of David" (Matthew 21:7-9). The enemies of Jesus were startled at this event and His cleansing of the Temple. They definitely plotted to bring His life to an end.

The leaders of the Sanhedrin did not want Jesus killed on the Passover day, but God directed that His crucifixion and death actually take place on the Passover day. He was nailed to the cross on Golgotha's hill. Here was fulfilled the part of the first Messianic promise which was given in the Garden of Eden pertaining to "the seed of the

Serpent *piercing the feet of the Seed of the woman."* Now instead of Jesus having established the kingdom of heaven, He *"had nothing"* for even His own disciples had denied Him and fled from the scene of Gethsemane.

This, the greatest tragedy of all history, followed with the Resurrection of Christ, resulted in the greatest victory ever gained in any of the world's greatest battles. Because the leaders of the Jews had rejected Jesus and charged Him with blasphemy before Caiaphas the high priest for claiming to be *the Messiah,* Jesus had prophesied the destruction of Jerusalem and their dispersion among the nations of the earth (Luke 21:22-27).

Notice at this point that Jesus had not cast the Jews aside forever, for He spoke of their return to the holy land at *the end of the age* in the parable of the Rebudding Fig Tree (Luke 21:29-33).

Here is where the Jews failed to acknowledge Jesus as their Messiah and stumbled at the *stumbling block* (Romans 9:32, 33) and therefore remained in unbelief as a nation during the entire period of this dispensation.

Attention has already been called once in this study to the fact that Dr. Silver utterly failed in his scholarly article published in the *Memoirs of Theodor Herzl* to make use of this most significant reference in the Old Testament (Daniel 9:25, 26) to "The Messiah." *Why this omission?* It was not because he was unaware of it being the *only reference* in the Old Testament regarding "The Messiah," but because he could not avoid facing the stern fact of the life and ministry of our Lord Jesus Christ, the only One who could declare the bold fact to the woman of Samaria, in reply to her declaration, *"Messiah cometh, which is called Christ; when he is come, he will tell us all things,"* "I that speak unto thee am he [The Messiah]" (John 4:25, 26).

Here is the Stone that Dr. Silver stumbled at. He well knew that he could not remove this Stone, "which had come down from heaven" (Daniel 2:34), so the only safe way of avoiding further discussion was to simply *bypass* or totally ignore the plain prophecy and *the only one* making reference to the coming of "The Messiah" as set forth in Daniel's vision of the "Seventy Weeks." This vision of the "Seventy Weeks," given to Daniel by the angel Gabriel, constitutes the most vital part of the Old Testament, on which depends the veracity of the entire New Testament with its frequent mention of Jesus being "The Christ" (The Messiah).

Dr. Silver could well know of the trial of Jesus before Caiaphas, the high priest, who gave the solemn command to Jesus: "I adjure thee by the living God, that thou tell us whether thou be the Christ [Messiah], the Son of God" — to which Jesus gave the *positive* answer: "Thou hast said . . ." (Matthew 26:63, 64).

Saul of Tarsus, the most zealous of all Jews, adhering to the law of Moses, had been taught "at the feet of Gamaliel." With that thorough training he went forth to persecute the Church, to torment and kill its followers (anti-Semitism). Jesus appeared to him in a vision on his way to Damascus. In this vision, Jesus said: "Why persecutest thou *me?*" When Saul inquired, "Who art thou?" the reply came: *"I am Jesus,* whom thou persecutest."

After being restored of his blindness, Saul "straightway . . . preached Christ [The Messiah] in the synagogues, that he is the Son of God" (Acts 9:4, 5, 20). In Paul's later teaching addressed to the Church of Rome, Paul could write: "I am not ashamed of the gospel of Christ [Messiah]: for it is the power of God unto salvation to every one that believeth; *to the Jew* first, and also to the Greek [Gentile]" (Romans 1:16).

With all this in mind, Dr. Silver, instead of dealing with the Person of "The Messiah," makes over fifty references in his learned treatise to *Messianism* — something impersonal, referring to the nation of Israel (being a Messianic nation because of its great sufferings during past centuries), thus totally avoiding any mention of Jesus as the Promised Messiah.

Notwithstanding the ignominious death of Jesus, the cross of the *Messiah* became the mighty power of God unto salvation to many millions through Christianity (Romans 1:16).

Let every true follower of Jesus pray unto God to bring the message of the *Messiah,* who having come in the life of Jesus Christ our blessed Lord is still to come a second time as the triumphant King of kings and Lord of lords, to Jew and Gentile alike. This Messiah will establish His Kingdom upon earth and reign as King over all nations, with a regenerated Israel as His chosen people to give forth the Gospel of the Kingdom until "all the families of the earth be blessed" (Genesis 12:3). The earth will be filled with the "knowledge of the Lord, as the waters cover the sea" (Isaiah 11:9).

✡ 3 ✡

THE GREAT HELP OF THE BRITISH EMPIRE IN THE FORMATION OF THE JEWISH STATE

FROM THE TIME that the British government undertook to carry out the Balfour Declaration, issued in November, 1917, there began an inflow of many thousands of Jews from many countries to make their home in Palestine. Great Britain, having the mandate over Palestine, increased or diminished the quota of immigrant Jews.

The British did not use military force to rob the Arabs of the land. The Zionist organization obtained millions of dollars of investment from Jews, the most of which was from Jews residing in the United States. With these vast funds large areas of land were purchased at high prices from the residing Arabs.

With the increasing population of Jews in the land of Palestine, there arose increasing jealousy and enmity between Arabs and Jews, resulting in numerous conflicts and warfare between them.

Considering that the Jews had purchased large areas of land, looking forward to forming a new State for the Jews in Palestine, over ten million Arabs became hostile to this project and openly stated that they would carry on warfare until the Jews were "driven into the sea." The Jews realized their need of organizing a strong military force with modern equipment in order to withstand the great force of the Arabs.

WAR BETWEEN ARABS AND JEWS

The Arabs began a great assault on the Jews but, overwhelmed by the superior forces of the Jews, they found it necessary to flee from their homes and seek shelter beyond the Jordan River. When the military forces of the Jews took the upper hand in Palestine, they took possession of the homes and property which the fleeing Arabs had left in Palestine.

This situation created large numbers of refugees in Trans-Jordan, and a vast and perplexing refugee problem developed for which a satisfactory solution has been most difficult to find.

48

On account of this contention between Jew and Arab, Great Britain found it necessary to withdraw its mandate over Palestine, thereby giving opportune time for the Jews to form the "State of Israel" and move its headquarters from Tel Aviv to Jerusalem on May 14, 1948.

This event marks one of the astounding results of World War II, in which can be seen the overruling providence of God the Almighty.

Now that the overruling power of the Almighty God was acknowledged by the founders of the State of Israel, it is appropriate to take notice of another spectacular event which had great bearing upon the formation of Israel that has been largely overlooked by historians of World War II.

This event is well known in studying the World War II between the Central and Allied powers. This event, to which your attention is now called, is known as, "The Evacuation of the British Army from Dunkirk."

It is not necessary to give much attention to the details which took place in carrying on the war between the Central and Allied forces during World War II.

To clarify the issue somewhat, it is enough to state that Adolph Hitler was the cause of this great World War to satisfy his greed for world-domination. He decided that he would make his first attack on Poland in 1939, without realizing that Great Britain and the United States would challenge his right to subdue a peace-loving people such as was Poland at that time.

Why Great Britain Entered World War II

It was a great surprise to Hitler that England sent large divisions of infantry across the English Channel to attack Germany, to hinder Hitler from subduing Poland. It was evident to Chancellor Winston Churchill that once Hitler would be victorious in subduing Poland, his next step would, of certainty, be to cross the English Channel with infantry and "Luftwaffe," bomb London and other cities, to destroy the British government and make it a vassal — an enslaved Nazi government under Germany. When the English and French armies were approaching the German frontiers, they became engaged in a fierce battle with Nazi troops, which with the Nazi Luftwaffe and tanks caused a terrible slaughter of British and French soldiers. The German divisions had pierced through the English divisions and reached the Belgian frontier. The British army found itself encircled by the Nazi troops. They were now facing utter defeat and the possibility not only of being captured and enslaved under Nazi government of Germany but of being slaughtered and even annihilated.

This brought utter despair not only to the hearts of the British soldiers but news of their desperate plight soon reached England. What could the people do with their husbands and sons in such a terrible plight?

PRAYER CHANGES THINGS

Just *one word* put into effect would not only bring the needed relief, but this *one word* would effect deliverance to their loved ones in a losing battle.

Found in the Bible, is it hard to know what that *one word* is? This *one word* was used under many critical conditions, as seen in the history of Israel.

That *one word* is PRAYER. In many homes is found on the walls a motto with but three words: "Prayer Changes Things."

The Word of God declares:

If my people, which are called by my name, shall humble themselves and *pray*, and seek my face, and turn from their wicked ways; then will I hear from heaven, and will forgive their sin, and will heal their land (II Chronicles 7:14).

It was Solomon who prayed:

When the heaven is shut up, and there is no rain, because they have sinned against thee; yet *if they pray* toward this place, and confess thy name, and turn from their sin, when thou dost afflict them;

Then hear thou from heaven, and forgive the sin of thy servants, and of thy people Israel, when thou hast taught them the good way, wherein they should walk; and send rain upon thy land, which thou hast given unto thy people for an inheritance (II Chronicles 6:26, 27).

Solomon put no limitation on prayer; he used the significant words regarding Israel's facing her foes in battle, stating:

. . . if their enemies besiege them in the cities of their land . . . Then hear thou from heaven thy dwelling place (II Chronicles 6:28, 30).

And if thy people Israel be put to the worse before the enemy . . . (II Chronicles 6:24).

Yes, the Bible teaches man that, in whatever plight he may be, God is able to bring deliverance, if the right conditions are met.

This plight of the British, encircled by the steel of Nazi panzers and soldiers, was indeed a most critical — yes, *the most desperate event of British history.* Winston Churchill was so stirred up with the danger of seeing the flower of the British army utterly annihilated that he called this the *"darkest hour of British history."*

THE DARKEST HOUR OF BRITISH HISTORY

This terrible plight of the British army brings to mind the great event of the *Exodus* of the entire nation of over three million people of Israel being delivered from Egyptian bondage. They saw the hand of God opening the Red Sea for them to pass through dryshod (Exodus 12:29-33; chapter 14).

This was the first Bible story that Theodor Herzl was made to recite in a school of Austria when but a lad of seven years. This was the story that foreshadowed the great mission he was to perform for dispersed Israel — to have them emigrate from many lands to wend their way to the *Promised Land.*

Notice the religious background that existed: the godless Nazi on the one hand, defying God, in exercising hatred to destroy *six million* Jews from the realm of Germany and its satellites; on the other hand, in this fierce conflict was Great Britain, which represented a Christian nation vitally interested in the welfare of the Jews to aid this dispersed nation to return to their homeland in Palestine.

God wrought a mighty deliverance in the *Exodus* event for Israel and God could work a mighty deliverance for the British army in this the *darkest hour* of their national history.

The Messiah had promised to Theodor Herzl in his dream when but a lad of twelve years, that He would do *"great and wonderful things for the Jews and for the whole world,"* and sure as Messiah's word is true, He was ready to work deliverance in this fateful hour of British history.

Yes, God proved Himself the God of battles on many occasions of Israel's history.

GREAT DELIVERANCES IN ISRAEL'S HISTORY

Did not Abraham with his household of 317 armed men win the Battle of the Kings for the rescue of Lot? (Genesis 14:9-16)

Did not Moses hold out his rod over the Red Sea to have it provide an opening for the vast army of three million people to be delivered from Egyptian slavery? (Exodus 14)

Did not Joshua make the sun to stand still in the valley of Gideon? (Joshua 10:12, 13)

Did not the Angel of the Lord slay 180,000 of the Assyrian army with a plague in one night for the protection of Jerusalem in the days of Hezekiah? (Isaiah 37:29-36)

Did not God preserve the three Hebrew children in the fiery furnace? and Daniel in the Lion's den? (Daniel 3:23-28; 6:20-24)

Did not God protect the Jews from being exterminated by Haman in the days of Esther? (Esther 8:13-17)

Did not Messiah still the storm on two occasions when the disciples were in utter despair? (Matthew 8:23-27; 14:23-32)

We now come to the inquiry as to how God wrought deliverance for the British army, encircled with a ring of bayonets and tanks ready to destroy them.

HITLER USED AS GOD'S SERVANT

In a most marvelous way, God used Adolph Hitler to accomplish this mighty deliverance. The German generals planned to use this opportunity to slay the British divisions, when suddenly they received orders from Adolph Hitler not to proceed with their plans, because he was giving orders for the Luftwaffe to destroy the British army. It was Goering, to satisfy his pride of the Luftwaffe, who persuaded Hitler to use the Air Force so that they would have the credit for the victory over the British army. God enveloped the entire area with a mist and smoothed the angry waves of the English Channel.

THE EVACUATION OF THE BRITISH FROM DUNKIRK AND ITS DIVINE PURPOSE

This made it possible for the British government to send warships and ferries and other ships and boats of every kind back and forth across the English Channel to evacuate the entire British divisions. This evacuation was carried out from May 26 to June 4, 1940, under the direction of Field Marshal John Gert and General Harold Alexander.

In this miraculous escape from Dunkirk, over 230,000 British troops were *rescued from the very jaws of death.*

God knew how to solve this most desperate problem by making the sea obey His orders. God made the elements of nature obey His bidding in providing mist in the air and calmness to the water of the English Channel.

In this way England was saved from national destruction and with her army could continue taking her part in World War II.

This miraculous evacuation proved to be an important link in *preserving the Jews of Palestine from being conquered by the Nazis and becoming a slave state under the rule of the Nazi government of Germany.*

Had the Nazi troops won the battle of Dunkirk, there is no question what the result would have been on the project for which Messiah had appeared in a dream to Theodor Herzl. The whole plan of founding the *"State of Israel" would have utterly collapsed and the dream would have proved a total failure.*

This evacuation of the British troops at Dunkirk was an important link in the dream of the Messiah that Herzl would do *"great and glorious things for the Jews and for the whole world."*

The evacuation of the British army from the battlefield at Dunkirk not only wrought, through the power of God, the preservation of the British government, but also, through this divine act, the preservation of the project of Zionism to form a State for the Jews in Palestine.

THE GREAT HELP OF THE BRITISH EMPIRE IN THE FORMATION OF THE JEWISH STATE

Notwithstanding that many contacts were made to secure effective support for Theodor Herzl's plan, the Dove of Peace could find no place in any government of Europe.

The leading of God, through the Messiah, enabled Theodor Herzl to find efficient response in the British government. Attention has already been called to this fact, but it is reiterated here to emphasize the fact that the British government was the only one to become in full sympathy with Theodor Herzl's plan.

Theodor Herzl realized that this government believed in the Bible, not only the Old Testament, as is the case with the Jews, but also the New Testament. Dr. William Heckler had convinced him that the teaching of the New Testament was *in full accord* with the hope and destiny held out for the restoration and redemption, as set forth in the Old Testament.

THE BENEFIT OF CHRISTIANITY FOR ISRAEL

No sooner had Theodor Herzl held his first Zionist Congress in Basel, Switzerland, in 1897, than decision was made to hold the second Zionist Congress in the city of London. Theodor Herzl had full confidence to accept counsel from Dr. William Heckler, though he knew that he was a converted Jew affiliated with the Episcopalian Church of England. Herzl had invited Heckler to deliver an address in the Zionist Congress in Basel, so now he had also invited Rev Heckler to address the Second Zionist Congress held in London.

Theodor Herzl had great respect for, and confidence in, the British government, because he found that the Jewish population in England enjoyed greater liberty and security than it had in any other government of Europe. With all the almost super strenuous efforts that Theodor Herzl had put forth for many years, he did not get to see the results that would come to fruition in the most efficient government—the British Commonwealth. The first real beginning for the long-sought-for solution to bring about immigration of the Jews to their homeland in Palestine, took place after the close of the First World War, fought through the years 1914 to 1918, when Great Britain issued the Balfour Declaration that laid a firm foundation for Israel's problem of forming a Jewish State in Palestine. Theodor Herzl was never known to express any dislike or caution regarding the Christian Church.

The teaching of the Old Testament was not sufficient to effect the formation of the Jewish State.

Contrary to the policy of Judaism, which ignores the greater need for help from the source of Christianity, God directed that to put the

plan of Theodor Herzl for the Jewish State into effect, another document was needed and welcomed by the leaders that followed Theodor
Herzl. This document, however, being the product of a distinct Christian
government, namely, that of the British Empire, thereby by this union,
prompted by divine compassion and love, a Gentile government was
led of God to be instrumental in giving to the Jews for the *first time* in
2,520 years the opportunity to be born into a nation — a nation of great
culture and high ideals; to give security and assistance in the formation
of the Jewish State.

It is for this reason that attention will now be directed to the two
famous documents that were given to make the dream of the Messiah,
of Theodor Herzl, a living reality. First, the document of the Balfour
Declaration, and second, the document of the State of Israel.

THE BALFOUR DECLARATION

London, England
November 2, 1917

Dear Lord Rothschild:

I have much pleasure in conveying to you on behalf of His Majesty's
Government the following declaration of Sympathy with Jewish Zionist aspirations, which has been submitted to and approved by The Cabinet.

His Majesty's Government views with favor the establishment in Palestine
of a national Home for the Jewish people, and will use their best endeavor to
facilitate the achievement of this object, it being clearly understood, that nothing shall be done which shall prejudice the civil and religious rights of existing
non-Jewish communities in Palestine, or the rights and political status enjoyed
by Jews in any other country.

I should be grateful if you would bring this declaration to the knowledge
of the Zionist Federation.

Yours sincerely,
Arthur James Balfour

This declaration made Great Britain responsible for conducting
the political relations within the borders of Palestine, allowing a certain number of Jewish immigrants to enter Palestine each year.

Because of increasing difficulties arising between Jews and Arabs
within Palestine, a new document was issued by Great Britain in 1934.
This commission brought about the partition of Palestine, giving the
coastal region mostly to the Jewish State and the Jordan region mostly
to the Arabs. In the following years there were many riots carried on
between Jews and Arabs.

The British government found it costly and difficult to carry out
its mandate over Palestine and, at last, conceded to give up its mandate,
which terminated on May 14, 1948. That very night the headquarters
of the Jewish government at Tel Aviv was moved to Jerusalem, and
the Jewish State was given the name of The State of Israel on May 15,

1948. The American government was the first to send its congratulations to the newly-formed State of Israel, with other nations following, including the United Nations.

Attention above was called to the famous declaration of the British government, called the "Balfour Declaration," November 2, 1917, which made it possible to lay the foundation for organizing Palestine as the homeland of the Jews.

Of far greater importance to the larger number of Jews that had already settled in Palestine was the declaration which was given forth by the State of Israel on the day that the Jewish government office was moved from Tel Aviv to Jerusalem to make it the Capitol of the newly-formed State of Israel.

Of great significance is the following portion of the declaration — a vital part of this newly-formed document issued by the State of Israel:

SECOND, THE DOCUMENT OF THE STATE OF ISRAEL

The State of Israel will be opened to the immigration of Jews from all countries of their Dispersion; will promote the development of the country for the benefit of all its inhabitants. It will be based on the precepts of *liberty, justice, and peace taught by the Hebrew prophets*. It will uphold the full social and political equality of all its citizens, without distinction of race, creed, or sex. It will guarantee full freedom of *conscience and worship*, education and culture. It will safeguard the safety, sanctity, and inviolability of the shrines and *holy places of all religions;* and will dedicate itself to the principles of the charter of the United Nations. . . . Our call goes out to *the Jewish people all over the world* to rally to our side in this great struggle for the fulfillment of the dream of generations — the redemption of Israel.

In this declaration of the newly-formed State of Israel, notice should be taken of four statements, or rather promises, that are most significant for the welfare of all the inhabitants of Palestine, including Arabs as well as Jewish citizens of the State of Israel.

1. *Promise is given to "safeguard the liberty, justice and peace taught by the Hebrew prophets."*

Such a thing as offering liberty to all the people of a nation was utterly unknown in the pagan world history. To Moses was given the message from God to *"proclaim liberty throughout* all the land unto all the inhabitants thereof"* (Leviticus 25:10).

The economic situation regarding property ownership was fully adjusted on this Jubilee year in Israel.

The Psalmist declared, *"I will walk at liberty"* (Psalm 119:45). But the greatest conception of liberty was shouted forth by the Hebrew prophets who declared that liberty must be based on *justice and peace* (Isaiah 61:1, 2; Jeremiah 34.8, 9).

2. *Promise of full freedom of conscience and worship.*

Man is made not only to live on a natural plane in a material universe, but he also is to live on a *supernatural plane* — not only in recognizing God as the Great Creator of the Universe, but also to render homage and worship unto Him. To Israel alone was given the right concept of *worship*. The words of Moses found in Deuteronomy 6:4, 5, should be instilled into the heart and life of every citizen of the "State of Israel" to *"Hear, O Israel: the Lord our God is one Lord: and thou shalt love the Lord thy God with all thine heart, and with all thy soul, and with all thy might."* To have the citizens of the "State of Israel" practice the right kind of worship means to render full allegiance and obedience to "love thy neighbour" (Exodus 20:17), as taught in the Ten Commandments.

3. *The sanctity of the holy places of all religions.*

This pertains to protecting the Moslem shrines in Palestine — of Jerusalem and Hebron, and of Damascus, and other places; but this promise is of great importance to the *Christian Church,* which has built sanctuaries over many sacred places as memorials to the ministry of the Lord Jesus Christ. These sanctuaries are seen in the Church of the Nativity at Bethlehem, the one built over Jacob's Well, the one at Ain Karim — the birthplace of John the Baptist, the one built in the Garden of Gethsemane, the one built in Jerusalem, and the one on Mount Olivet. These all are sacred places, attracting thousands of tourists there to worship Christ as their Lord.

4. *Promise to fulfill the dream of generations, namely the Redemption of Israel.*

The word *redemption* is a word that connotes great blessing to Israel along all material lines, as set forth in Deuteronomy 28:1-14, where God promised to bless them "in the city and in the field, in the fruit of their body and the fruit of their ground, to assure victory over their enemies in time of war, to make Israel the head and not the tail of all nations and to establish Israel to be *a holy people."*

THESE PROMISES OF "THE STATE OF ISRAEL" FULFILLED BY ISRAEL'S MESSIAH

These promises have never, as yet, been fulfilled in the history of Israel. In compliance with God's promise of *redemption,* it involves not only putting an end to their world-wide dispersion and bringing them back, but possessing, eventually, all the land from the Nile to Tigris and Euphrates rivers promised to Israel (Genesis 15:18; Isaiah 35).

Redemption for Israel involves for Israel to have God create a new heart (Psalm 51:1-10) through the atoning sacrifice promised through the Messiah John 3:1-16; Romans 11:25, 26). The *Redemption of Israel* means a saved nation through the atoning sacrifice of their long-promised Messiah (Deuteronomy 28:1-16; Isaiah 55:1-7).

When these four promises, given forth by the "State of Israel," will be fully observed Israel will become the "wonder of the world," because of its standard of liberty, justice, and truth among the nations of earth under the reign of Israel's Messiah as King and Ruler of all nations (Isaiah 9:6, 7).

Chaim Weizman was elected as first President of the State of Israel and David Ben Gurion as first Minister of the State of Israel. It was incumbent upon Ben Gurion to read the entire Proclamation of the State of Israel.

✡ *4* ✡

THE IMPACT OF DR. JOSEPH KLAUSNER

THE WORD OF GOD relates a number of instances where God provided opportunity of training to those who were destined to fulfill a work of great importance in carrying out God's plan for the benefit of mankind.

A most fascinating story along this line is that of Joseph, who in his long imprisonment received the needful training to become the ruler of Egypt next to Pharaoh. By storing up food during seven years of plenty he was able to provide food for the people of Egypt during the seven years of famine, and especially to bring Jacob and his family to Egypt there to receive training to become a great nation (Genesis 41:14-28).

Other examples can be cited, such as that of Moses in Pharaoh's palace, David in Saul's household, and Daniel taken captive to Babylon and there rising to the highest position in the rulership of that realm (Daniel 1:3-21). Notice should also be taken of the providential manner that God was directing Queen Esther to save her people, the Jews, in Medo-Persia from utter extermination.

The most noted example of providential training in life is that of Paul who, in addition to his classical training in the schools of Tarsus, was given the opportunity to sit at the feet of Gamaliel. This last opportunity became the one outstanding factor in propagating the Christian faith in various parts of Asia Minor and in Macedonia, Greece, and Rome, contributing thirteen epistles to the writings of the New Testament (Acts 26:4-17).

Attention has been called to these notable examples in Bible history for everyone to see how the providence of God rules in the affairs of mankind.

Of special interest is it to see this same principle of divine providence being carried out in the building of "Messiah's Israel." For many centuries the Jews in their dispersion among the nations of earth have been calling upon God to bring them back to their own land where they could work out their own destiny of making Israel the center of culture and religious freedom for the Jewish nation.

In our study of "Messiah's Israel," attention has been given to the study of Ezekiel's vision of the "dry bones." Can the Jews, after twenty centuries of exile, again become an independent nation in their own homeland of Palestine (Ezekiel 37:3-10)? Baron Hirsch and Lord Rothschild had spent millions and millions of dollars to organize Zion colonies for the Jews in Palestine and Argentina. They could not awaken the masses of Jews in Europe to bring them out of their age-long slumber and indifference toward assimilation with other nations. The Jews had thereby lost their God-given heritage handed down from the days of Abraham, God had given the promise to Abraham to make of him a great nation, by whom all the families of the earth were to be blessed (Genesis 12:1-3).

How was this to be brought about that Israel should again become a great nation? God alone had the answer to this perplexing problem. It was "Messiah" who declared that "I will build again the Tabernacle of David."

To Theodor Herzl was given the vision of the Messiah, who gave to him a special commission as a lad of but twelve years of age, that He would do "great and wonderful things through him for the Jews and for the whole world." Yes, it was Messiah who was preparing Theodor Herzl for his great world mission of founding the Zionist movement, which eventually resulted in the birth of the State of Israel in 1948, in the land of Palestine. Many noble men put their hands to the plow and labored vigorously to carry out the ideals for which the State of Israel was born.

THE HEBREW BIBLE TAUGHT IN "ISRAEL'S" SCHOOLS

The Hebrew language having been revived and taught in the educational institutions of Palestine in order to weld the citizens of the State of Israel into one united people, enabled them to work together for the upbuilding of the State of Israel in the land of Palestine.

What was needed was the culture of the spiritual life in Israel. How was the spiritual life of Israel to be restored? This was to be done by the *study of the Hebrew Bible* in all the schools of Palestine. Yes, the Bible is being taught, but it is only the Bible of the Old Testament. Was it God's will that Israel should remain ignorant of the life and work of the Messiah, who had been promised so distinctly by the prophets of the Old Testament?

It is true that the Church has been active in many ways to give the Gospel of the Lord Jesus Christ and also many helpful tracts to the people of Palestine.

Wonder of wonders happened in God's bringing to Palestine among the millions of immigrants one distinct man *born in Russia* in 1875, trained in the universities of Europe not only in the classical languages of Latin and Greek, but also in Hebrew and the Semitic languages. For years, in the studies that he was pursuing in the universities of Europe, this scholar was interested in the study pertaining to the "Messiah." He was not doing this from the Christian standpoint but only from the Jewish standpoint to understand the meaning of the life of Jesus the Messiah.

THE MESSIAH LED DR. JOSEPH KLAUSNER TO THE STATE OF ISRAEL

This great scholar was Dr. Joseph Klausner, doctor of philosophy and Semitic languages, who came to Palestine in the year 1920. Prior to coming to Palestine, Dr. Klausner held important positions as professor in Odessa, Russia. He saw the dangerous position of the Jews in Russia, many being killed and large numbers being sent to concentration camps and ghettos of Europe. He saw that the same fate awaited the Jews in other parts of Europe. He became interested in the Zionist movement, organized by Theodor Herzl, who set the goal for the State of Israel by his famous document, *The Jewish State,* in 1896.

England had already issued the Balfour Declaration for the millions of scattered Jews throughout the world to have liberty and security in Palestine as their homeland for all kinds of emigrants — architects, manufacturers, artists, physicians, learned men in the teaching profession, and among these we find Dr. Klausner.

I believe that "Messiah" had chosen this great scholar to make his abode in Palestine, where he could be in direct contact with vast numbers of his countrymen.

It was in 1920 that Dr. Klausner made his permanent home in Palestine, where he affiliated himself with the Hebrew University as professor of Semitic languages. He wrote large numbers of articles pertaining to Judaism for various magazines. He published numbers of books in Hebrew, among which was a massive work of three volumes on the subject, *The History of the Jews.*

TWO EPOCHAL BOOKS FOR JUDAISM AND CHRISTIANITY

Dr. Joseph Klausner also published two far-reaching volumes dealing with the relationship between Judaism and Christianity. For many years he had been gathering material from ancient and modern Jewish leaders pertaining to the relationship between Judaism and Christianity. The two volumes referred to are *Jesus of Nazareth* and *From Jesus to Paul.* Our interest here is confined primarily to Dr. Joseph Klausner's volume on *Jesus of Nazareth.* It was first published in Hebrew in 1922, and in 1925 was translated into English by Herbert Danby, D.D., a Christian scholar.

Some conception of how Dr. Klausner presents the life of Jesus is given in the following excerpts. This unusual book contains a vast amount of material not found in any modern life of Jesus.

I have selected the following five subjects from Dr. Klausner's presentation of Jesus:

1. The Triumphal Entry Into Jerusalem
2. The Garden of Gethsemane
3. Jesus' Trial Before Caiaphas
4. The Trial Before Pilate
5. The Resurrection of Jesus

Notice the meticulous care, combined with love and admiration, with which Joseph Klausner deals with the mystic writer on these and many other details of the life of Jesus.

The following selections are from the book entitled, *Jesus of Nazareth,* that was written in Palestine primarily for the Jewish settlers:

1. THE GARDEN OF GETHSEMANE. The whole story bears the hallmark of human truth; only a few details are dubious. It must have been transmitted by the Evangelists (or their sources) directly from Peter, James, or John with such simplicity and conviction, that even the ideas or tendencies of Pauline times could not obscure their memories. The sorrow and sufferings of the solitary Son of Man, profound as they are, leave on every sympathetic heart, be it the heart of a believer or unbeliever, such an impression as may never be wiped out. (Page 332)

2. JESUS' TRIAL BEFORE CAIAPHAS. Throughout the entire inquiry Jesus remained silent. At the moment such silence was best suited to his frame of mind. Jesus did not resemble in his preaching those other rebel messiahs of the time, and it was difficult to get at the truth as to his real character. The High Priest, therefore, put the direct question to Jesus, "Art thou the Messiah?" Mark here adds the words, "the Son of the Blessed." This is not a Hebrew expression and must be a later addition. It is scarcely an abbreviation of habitual "the Holy One, blessed be he." Matthew records it in more solemn form: "I adjure thee by the living God, that thou tell us whether thou be the Messiah, the Son of God.

Jesus was convinced of his messiahship; of this there is no doubt. Were it not so, he would have been nothing more than a deceiver and imposter and such men do not make history; they do not found new religions which persist for two thousand years and hold sway among five hundred million civilized people. (Emphasis by the author) When this challenge came from the High Priest, a challenge which he had already answered affirmatively at Caesarea Philippi and Bethphage, it was impossible but that the soul and feelings of Jesus, a mystic, a dreamer, and an enthusiast, should be stirred to their depths. There is no doubt that he returned a positive answer.

According to Mark's version, he answered: "Thou sayest," derived from the answer of Jesus to Pilate. Then according to all the Synoptic Gospels, Jesus added: "Ye shall see the Son of Man sitting at the right hand of the Power, and coming with the clouds of heaven." Could his enthusiastic belief in himself have led him to such lengths as to make use of this startling reference to himself? The two expressions, "Son of Man" (frequently on his lips) and "at the right hand of Power" . . . a peculiar expression in Hebrew for the Deity, show that the answer is perfectly in accord with Jesus' spirit and manner of speech.

To the High Priest the answer was sheer blasphemy — a Galilean carpenter styling himself "Son of Man" in the sense of the book of Daniel, and saying that he should sit "on the right hand of God and come with the clouds of heaven." The High Priest rent his garment, the custom of the judge who heard blasphemous words. According to the rule of *Mishua*, Jesus was not worthy of death since the "blasphemer is not guilty till he have expressly pronounced the Name," and Jesus, like a scrupulous Jew, said "Power" instead of "Yahweh." We have, however, pointed out: (a) that this was a court of law, mainly composed of Sadducees, whose President, then High Priest, was a Bethusean, and (b) that, even in Jesus' time, the Pharisees had not yet laid down the rule of procedure in the precise form which they receive in the Mishna.

After rending his garments, the Bethusean High Priest turned to the members of the Sanhedrin and asked, "What further need have we of witnesses? Ye have heard the blasphemy, what think ye?" And the Gospels add, "and they all condemned him to be worthy of death." But since there had not been actual blasphemy, it is difficult to believe that even in the opinion of the Sadducees Jesus was worthy of death, since they would see in his words nothing more than a rash fantasy; he had not "pronounced the Name" and he had not beguiled others into worshipping other gods.

At this stage there begins a long series of statements by the Evangelists, having as their object to make all the Jews (leaders, priests, scribes, and the entire Jewish population) responsible for the death and torture. Therefore, they emphasize the fact that not even one of the members of the Sanhedrin took the part of Jesus, though there was certainly one of them, Joseph of Arimathea, who was not opposed to Jesus. To pile up the Jewish guilt, all the Synoptic Gospels record how even in the presence of the judge the servants or attendants (the judge, too, according to Mark and Matthew) spat in the face of Jesus, covered his eyes and struck him with their fists and said, "Prophesy unto us, who is he that struck thee?" and they buffet him on the cheek . . .

They, therefore, bound Jesus (from which it is to be presumed that he was not bound during the judicial inquiry), and brought him to Pilate and explained to him that the Sanhedrin had condemned Jesus for assuming the role of Messiah, i.e., King of Jews; such was all the meaning that "Messiah" would convey to Pilate, the Roman. (Pages 242, 243, 244)

3. JESUS' TRIAL BEFORE PILATE. When Pilate came to Jerusalem to be present during the time of the Passover, he did not live in the Citadel of Antonio but, according to the evidence of Josephus, in the palace of Herod (one of the three towers, one of which survives under the title of "Tower of David," though it is really the "Tower of Phanael," where was a "garrison" or large barracks). Jesus was tried before Pilate in a place called the Praetorium. The Fourth Gospel calls Pilate's judgment seat by the Aramaic term "Gabbatha," in Greek meaning "stone pavement."

But all four Gospels are unanimous in relating how at every festival Pilate used to liberate to the Jews any one prisoner whom they desired. On this occasion another rebel, a zealot, Barabbas by name, who had committed murder, was waiting to be crucified. Pilate wished to liberate the "King of the Jews," Jesus, since he knew that only "for envy" had the chief priests betrayed him (but how did he know it?). The chief priests (as though they did not have more urgent business on the eve of the Passover and the eve of the Sabbath) incited the people to demand that Barabbas, and no other, should be set free.

And this the people did. On Pilate's asking, "And what shall I do to him whom ye (and not Pilate or even Jesus himself) call 'King of the Jews'? Why, what evil hath he done?" They continued to cry out, "Crucify him!" Then the helpless Pilate was "compelled" to do the people's will, and to free Barabbas. Jesus he scourged and gave up to be crucified.

A more important point, however, is the fact that the right to free a criminal after condemnation belonged only to the Emperor and it is, on the whole, most unlikely that in all his four books Josephus found no opportunity to mention such a noteworthy custom as that of liberating a prisoner before the Passover. A few of the priestly caste had condemned Jesus to death and given him up to Pilate, primarily because of their dread of this same Pilate, and only incidentally because of their annoyance at his "cleansing of the Temple," and because Jesus mocked "at the words of the wise," and spoke ill of the Temple and, what was more serious, because of his blasphemy in thinking himself the "Son of Man coming with the clouds of heaven," who should sit at the right hand of God.

Through fear of the Roman tyrant, these who were then the chief men among the Jews delivered up Jesus to this tyrant. Jews took no further part in the actual trial and crucifixion. Pilate, the "man of blood," was responsible for the rest. The Jews as a nation were far less guilty of the death of Jesus than the Greeks as a nation were guilty of the death of Socrates. *But who now would think of avenging the blood of Socrates, the Greek, upon his countryman, the present Greek race? Yet these nineteen hundred years past the world has gone on avenging the blood of Jesus, the Jew, upon his countrymen, the Jews, who have already paid the penalty, and still go on paying the penalty in rivers and torrents of blood.* (Pages 245, 247, 248 — emphasis by the author)

4. THE CRUCIFIXION OF JESUS. Crucifixion is the most terrible and cruel death which man has ever devised for taking vengeance on his fellowmen. . . . Crucifixion was, therefore, a penalty characteristic of the Romans . . . . it is well known that the Roman officials frequently crucified Jews. . . . There was no real justice in the case of Jesus. Neither the Sanhedrin nor Pilate probed deeply enough to discover that Jesus was no rebel, and a Sanhedrin court of law would not pay scrupulous regard to the fact whether Jesus was or was not a "blasphemer," as "false prophet," or any inciter to idolatry, in the Biblical sense.

Of the charge which the Sanhedrin brought against Jesus — blasphemy and Messianic pretentions — Pilate took account of the second only. Jesus was the "King, Messiah," and so from Pilate's standpoint (since he could have no notion of the spiritual approach to the Hebrew messianic idea), he was "King of the Jews." This was treason against the Roman Emperor, for which the Lex Juliana knew but one penalty and punishment — death. The prescribed death of rebel traitors was crucifixion. The superscription of the Cross was in three languages — Aramaic, Greek, and Latin. . . . The "King of the Jews" is common to all Gospels. *The inference is clear* that Jesus was crucified as "King, Messiah," which for non-Jews could only mean, "King of the Jews." (Pages 349, 350)

This renders untenable any hypothesis to the effect that Jesus never declared himself as Messiah even at the last, and that he remained no more than a Pharisee "Rab," an "apocalyptic prophet," or, a "forerunner of the Messiah." He was delivered up to Pilate as a false Messiah, and as such he was crucified by Pilate. . . .

The Messiah was crucified (the Son of man was hanged, and so became a "curse of God") by uncircumcised heathen, and yet no help from on High. The great and gracious God, Father of all men, his own heavenly Father, especially near to him, his beloved Son and Messiah — his heavenly Father came not to his help, nor released him from his agony, nor saved him by a miracle

Joseph bought the graveclothes, wrapped up the body and placed it in a tomb hewn in the rock . . . . at the mouth of the tomb a heavy stone was rolled . . . . And so the burial ended. Here ends the life of Jesus, and there begins the history of Christianity. (Pages 353, 355)

5. THE ETHICAL TEACHING OF JESUS. The main strength of Jesus lay in his ethical teaching. If we omitted the miracles and a few mythical sayings, which tended to deify the Son of Man, and reserved only the moral precepts and parables, the Gospels would count as one of the most wonderful collections of ethical teaching in the world. . . . The tragedy of his dreadful death, which came upon Jesus wrongly (though in accordance with the justice of the time), added a crown of Divine glory both to the personality and to the teaching. Later arose the legend of the resurrection heightening every virtue — and Jesus the Jew became half Jew and half Gentile, and began to hold that supernatural rank which is his today among hundreds of millions of mankind. (Pages 408, 414)

These selections, taken from the book, *Jesus of Nazareth,** manifest a deep insight and understanding of Dr. Joseph Klausner. They were written with an unbiased mind and sympathetic heart, that cause one to wonder how this profound Jewish scholar could ever relate these epochal events in the ministry of the "Messiah" with such reverence and devotion of spirit as is seen in this great volume.

I recommend highly that every reader purchase the book, *Jesus of Nazareth*.

THE IMPACT OF DR. JOSEPH KLAUSNER ON THE STATE OF ISRAEL

Dr. Joseph Klausner stands forth in the history of Judaism as a pillar of great strength. He was not afraid to take for his main theme of scholarship the publishing of the book entitled, *Jesus of Nazareth*.

The attitude of Jews of past centuries was that of utter repudiation and contemptuous mention of Jesus as the promised Messiah for the Jews and for the world. Torrents of blood were shed of Jews by the hands of professed followers of Jesus. This fact had blinded their eyes with unbelief so that they could see nothing good in the life and teaching of Jesus.

Whatever there is to be said of Dr. Klausner's concept of the life of Jesus, he had commanded great respect and attention as a scholar of profound knowledge. He used it to clarify the difference existing between Jews and Christians regarding the claims of Jesus as being the promised Messiah set forth both in the Old as well as the New Testament.

His book was not intended for the Christian world, but solely for the Jews. The proof for this is that the mammoth volume was written in Hebrew. The writing of this extraordinary volume was the first time that a Jewish scholar has ever attempted to give to the Jews an astound-

* These quotations are given by special permission of the publishers of the book, *Jesus of Nazareth*, The MacMillan Company, New York, 1959.

ing work of scholarship on the life of Jesus. Dr. Klausner's purpose was to remove the age-long bitterness and even hatred which Jews showed at even the mention of the name of Jesus.

DR. KLAUSNER'S GREAT INTEREST IN THE MESSIAH

What had moved Dr. Klausner to use the word *Messiah* for an appellation of Jesus repeatedly was not to prove that he was a disciple of Jesus, defending His teaching and His claims to being the promised Messiah.

While he could strongly affirm the declaration of Jesus' innocence made repeatedly by Pilate, yet he finds at least one barrier: "Judaism cannot accept Jesus as their national Messiah." The reason they cannot fully accept the Sermon on the Mount is that Jesus taught that His teaching superseded that of Moses.

Another barrier to Judaism's acceptance of the teaching of Jesus was His statement that "The Father in Heaven makes his sun to shine upon the righteous and evil, and sends His rain upon the righteous and the wicked." The attitude of Judaism is that God executes judgment upon the wicked instead of sending blessings upon the wicked.

It is not the purpose of this writer to enter into any theological differences between the teaching of Judaism and that of Christianity.

THE ETHICAL TEACHING OF JESUS

It is the right of this writer, however, to examine the reasons why Dr. Klausner accepts mainly the ethical and parabolic teaching of Jesus. In so doing he is depriving Jesus of the right to claim Himself as being the only Messiah that had ever met the Bible requirement of deity to that of humanity of Jesus.

Whatever shortcoming may be found by any critic of Dr. Klausner's most useful book, it fills an epochal need in elaborating on the theme of this book. It is the contention of this writer that the State of Israel could never have come into existence without collaboration of a Divine Messiah, as appeared in Theodor Herzl's dream and as being fulfilled in the world-wide work of the Zionist movement.

Wonderful as are the writings of Dr. Klausner, attention is now called to a definite weakness that is manifested in this majestic presentation of the life of *Jesus of Nazareth* by its author. One proof of the intensive study of the New Testament made by Dr. Klausner in his book under consideration is the vast amount of quotations and references to the Four Gospels and some other portions of the New Testament. Herein lies a weakness in the references given in that Dr. Klausner cannot go on beyond the trial and crucifixion and death of Jesus.

With reference to the resurrection of Jesus from the dead, Dr.

Klausner accepts it more as *a mere vision than as a living reality,* that Jesus arose from the dead in a bloodless body, yet one having "flesh and bones" (Luke 24:39), yet endowed with immortality, which made it possible for Jesus as the "Son of Man" to ascend to Heaven and be "seated at the right hand of God" (Mark 16:19). Dr. Klausner desires to see the day that the ethical codes of Jesus "be stripped of wrappings of miracles and mysticism" — then the glory of Jesus will indeed *be accepted by Judaism.*

Now, going to the task of examining the *516 references* (five full double-column pages) given of the life and teaching of Jesus in the *Four* Gospels: of these, *198 are given in the Gospel of Matthew, 168 in the Gospel of Mark, 128 from the Gospel of Luke, and only 22 references in the Gospel of John.*

THE EMPHASIS OF MESSIAH'S DEITY

From the three chapters, Matthew 5, 6, and 7, are given *28 references,* but from the entire Gospel of John only 22 references. In deciding the literary value of the Four Gospels, Matthew has 60% new material, Mark 10% new material, Luke 40% new material, but John has 90% new material. The Gospel of John was written at the close of the first century, after the Synoptic Gospels had all been written.

Is it reasonable for one writing the story of the life of Jesus to set aside the valuable contents of this Gospel that was written primarily to establish the deity and divinity of Jesus? It is important to see what chapters were omitted from this Gospel and why they were omitted.

In the fifth chapter of John the story of the impotent man at the pool of Bethesda is followed by a discourse of Jesus in which He states that the "Scriptures (Old Testament) testify of Me" (verse 39). Jesus told His enemies, "Had ye *believed Moses,* ye would have believed me: *for he wrote of me.* But if ye believe not his writings, how shall ye believe my words?" (verses 46, 47). Chapter 6 is omitted, relating the story of the feeding of the five thousand, followed by a long discourse of Jesus, in which He declared that He was the *Bread of God which came down from Heaven, and giveth life unto the world* (John 6:51). Jesus said, "He that eateth my flesh, and drinketh my blood, dwelleth in me, and I in him" (verses 49-58). Chapter 9 is omitted, telling the story of the man born blind, followed by the statement that when Jesus declared that He was the Messiah, the blind man whose sight had been restored so that he could see worshiped Him (verse 38). Chapter 10 is omitted, giving the teaching of Jesus' being the Good Shepherd. When Jesus declared, "I and my Father are one," the Jews took up stones to stone Him (John 10:30, 31) for being guilty of blasphemy.

The greatest omission is leaving out the entire chapters — 13, 14,

15, 16, and 17 — which constitute the discourse of Jesus in the Upper Room in Jerusalem, giving His last and greatest legacy of five distinct promises of the Holy Spirit, the Third Person of the Divine Trinity; and four distinct promises to henceforth pray in the name of Jesus, and finally ending with Jesus' High Priestly prayer, which constitutes the "Holy of holies," the inmost sanctuary of Jesus' life as Man's Saviour and Redeemer.

Dr. Klausner considered it wise for him to omit these chapters, which most emphatically set forth the Deity of Jesus as the Son of God, and the Deity of the Holy Spirit as the Guide, Counselor, Convictor, and Teacher for the followers of Jesus. He knew that to use the Fourth Gospel as minutely as he did the Sermon on the Mount or the three Synoptic Gospels, would destroy the *Monotheism of Judaism* and in its place substitute the Trinitarianism of Christianity.

The Gospel of John deals primarily with the place that Jesus holds as the *Messiah,* the Founder and Builder of Israel and the Kingdom of God, whereas the Synoptic Gospels emphasize to a larger extent the *humanity* of Jesus, obtained through the Virgin Birth, giving His life to "do good" in healing the sick and raising the dead.

The Gospel of John deals with the *Messiah's* being in the beginning as the Word (the eternal *Logos* — John 1:1-3). He not only was "with God," but He "was God" (John 1:1, 2) and therefore He was able to make "all things" (in the entire universe). "All things were made by him; and without him was not any thing made that was made" (John 1:3). Now look at verse 14, that declares that "The Word was made flesh, and dwelt among us, (and we beheld his glory as of the only begotten [virgin birth] of the Father,) full of grace and truth" (John 1:14).

ISRAEL BOUND INSEPARABLY TO THE MESSIAH

Jesus is therefore bound inseparably to Messiah. Jesus came "to the lost sheep of *the house of Israel"* (Matthew 10:6 and 15:24) and Israel is bound inseparably to its Founder, "the Messiah." *Messiah and Israel belong to each other.*

Therefore Israel, still in its unbelief, not only in its dispersion but also in the "State of Israel," needs to be taught the *whole* message of the Gospel — not only those parts dealing with the *ethical* teaching of right living but especially those parts pertaining to the *redeeming work of the Messiah.*

Dr. Joseph Klausner has laid the foundation for this presentation of the Messiah in proving to the Jews of Palestine through his book, written in Hebrew, *Jesus of Nazareth*, that from the human view, Jesus was the "Messiah." Israel needs not only a human but it needs especially a *Divine Messiah,* and this it can only obtain by having access to the whole *New Testament,* with its glorious message of fulfillment of the Old Testament Scriptures pertaining to the Coming Messiah.

It is praiseworthy that the Old Testament is being taught in public schools of Palestine according to the law of the State of Israel.

It is also praiseworthy that at this writing one hundred thousand copies of the entire Bible in Hebrew, Old and New Testaments, are being printed for free distribution in the cities and villages of Israel for those who have a desire to read it.

In both cases just mentioned, the State of Israel is being prepared to become a greater Messianic power for Jews scattered throughout the world to bring to them the full knowledge of God's plan of Redemption.

JUDAISM DAILY PRAYS FOR THE MESSIAH

Right here is a delicate situation when approached on this subject in Judaism. It is true that Judaism daily prays for the coming of the Messiah. This prayer, recorded in the *Standard Prayer Book,* reads as follows, on page 109: "I believe with perfect faith in the *Coming of the Messiah,* and though He tarry, *I will wait daily for His Coming."*

This prayer, though offered with a sincere heart, is not offered according to the Old Testament. The Old Testament (Daniel 9:25-27) represents the Messiah as coming at a definite period on earth — 483 years after the rebuilding of the wall of Jerusalem by Nehemiah, which is dated 445 B.C. These 483 years arrive at A.D. 32, pointing directly to the greatest spectacular event in Jesus' ministry, namely, His Triumphal Entry into Jerusalem (John 12:12-16). The statement of Daniel of the Messiah being "cut off" (Daniel 9:26) dates directly to the crucifixion of Jesus. The Coming of the "Messiah," foretold by Daniel, *covers the complete ministry from the beginning to the end.* Is there any justification for "waiting" any more for His appearance as the Messiah?

Dr. Joseph Klausner has answered this question. In writing his supreme book in Hebrew, the equal of which never had appeared, he never questions the right of *Jesus' being called the Messiah.* He also allows the legitimate right of Jesus calling Himself the "Son of Man."

One of the strongest proofs given by Jesus concerning His Deity is His frequent use of the word *sent,* or rather the words being *"sent from the Father,"* which occurs thirty-two times in the four Gospels. It is noteworthy that of these *thirty-two,* only *six references* are given in the *three Synoptic Gospels* — two in Matthew, two in Mark, two in Luke. This meaningful word, *sent,* is given *twenty-two times* in the *Gospel of John — four times as many as are found in the Synoptic Gospels.*

At any rate, it can be seen from the record of the life of Jesus as set forth in the Gospel of John that Jesus did not hide His Messiahship under a bushel, but clearly and boldly in His controversies with His adversaries testified that He was *"sent from the Father"* into this world.

This meant definitely that He existed before coming into this world as being the "Son of God."

In order to clarify this great issue of Jesus' using the word *sent* twenty-two times in the Gospel of John, referring to Himself as being the Divine Messenger to this sin-cursed earth to fulfill the destiny of His being the Messiah — the following ten distinct references of Jesus' use of the word *sent* are herewith given.

1. ". . . My meat is to do the will of him that *sent me,* and to finish his work" (John 4:34).

2. "Verily, verily, I say unto you, He that heareth my word, and believeth on him that *sent me,* hath everlasting life, . . ." (John 5:24).

3. "I came *down from heaven,* not to do mine own will, but the will of him that *sent me"* (John 6:38).

4. ". . . I am not come of myself, but He that *sent me* is true . . ." (John 7:28).

5. ". . . he that *sent me* is with me . . ." (John 8:28, 29).

6. "I must work the works of him that *sent me,* while it is day: the night cometh when no man can work" (John 9:4).

7. ". . . the Father which *sent me,* he gave me a commandment, what I should say, and what I should speak" (John 12:49).

8. ". . . he that receiveth me receiveth him that *sent me"* (John 13:20).

9. ". . . the word which ye hear is not mine, but the Father's which *sent me"* (John 14:24).

10. "But now I go my way to him that *sent me* . . ." (John 16:5).

These 10 out of the 22 references of the term Jesus used of Himself in the Gospel of John as being *sent* from the Father in Heaven are sufficient to prove His Deity and Divinity as being the *"Messiah"* foretold by the prophet Daniel in Daniel 9:25, 26, and even before Adam, and even before the creation of the universe, for we have proof, given in Revelation 13:8, that the "Lamb" (Messiah) was "slain from the foundation of the world."

Notice that it was not the *"Son of Man"* that "was God" before the foundation of the world. It was the "Son of God" as the second Person in the Trinity, that was "with God" and that "was God" (John 1:1).

The "Son of God" did not become the "Son of Man" *except by the virgin birth* (Isaiah 7:14). Of thirty-two years of Jesus' life, only three-and-a-half were given to His ministry as the Son of Man, as Jesus declared that the "Son of Man is come to seek and to save that which was lost" (Luke 19:10).

THE COMING OF THE MESSIAH IN THE BOOK OF DANIEL

Attention has been called to the fact that the Book of Daniel sets forth the coming of the Messiah as coming *into Jerusalem* acclaimed as King with hosannas by the multitude (John 12:13).

Jesus in His reply to Caiaphas' inquiry as to whether He was the "Messiah" (Matthew 26:63-65), affirmed that He was the "Christ [Messiah], the Son of God." Caiaphas considered it unnecessary to refer to Jesus as the "Son of Man," for He was right before the High Priest.

THE SON OF MAN SEATED AT THE RIGHT HAND OF GOD

Notice Jesus' further great announcement of Himself that He would take His rightful place in Heaven above the angels, cherubim, or seraphim. Jesus, as the Son of Man, had never been in Heaven but only on earth during the entire time of thirty-two years, but now, on the very day that He was summoned before the Council, He could say: "Hereafter shall ye see the *'Son of Man'* [Daniel 7:13, 14] sitting on the right hand of power." Then He said further of the "Son of Man" that He would be coming in *clouds of heaven"* (Matthew 26:64).

That is exactly what the Scriptures had foretold of the Messiah in Daniel 7:14. He must first finish His work as *Messiah on earth* before the Son of Man will come in the "clouds of heaven" to be seated on David's throne in Jerusalem to establish His Messianic kingdom (Isaiah 9:6, 7).

The chronological order of Messiah's coming as set forth in the Old Testament is:

1. The *Virgin Birth of Jesus* (Isaiah 7:14) announced to the shepherds *as Christ* (the Messiah) (Luke 2:4).

2. The *earthly ministry of the Messiah* set forth in Isaiah 61:1 and Luke 4:18.

3. The Triumphal Entry into Jerusalem (Daniel 9:24-26; Zechariah 9:9; Matthew 21:1-9).

4. The *Crucifixion of the Messiah,* King of the Jews (Isaiah 53; John 19:6, 7).

5. The *Resurrection of the Messiah* (Psalm 30:12; John 20:1-9).

6. The *Ascension of Messiah* (Psalm 24:7-9; Luke 24:49-53).

7. The *Second Coming of the Son of God* as Messiah, the Son of Man (Daniel 7:13, 14; 7:27; Isaiah 9:6, 7; Daniel 2:45; Matthew 26:64).

This is the goal that the "State of Israel" must reach to be "Messiah's Israel." Messiah will not perpetuate the democratic government which Zionism has chosen for the "State of Israel." The nature of government must be of a higher, better, more enduring order than that of any government on earth that has ever existed. It must be a *One Man* (Messiah) form of government — a theocracy, that will rule with "a rod of iron" in justice and righteousness. All world-dominions will give place to the rule of the Messiah (Isaiah 9:6, 7). Israel will then be the head of all nations.

ISRAEL DESTINED TO BE THE HEAD OF ALL NATIONS

Now read Deuteronomy 28:1-10; Isaiah 35; and Isaiah 62:1-7. This will be "Messiah's Israel" in deed and in truth.

Earlier we called attention to various persons in the Scriptures who proved themselves providential characters in the plan of God.

This claim was also made by the writer for Dr. Joseph Klausner. It is true that Dr. Klausner did not obtain through his intensive study of the Scriptures a full vision of the Messiah. However, that does not diminish the tremendous value of his book on *Jesus of Nazareth*.

Dr. Joseph Klausner's contribution of a sound, impartial inimitable view of the Messiah for Judaism will never be forgotten in the annals of the State of Israel.

An important Bible character that can be applied to Dr. Joseph Klausner is that of Nicodemus, who was the only member of the Sanhedrin who ever had the courage to openly defend Jesus in the Sanhedrin (John 7:45-53) and later, with Joseph of Arimathaea, gave a royal burial to Jesus (John 19:39).

It can be truly said of Dr. Joseph Klausner that he was and still is the *Nicodemus of Judaism* for his fearless courage to make the State of Israel realize their need of making the life and teaching of Jesus a vital part of the knowledge and culture to be imparted not only to the residents of Palestine, but also to revitalize the spiritual culture of his countrymen of the Diaspora, the scattered Jewish nation throughout the world.

It was said of Esther in the time of Israel's greatest devastating calamity and disaster, by Mordecai, her uncle, "Who knoweth whether thou art come to the kingdom for such a time as this?" (Esther 4:14-16).

Of Dr. Joseph Klausner no one need have any doubt that God brought him into the State of Israel "*for such a time as this*," to pour out his mind and heart in teaching the State of Israel the need for a fuller understanding of Jesus' being the Messiah. In the closing chapter of his book, *Jesus of Nazareth*, Dr. Klausner declares that "No Jew can overlook the value of Jesus and His teaching from the point of view of universal history."

DAVID BEN GURION'S INTENSE INTEREST IN THE BIBLE FOR THE BIBLE LAND

DAVID BEN GURION was born of Jewish parents in the town of Plinsk, Poland, in the year 1886. His father's name was Gorgton Green. He followed the profession of law. David was the sixth child in the family. His parents were devout Jews seeking to bring up their children in the Jewish faith. They believed that the Hebrew language should be used not only in the synagogue to worship God, but that it was necessary to teach their children the Hebrew tongue at home so that they would grow up to be devout believers in the teaching of Moses and the prophets.

Russia, the original home of the family, was known in the nineteenth century for engaging in anti-Semitism. Large numbers of Jews became a prey to their hatred and were massacred, their bodies being laid in the streets like cords of wood. Many of the Jews belonged to the "Lovers of Zion," made up of a small gathering of Jews that had a great love for Palestine, their homeland. The father of David was greatly interested in getting the Jews of their city to come to his home to learn more of what the Old Testament taught about the Jews being given Palestine as their homeland and that support should be given to the colonies that Lord Rothschild was organizing in Palestine.

David's mother passed away when he was in his teens and it was left to the father to bring up his family in the Jewish faith in the face of the rage of anti-Semitism that was raging in Russia at that time.

The father determined to leave Russia and take his family to Poland, where they would have more protection and liberty.

Realizing that David was a gifted child, he sought to train him to be either an editor or a lawyer. He gave him help in public speaking, so that he could talk freely to others on the great issue of Socialism, that promised to give to the Jews a greater measure of liberty for the common people, including the Jews that were confined in ghettos in many of the cities of Eastern Europe.

72

How David Ben Gurion Became Interested in Palestine

David was becoming an exciting orator to arouse interest not only for Socialism but also for the Jews to return to their own homeland in Palestine. His father had received a copy of Theodor Herzl's book, *The Jewish State,* while yet in Russia.

At this time two great events influenced David's life: one, the revolution in Russia that brought about the downfall of the Czar's regime and gave birth to a new form of government — communism; the other, the issuance of the Balfour Declaration in 1917.

Wrestling between these two great movements, David decided to go to Palestine to devote himself to taking his place among the common laboring people in Palestine. His father protested strongly at his son's giving up his educational advantages in Poland to become only a laboring man. David persisted in carrying out his plan and with a company of other Jewish lads went to Palestine. He loved the sacred soil of the Holy Land and determined that he would devote his energy to promote the cause which had avowed to build Palestine as a homeland for the Jews.

Having a great gift for writing as well as for oratory, he was induced to found a new socialistic magazine in Jerusalem. He was to join the editorial staff. In writing his first article for this magazine he wanted to conceal his identity, and instead of signing it with his rightful name, David Green, he chose to sign it *David Ben Gurion,* Ben being the Hebrew for *son,* and Gurion in Hebrew designating a *young lion.* From that time on he became known the world over as *David Ben Gurion.*

In working out his destiny, he proved his capacity for leadership as a lion known for sagacity of powerful statesmanship, becoming known as one of the "ten greatest world leaders."

He organized the Jewish army, bringing it to a high standard of efficiency and patriotism. As time went on he held the highest offices in the newly-formed State of Israel. He was among the first to sign the Declaration of Independence on May 14, 1948, and since then has filled the office of Secretary of Defense, The Jewish Agency, and other great offices in the government of Israel.

The State of Israel Not a Religious Institution

Let the reader now remember this, that the *State of Israel* was not founded as a religious institution nor for a Messianic State. Theodor Herzl distinctly disclaims this. He promised liberty and freedom for every citizen of the *State of Israel,* be he Christian, Arab, or Jew. Nor can it be said of Chaim Weizman, nor of David Ben Gurion, that they sought in any way to project the religious issue as the one of greatest importance.

One, therefore, cannot be surprised that many things have happened in the *State of Israel* that are not in accord with justice or righteousness, as is seen in the perplexing problem of the vast number of refugees eking out a bare existence at the borders of the Jordan river.

This writer has no calling of God to discuss issues, dealing with such perplexing problems as that of the relationship of Israel with the Arab people.

There are those who claim that David Ben Gurion is largely responsible for the refugee problem.

Be that as it may, there is no question as to the high esteem that Ben Gurion has held in the State of Israel as well as in the whole world.

Whatever failings and imperfection David Ben Gurion has manifested during his long career of more than sixty years, he enjoys the highest esteem of his fellow-citizens in the State of Israel. As an evidence of that well-earned esteem, attention is now called to a citation which he received from the Hadassah Hospital in Jerusalem.

This citation is recorded in the last sentences of the splendid *Biography of David Ben Gurion, An Extraordinary Man,** written by Robert St. John, published by Doubleday and Company, Garden City, N.Y., 1959, as follows:

> Man of action, and man of thought, his life has been dedicated to the survival of the Jews as a people, the establishment of Israel as a State, and to the rights of man everywhere.
>
> What insight derived from wisdom, what perseverance and courage!
>
> Inspired by prophetic vision, guided always by spiritual teachings of the Holy Bible, he has translated the moral concepts of our ancient heritage into a humane and democratic leadership, thus assuring for Israel and himself a unique and honorable place in the history of man's struggle for freedom.

Do you notice in the above citation of the Hadassah Hospital that special emphasis is called to David Ben Gurion's having been guided by the *"spiritual teachings of the Bible"?*

In the closing chapter of the biography of David Ben Gurion, Robert St. John furnished a most interesting story of a Bible Quiz, which is conducted annually in Palestine, in which David Ben Gurion showed a special, vital interest.

Not at any time in Israel's long history has any such performance been given as was done on this tenth anniversary of the *State of Israel.* The Prime Minister proved his great interest in calling Amos Hachman, the winner, to his office, himself knowing how to ask a difficult question, to which the right answer was immediately given.

* Used by permission.

The Old Testament Scriptures in Hebrew are made a vital study in the schoolrooms of Israel. They put many nations, including America, to shame. Yes, America will do well to make the Bible a vital part of our national school system. There was a day in American history when Bible events were taught in the public schools. Our colleges and universities were organized for preparing men for the ministry. The trend today in American education is to exclude the Bible and give way to our young generation.

In closing this study of Israel's vital interest in the Bible, it should be known that large numbers of Hebrew Old and New Testaments are being printed and distributed in country villages and cities of Israel, with a good response from many. They read not only the Hebrew Scriptures of the Old Testament, but especially those of the Hebrew New Testament. Thus the Israeli readers will read not only the two Messianic references found in the Old Testament (in Daniel 9:25) but also the numerous references to Messiah (i.e., *"Christ"* in the Greek) in the New Testament.

A new day is dawning in Israel — that of the hunger after the Bread of Life, given fully in the New Testament Scriptures.

DAVID BEN GURION'S LOFTY IDEALS FOR THE STATE OF ISRAEL

The outcome of the rise and development of Israel is primarily the result of the dream given to Theodor Herzl when but a lad of twelve years, in which he had a vision of the Messiah, who promised to do "great and wonderful things for the Jews, and for the whole world."

During the thirty-four years of Theodor Herzl's labors, implanting the idea of a Jewish State in Palestine in spite of the criticism and rejection of his plan, he succeeded primarily through his publication of but one document to interest the three greatest, most effective men of great talent and ability to fill a tremendous part in the real, living State of Israel, founded in 1948, which happened about a half century after Theodor Herzl's death in 1904.

THE WORK OF THE TRIUMVIRATE TO BUILD THE STATE OF ISRAEL

The three greatest characters in the building of the *Jewish State,* were, undoubtedly, those of Chaim Weizman, David Ben Gurion, and Joseph Klausner. In their special fields of research, they contributed an immense wealth of knowledge to make the *Jewish State* "a place of culture" not only for Palestine but as an example of efficiency to the whole world.

The first of these three great men to come to Palestine was David Ben Gurion, who reached the shores of Palestine in 1910, whereas Joseph Klausner did not move to Palestine until 1920. Chaim Weizman did not take an active part within the *State of Israel* until the years from 1932-1952, during which he became President of the Hebrew University. He was teaching science in universities long before he came to Palestine and was active as head of the World Zionist Movement a number of years, but at last he gave his whole effort to raising the standard of education for the *State of Israel*. As for Ben Gurion, he had already absorbed Theodor Herzl's famous document of the *Jewish State* in Russia before 1910.

These three men, who collaborated together, may rightly be called the *Triumvirate of Jerusalem*. Of these three, Joseph Klausner was definitely the most religious; whereas Weizman gave the first clue to Jewish independence in Palestine. He enabled the British government to know how to make *TNT* through a simple method — that of using chestnuts as the main ingredient.

This brief study of these three great men resolves that of them Ben Gurion becomes the chief for his directing service to Palestine as Minister of Defense and Prime Minister for more or less sixty years, so that, in other words, Ben Gurion had an opportunity to absorb the useful services in the State of Israel of Chaim Weizman (between 1894 and 1952) and Joseph Klausner (to the age of 78 years).

Dr. Klausner's wonderful service as President of the Hebrew University lasted from 1920-1958. He was born in 1874, making his life-span that of 75 years. We find in this brief study that Ben Gurion had 51 years of residence in Palestine, while Weizman had 29 years, and Joseph Klausner was in residence in Palestine 41 years. This makes Ben Gurion to have been active the longest of any of this triumvirate.

THE LOFTY IDEALS OF DAVID BEN GURION

Now we come to the vital matter of this chapter on Ben Gurion — that it was left to his honor as the Senior Worker for Palestine either to direct or to supervise the great supplement on *Israel* in the November, 1961, issue of the *Atlantic* magazine, with its leading article written by Ben Gurion.

Excerpts from an article, entitled
THE KINGDOM OF THE SPIRIT
by David Ben Gurion
Published in *The Atlantic Magazine* of November, 1961

1. In ancient times our most important neighbors were Egypt and Babylon. The struggle with these mighty neighbors was political and military as well as cultural and spiritual. Israeli prophets spoke out against the spiritual influence of these neighbors on Israel's religion, moral conception, and social patterns. They advanced faith in one God, the unity of the human race, and the dominion of justice. Today the Jewish people, having held their own, appear again in the same area in which they evolved. The entire environment in the region has been

completely transformed since Bible days. The languages, religions, and civilization, and the very names of the ancient Middle Eastern people, have disappeared,
yet Israel though largely uprooted for two millenniums continued its ancient traditions of language, faith, and culture as it were uninterruptedly.

2. The Jewish people's most difficult test came, however, after the birth
of Christianity. Unlike the culture of Egypt, Babylon, Greece and Rome, Christianity was not foreign to Judaism. It stemmed from Jewish people, its inspiration was from a Jew, whose ideas belonged within the framework of Jewish con-
cepts of his day. The new faith was given its direction away from Judaism by
Saul of Tarsus. Called Paul, he was the son of a Jewish citizen of Rome, living
in Syria. He was brought up in the spirit of Judaism and was a zealous Pharisee;
but as a Diaspora Jew he had absorbed something of Hellenistic culture. Once
a fanatical opponent of the Christians he saw the light, came to believe in Jesus
as the Son of God, and gave new direction to the sect . . . .

3. Many of the Western Jews accepted an assimilation movement, which
threatened to overwhelm the Jewish people. The Jewish historic will withstand
even this powerful challenge. Emancipation instead led to new expressions of its
national character and Messianic yearnings. Much of Jewry divested itself of its
theocratic garb and adopted a secular outlook, but its attachment to its historic
origin and its homeland became stronger; its ancient language awoke to new
life, a secular Hebrew literature was created and there arose the movement of
"Chibbet Zion" (Lovers of Zion) and Zionism. The emancipation which came
from without was transformed into self-emancipation – a movement of liberation
from the bonds of dependence on others and life in foreign lands and the first
foundation was laid for the resuscitation of the national independence in the
national homeland. . . . In 1917 the Balfour Declaration was issued. For the first
time since the Destruction of the Temple, the Jews were recognized by a world
power as a separate nation, and they were promised the right to return to their
land. The League of Nations, established at the end of World War I, gave international confirmation to the Balfour Declaration and recognized the historic
connection of the Jewish people with their ancient homeland. . . .

4. The Jewish people, after two thousand years and tribulation in every
part of the globe, having arrived at the first step of renewed sovereignty in the
land of their origin, will not abandon their historic vision and great spiritual
heritage – the aspiration to combine their national redemption with universal
redemption for all the people of the world. Even the greatest tragedy ever
wrought by man against a people – the Hitlerite holocaust which destroyed one-
third of the Jewish people, did not dim the profound faith of the Jews, including
those who went to their death in the ovens of Europe, in their national redemption and in that of mankind.

5. The Jewish people will not submit to foreign bondage or surrender to
the great and powerful in determining their future and their road to the vision
of the Latter Days. In the State of Israel there is no barrier between the Jew
and the man within us. Independence is indivisible.

6. The faith of the Jewish people in the superiority of the spirit is bound
up with their belief in the value of man. Man, according to the faith of the
Jewish people, was created in the image of God. There could be no more profound, exalted, or far-reaching expression of the great importance and value of
man than this, for the concept of God in Judaism symbolized the apex of goodness, beauty, justice, and truth. Human life in the eyes of the Jewish people
is precious and sacred. The sons of man, created in the image of God, are equal
in rights. They are an end in themselves, not a means. It is no wonder that the

sages of the people based the law on one great principle: "And thou shalt love thy neighbor as thyself." Love of one's neighbor applies not only to Jewish citizens — "the stranger that sojourneth with you shall be unto you as the home-born among you, and thou shalt love him as thyself; for ye were strangers in the land of Egypt." . . . Unlike the other ancient people, ours did not look backward to a legendary Golden Age in the past, which has gone never to return, but turned their gaze to the future — to the Latter Days, in which the earth will be filled with the knowledge as the waters cover the sea, when nations will "beat their swords into plowshares," and nation shall not lift up sword against nation, or learn war any more.

That was the historic philosophy which the prophets of Israel bequeathed to their own people and through these people to the best of all nations.

This expectation and faith in the future stood by our people during the tribulation of their long journey through history and have brought us to the beginning of our national redemption, when we can also see the first gleams of redemption for the whole of humanity.

AN ANALYSIS OF DAVID BEN GURION'S GREAT DOCUMENT

This article of Ben Gurion on the "Kingdom of the Spirit" must be considered as a rare classic for all future in the annals of Israel's history. In order for the reader to be able to consider the high points of the great document, a brief analysis follows:

1. Israel's prophets spoke out against their being influenced by Egypt and Babylon.

2. Israel's belief of worshiping one God and the majesty of the unity of man.

3. Israel, though uprooted in the Diaspora, maintained her old traditions.

4. Christianity stemmed from a Jew, whose teaching was within the framework of Israel's tradition.

5. Paul led away Christianity from the teaching given in Judaism.

6. Paul, "After he saw the light," believed in Jesus as the "Son of God."

7. Many Jews weakened their faith by assimilation with other nations.

8. *Emancipation of the Jews gave new expression to Messianic yearning.*

9. Attachment to their homeland in Palestine caused a great awakening in the Diaspora.

10. The secular Hebrew language was created in Palestine.

11. The Jews in the Diaspora awakened through Zionism to a longing for their homeland in Palestine.

12. The Balfour Declaration enabled the Jews for the first time to recognize their independence from other nations.

13. The Jews were given national recognition to return to their homeland.

14. The League of Nations and many nations recognized the independence of Israel as a separate nation.

15. Israel in Palestine will not abandon her spiritual heritage.

16. *Israel's national redemption is bound up in the redemption of the world.*

17. The concept of God in Israel symbolizes the apex of "goodness, truth, and beauty."

18. The great Law given to Israel by Moses was unknown in the pagan world.

19. This law has no parallel in all the nations of antiquity.

20. Israel looks forward to the "last days," to the "Golden Age" of a warless world.

David Ben Gurion in this document has combined the ideals of its officials and citizens into one of charming beauty and greatness. A remarkable feature of Ben Gurion's document is that he has held himself totally in the background though, in fact, he is the most important factor in creating the ideals for Israel's undertaking to build a State in Israel in many features totally different from other nations. Not a single reference is made to himself as being the Prime Minister for Israel for 11 of the 13 years that this government was established in Palestine.

DAVID BEN GURION'S RECOGNITION OF THE COMING MESSIAH

Israel with its Mosaic Theocracy does not pretend today to be a Theocracy, but a secular state which gives full liberty along rightful lines to its citizens.

In looking over the twenty points of this rare document, can it be established which one of them is the most important?

The writer considers No. 8 the most important of all in this document, because it is the only place where some *recognition is given to the Messiah*.

It is worthy of praise that a number of references are made in Ben Gurion's document to the heritage given to Israel by the sages and prophets of old.

But the question now arises: What was this heritage which was left by the prophets to Israel?

It can be easily established that of the three great offices given to Israel — those of prophet, priest and king — the prophetic one proved the most significant of them all. Though false prophets arose in Israel, as the prophets of Baal in Elijah's time, that brought about the spiritual and national ruin of the nation, yet down through the history of Israel the prophetic office remained untainted, because God inspired men to deliver a message never told by any false prophet. That message, whether given by Abraham, Isaac, Jacob, Joseph, Moses, David, Elisha — one and all the prophets of Israel, centered their message upon the one vital factor of man's sinfulness and the deliverance from all its effects through the Coming Messiah.

This message of the Coming Messiah, which was first given in the Garden of Eden, runs through all the sacred Scriptures as a scarlet thread, foretelling man's redemption through blood atonement of only one Person, the Son of God, sent from heaven to this sinful earth, our Lord Jesus Christ, who only is referred to as "God-provided Messiah."

The Prayer Book of Judaism embodies a *Daily Prayer for the Coming Messiah,* "And though He tarries, I will wait daily for His Coming."

JUDAISM AWAITING THE COMING MESSIAH

Judaism is expecting a Golden Age of a warless world through the Coming Messiah. This fact is absolutely correct, that through Messiah the long-awaited Messianic Age will dawn with the visible appearing of the Son of God to this earth to sit on the throne of David to inaugurate a distinctly Messianic age for a thousand years (Revelation 19:16-18; 20:1-6).

Prime Minister Ben Gurion does not make mention that Messiah has already come to make atonement and exclaimed as His last words: "It is finished," spoken on the cross of Calvary's hill (John 19:30). *Finished* means that nothing is to be added. It means completeness of Messiah's task.

It is not difficult to designate the exact time of Messiah's appearance on earth. God designated it clearly through the prophet Daniel in chapter 9, verses 25-27, where it states that the beginning of the "Seventy Weeks" is the building of the walls of Jerusalem in 445 B.C. Now 69 of the "Seventy Weeks" means 483 years from the starting point, which reaches to the year A.D. 32 to the year, month, and day when the Triumphal Entry of Jesus took place. It consequently includes the whole life and ministry of Jesus as the *promised Messiah.* The Virgin Birth, foretold by Isaiah the prophet in Isaiah 7:14, was fulfilled in the birth of Christ, the Messiah.

JUDAISM AWAITING THE WORLD'S REDEMPTION THROUGH THE MESSIAH

The closing of Jesus' ministry, including His crucifixion and death, is completely set forth in the fifty-third chapter of Isaiah.

The reason that Ben Gurion awaits the Messiah in the "Last Days" is that there are a great many more prophecies in the Old Testament which deal with Messiah's appearance in glory to establish the Messianic

Kingdom over all the earth. Only a few will be referred to here: II Samuel 7:12, 20-29; Psalm 2; Psalm 8; Psalm 47, and many others; Isaiah 2:1-4; Isaiah 60 to chapter 62; Daniel 7:13, 14. The latter passage was claimed for Himself by Jesus in His trial before Caiaphas in answer to his question, "Art thou the Messiah?" Jesus knew definitely that it was His mission to proceed with establishing His Messianic Kingdom upon earth. He declared that it would be a long time until His time in glory.

Then will Messiah come in the Last Days to bring to fulfillment what Ben Gurion set forth in his lofty ideals when Israel's national redemption will have been a great foretoken of the redemption of the whole world, when the "earth will be filled with knowledge, as the waters cover the sea."

Then will the "desire of the nations" have a rule of justice and truth that will blossom into "a new heaven and a new earth, wherein dwelleth righteousness" (Haggai 2:5-9), when peace will come to all nations.

Israel is the only nation that has had the courage to declare that these blessings of joy and happiness await the nations of earth through Messiah's coming to have a real, vital Kingdom upon earth.

Ben Gurion has had the wisdom and courage to declare to all the nations of earth that he believes that only with the coming of the long-awaited Messiah will come peace upon the nations of earth.

This is a sublime task for the *State of Israel* that they uphold the Commandments, Covenants, and Prophecies of the Old Testament, given to Israel of old, and teach their youth through the reading of the Old Testament in the Hebrew language. The State of Israel is being built on a stable foundation that will lead on to a time of justice, truth, and righteousness for all the nations of earth. Then the angels can sing with greater power the song, "Glory to God in the highest, and on earth peace, good will toward men" (Luke 2:14).

✡ 6 ✡

THE JUBILEE CELEBRATION OF THE STATE OF ISRAEL

ATTENTION HAS BEEN CALLED in a previous chapter to a national program that was given to the people of Palestine from Jerusalem to give evidence in a special Bible contest that aroused the interest of millions of people in Palestine. That program was given under the auspices of the State of Israel.

That "Bible Quiz" Program was based on the Old Testament which is the most important subject in the education of the State of Israel. Never has any other program aroused its youth to such dedication in the study of the Bible, to have its youth engage in a quiz made up of difficult questions. There is likely to be but little juvenile delinquency, if any, in a nation like the State of Israel where the Bible is given its first place for the purpose of instilling the fear and love of God into the minds and hearts of its youth.

The ultimate motive that the State of Israel teach its youth the Word of God, is not merely to give its youth an abstract knowledge of God Almighty, but to give them some new kind of knowledge than what mankind has ever known before on how to make of life a success in everything that man undertakes.

There is only one passage in the whole Bible that gives the formula for enduring success, for a nation or individual. This passage is found in Joshua 1:8, namely as follows:

(1) This book of the law shall not depart out of thy mouth; but thou shalt meditate therein day and night, that
(2) thou mayest observe to do according to all that is written therein:
(3) for then thou shalt make thy way prosperous
(4) and then thou shalt have *good success.*

Unless an individual or a nation is taught how to serve the Lord and obey His commandments, he cannot make of life a *good success.*

We now come to the question that the State of Israel had to face. When God called Abraham out of a pagan world to follow Him, it was for the purpose of making of his posterity "a holy nation" that would be able to prove to the world how to make a *good success* in the functioning of various occupations in the national life. When God brought Israel out of Egyptian bondage He promised to give them a land flowing with *milk and honey.* Milk and honey are the very best of foods.

In Deuteronomy 28, God enumerated the many blessings in store for Israel to make "a good success" of their living on the soil of Palestine, the Promised Land.

Israel was promised that they would be blessed in the field (agriculture) and the increase of their cattle. They would be blessed in basket and store, and victory of their enemies. They would be made the head of all nations and not the tail (Deuteronomy 28).

The Bible is the blueprint of man's history. It carries on its pages the stamp of reality. Many of its prophecies regarding Israel's history have already been fulfilled.

This was made evident in the most excellent television program sent out to the world on the day of the fourteenth anniversary of the State of Israel, May 15, 1962. The program, a Jubilee Celebration, gave evidence (lesson from the book of Psalms) of a mastermind's having selected not only the best talent but sacred songs given by a highly efficient Cantor and others constituting the choir.

However interesting was this sacred music and song, of still greater interest and importance was the fact of the use of the sacred Scriptures. The phenomenal feature of this world-wide television program was that it made frequent use of responsive reading by the vast audience. of beautiful selections from the Psalms and the prophets of old, setting forth God's promises to Israel, of a latter-day Israel made up of returned exiles from 75 different countries, now settled in Palestine. They gave evidence of God's fulfillment in deserts blossoming "as the rose." Special mention was made of Theodor Herzl, the founder of the Jewish State, and of David Ben Gurion, the Prime Minister of the State of Israel.

The writer is bold in stating no nation has ever used the wonderful and beautiful selections as given in this program. Such a program, giving forth many selections from the Bible, must demand the respect of the vast audience of millions listening in Palestine and other countries.

Yet, with all due praise to those who took part in the rendition of this sublime program, in which God was given the honor and glory for the tremendous success which He gave to the miracle nation of a restored Israel, it is not wrong to state that something was lacking in the program that was given on this anniversary of the birth of the State of Israel.

What was it that was lacking in the beautiful, sublime program celebrating the birth of a miracle nation such as the State of Israel today?

The lack in this program can be stated in but *one word* — *Messiah*.

The omission of this one word from the program given on the annual celebration of the foundation of the State of Israel is of tremendous importance, since the word *Messiah* forms the key to unlock the massive divine vault of Scripture revelation, that contains not only the promises given to Israel but, as stated by God to Abraham, was to reach unto all lands and nations, to give forth blessing to "all the families of the earth" (Genesis 12). This word *Messiah* is repeated in Hebrew but twice — in the New Testament the Hebrew word Messiah also occurs but twice — so that Judaism and Christianity have the same claim for God's redemptive work of salvation through the suffering and atoning death of Jesus, the Son of God.

It can be said that this jubilee anniversary program, given in the city of Jerusalem, gave evidence of believing the Scriptures of the Old Testament regarding the *material and temporal* earthly affairs of Israel and giving no evidence of a spiritual regeneration, preparing God's chosen people, the Jews, to be ready to enjoy eternal blessings promised in both the Old and New Testaments.

God grant that the veil of unbelief still resting on the people of Judaism may be taken away and that the Messiah, mentioned more than 500 times in the New Testament as *Christ,* will be recognized and accepted by a regenerated newly-born nation as the Messiah for whose coming Israel prays daily in its Prayer Book, which teaches Israel, the State of Israel, "to pray daily for the Coming of the Messiah, though He tarry long."

When Messiah comes in glory there will be a real, vital unity between believers of Judaism and of Christianity; and hallelujahs will ascend to the Messiah not only from the State of Israel but from all lands and nations, as the Prophet Habakkuk declared that the earth will be filled with the "knowledge of the glory of the Lord, as the waters cover the sea" (Habakkuk 2:14).

Great as was the liberation of the oppressed children of Israel out of the bondage of Egypt, it did not bring them to the Promised Land until they had passed through forty years of wilderness journey. However, with regard to the birth of the State of Israel, we have a nation giving birth over night, already equipped to carry on its political, cultural and economic aspects of national life. Such a movement from bondage to liberty has never happened in earth's history.

How did this singular, tremendous event come to pass? There is only one answer that gives a clue to untangling this Gordian knot about the birth of the State of Israel, and that is the wonderful dream that was given of the Messiah to Theodor Herzl.

Now the query comes as to what impression this strange dream made upon this lad of twelve years? The strange answer to this query is that never in his life up to six months before his death did he give utterance of the dream itself without any comment whatever but to an intimate friend. For more than thirty years Theodor Herzl carried this secret in his own mind and heart.

As in the Biblical case of Joseph, Theodor Herzl thought his revealing this dream to his family, or to Rabbis, or speaking of it in Zionist Congress, would only bring ridicule from everyone.

Eighteen words of this dream constitute a string of costly diamonds, that have great meaning for the future. This dream constituted an embryonic seed which developed finally through divine guidance in the endeavors of Theodor Herzl's contacts with the great leaders of Europe, which ultimately ripened into the birth of the State of Israel in 1948.

This dream, but an acorn in its inception, grew, through tremendous labors and trials of Theodor Herzl; those of his successors through the years in the Zionist Congresses, despite the agitation, animosities and myriad other stumbling blocks, to be the mighty oak, the State of Israel, born May 14 and 15, 1948.

Here the decision will have to be made by Israel as to what their attitude will be when their many prayers for the coming of the Messiah will be answered in the coming in glory of the Messiah.

Then Israel will mourn for having rejected Him for these twenty centuries. Then, and not until then, will the words of Paul be fulfilled, that "all Israel shall be saved" (Romans 11:26).

Israel will have its greatest mission in having an important part in the millennial reign of our Lord and Saviour Jesus Christ.

Then during the thousand year reign of our blessed Lord, Theodor Herzl's dream of the Messiah doing "great things for the Jews and for the whole world" will be literally fulfilled.

Israel will have a perpetual jubilee celebration throughout the millennial reign of Christ, when Christ (the Messiah) will be acknowledged as King of kings and Lord of lords forever over all the nations of earth.

✡ 7 ✡

THE APPLICATION OF GOD'S SEVEN COVENANTS TO ISRAEL

PREVIOUSLY WE HAVE DISCUSSED those references in the Four Gospels to Jesus Christ as the Messiah. After the completion of Jesus' ministry, that took place with His ascension to heaven, the New Testament relates three definite instances where Jesus appeared and made Himself manifest as the Messiah. The first is the story of Stephen's martyrdom in Jerusalem, on which occasion Stephen declared, at the conclusion of his address, that "Behold, I see the heavens opened, and the Son of man standing on the right hand of God."

But he, being full of the Holy Ghost, looked up stedfastly into heaven, and saw the glory of God, and Jesus standing on the right hand of God, and said, Behold, I see the heavens opened, and the Son of man standing on the right hand of God (Acts 7:55, 56).

The second incident is that of the conversion of Paul . . . when, on his way to Damascus persecuting the Church, he was suddenly surrounded by a great "light from heaven."

And he fell to the earth, and heard a voice saying unto him, Saul, Saul, why persecutest thou me? And he said, Who art thou, Lord? And the Lord said, I am Jesus whom thou persecutest: it is hard for thee to kick against the pricks. And he trembling and astonished said, Lord, what wilt thou have me to do? And the Lord said unto him, Arise, and go into the city, and it shall be told thee what thou must do (Acts 9:4-6).

The tenth chapter of Acts records the vision that was given to Peter of a sheet let down from heaven, filled with "wild beasts and creeping things." Peter heard a voice from heaven saying, "Rise, Peter, kill and eat." When Peter refused to eat any of the unclean animals, the voice from heaven said, "What God hath cleansed, that call not thou common." This was done three times: and all were drawn up again into heaven. The vision was given to Peter to assure him that the Gospel of God's salvation was not only for Cornelius and his household, but also for all Gentiles (Acts 11:17, 18).

The third instance of Jesus appearing after His ascension to heaven is that recorded by John, the beloved disciple, of Jesus while on the Isle of Patmos, when he received the majestic vision of Jesus:

> I was in the Spirit on the Lord's day, and heard behind me a great voice, as of a trumpet. . . . And I turned to see the voice that spake with me. And being turned, I saw seven golden candlesticks; and in the midst of the seven candlesticks one like unto the Son of man, clothed with a garment down to the foot, and girt about the paps with a golden girdle. His head and his hairs were white like wool, as white as snow; and his eyes were as a flame of fire; and his feet like unto fine brass, as if they burned in a furnace; and his voice as the sound of many waters. And he had in his right hand seven stars: and out of his mouth went a sharp twoedged sword: and his countenance was as the sun shineth in his strength. And when I saw him, I fell at his feet as dead. And he laid his right hand upon me, saying unto me, Fear not; I am the first and the last . . . . (Revelation 1:10, 12-17).

Now that the term *Messiah* has been clarified in the light of the Scriptures, before seeing its effect upon the life of Theodor Herzl, it is necessary to look into the meaning of another word of Holy Writ; namely, that of "covenant."

The word *covenant* is not used in relating the dream given to this lad of twelve years, Theodor Herzl. And if it had been mentioned it would have been foreign to his understanding. Nevertheless, as one examines this dream, or vision, of the Messiah, we see that a mission was being made known that this lad was to perform. And he alone, of the entire human family, was the one selected especially for the task of having great things done by the Messiah for the Jews.

THE MEANING OF THE WORD 'COVENANT'

The Biblical name for a compact between two persons is called a *covenant,* whether between God and man, or between two or more persons. The word *covenant* is used frequently in the Old Testament, and also a few times in the New Testament, to validate important transactions.

To understand God's dealings with mankind, one should understand also the meaning of the seven distinct dispensations: (1) Innocence, (2) Conscience, (3) Human Government, (4) Promise, (5) Law, (6) Grace, (7) Kingdom. In all of these, God was testing man during various periods of time as to their obedience to do the will of God. And according to the Word of God, all seven dispensations ended in failure of man to prove faithful to God's promises.

In the face of these repeated failures, the question then arises as to how God's plan of redemption can be proven to be successful in establishing the kingdom of God upon the earth so that the "earth will *be filled* with the knowledge of the Lord as the waters cover the sea."

Man's failure does not spell God's failure. While it is well for one to understand the *seven dispensations,* which are all conditional on man's obedience to God, it is more necessary for man to know of God's covenants that are wholly unconditional, since they depend upon God's power overruling the weakness and failings of mankind, and wholly and solely upon God's faithfulness. The divine covenants may be referred to as (1) Edenic, (2) Adamic, (3) Noahic, (4) Abrahamic, (5) Mosaic, (6) Palestinian, (7) Davidic, (8) New.

THE ABRAHAMIC COVENANT

In each of these there stands out some distinct great promise of God that He will positively fulfill, to prove His faithfulness. The first three prove God's faithfulness to mankind in general; but the fourth, Abrahamic, is dealing with a specific race, or nation, which is known as *Israel.* In dealing with the specific problem of Messianic origin of the State of Israel, it is necessary to get in mind the whole scope that God has in mind with regard to Israel as a nation. This is given in the *Abrahamic Covenant* that through Abraham's Messianic Seed all the families of the earth are to be blessed (Genesis 12:1-3).

God said to Abraham, "I will make of thee a great nation . . . and I will bless them that bless thee, and curse him that curseth thee." The fundamental purpose that Theodor Herzl had in mind was to make the State of Israel a great center of education, culture, moral character, industry, and commerce on a high standard, all of which will affect the welfare of mankind. What is omitted in this plan of Theodor Herzl in his "document of the State of Israel" is the spiritual aspect of the covenant that God made.

It should not be overlooked that God's promise to give the land of Palestine to Israel was validated to Abraham by sacrifice of a heifer, goat, ram, turtle dove, and young pigeon:

And I will establish my covenant between me and thee and thy seed after thee in their generations for an everlasting covenant, to be a God unto thee, and to thy seed after thee. And I will give unto thee, and to thy seed after thee, the land wherein thou art a stranger, all the land of Canaan, for an everlasting possession; and I will be their God (Genesis 17:7, 8).

In this everlasting covenant God does not give to Abraham's seed, Israel, merely the land of Palestine for an *everlasting possession,* but the actual area of Israel's land possession was to reach out to an area twenty-five times greater in size; namely from the "river of Egypt to the great river, the river Euphrates" (Genesis 15:18). This large area, as some say, of a good-for-nothing desert, is already proving an astonishing source of wealth through the increase in oil wells.

However, it awaits a greater source of wealth through the restored fertility of the soil, so that "the desert shall rejoice, and blossom as the rose. . . . It shall blossom abundantly" (Isaiah 35:1, 2), and thus become the habitation of a regenerated, restored Israel, of which God will say, "I will be their God" (Genesis 17:8).

This will bring about the fulfillment not only of the Abrahamic and Mosaic covenants, but also that of the *Palestinian Covenant.* The State of Israel is only in its kindergarten, or initial stage of beginning. What will result in a theocracy ruled over by the promised Messiah?

THE DAVIDIC COVENANT

This is more clearly seen in what is known as the *Davidic Covenant,* set forth in II Samuel 7:8-17, and also in Psalm 89:32-37. In these two great chapters a greater glory awaits the present State of Israel by the fulfillment of the promise made by God to David. It is more than a coincidence that in connection with the birth of the State of Israel, the founders wisely chose the right name for their project. They could have chosen the name of *Judea,* used for centuries, but the founders of Modern Israel well knew that that title never represented all the tribes of Israel, but only a small portion — that of Judah and Benjamin.

There is a movement, named *British Israelism,* which contends that the Anglo-Saxon race represents the lost Ten Tribes of Israel and, from their standpoint, the Jews are composed of a remnant of Judah with a mixture of other races.

The leading Jews have always contended that they represent all twelve tribes. The writers of the New Testament hold that the words *Jews* and *Israel* refer to, and include, all twelve tribes of Israel. The modern Jews gave the proof for this contention in that they named their newly founded state by the name given by God to Jacob when he wrestled with the Angel of the Lord — Messiah, when Jacob pleaded with Him saying, "I will not let thee go, except thou bless me." And the needed blessing was given to Jacob and his name was changed from that of Jacob, a "supplanter," to that of *Israel,* for he was told,

"As a prince hast thou *power with God* and with men, and hast prevailed.

And Jacob called the name of the place Peniel: for I have seen God face to face, and my life is preserved (Genesis 32:30).

THE NAME 'ISRAEL' CHOSEN FOR THE NEW NATION

The name chosen for the State of Israel was chosen in preference to other names. The name given was Israel — the name given by God Himself; *Israel* meaning "prevailed with God."

The State of Israel gives evidence of God's favor and blessing although the full recognition of dependence upon God is still put in the background, instead of putting emphasis on the letters *El* in the word *Israel,* which means *God.* The full recognition of God will be realized in Israel's future development.

Thou hast given a banner to them that fear thee, that it may be displayed because of the truth (Psalm 60:4).

He brought me to the banqueting house, and his banner over me was love (Song of Solomon 2:4).

THE FLAG OF DAVID

Another matter in the founding of a nation is the making and choosing of a design, or flag, that expresses to some extent the principles of its government. In this also, as in choosing its name from the Old Testament, the founders of the State of Israel have taken for its "banner," or flag, the *Flag of David,* with its six pointed star, made by two triangles intertwined. These two triangles represent the two greatest truths contained in the Bible — that of God and Man. The triangle reaching from the top to the base represents the Hebrew uni-plural name for God, *Elohim.* This triangle, composed of three lines of equal length, represents the Divine Trinity of the Father, the Son and the Holy Spirit. In the Old Testament, God is represented as being the Father of the nation of Israel; the Son is represented by the term Messiah, as the promised Saviour and Redeemer of mankind; and the Holy Spirit as the One enduing God's servants with Divine power to carry out their calling in God's service. This upper triangle reaches down from Heaven to, and through, the lower triangle of Man with his three lines setting forth the tripartite nature of Man's spirit, soul, and body.

This triangle reaches up into the upper triangle to obtain continued sustenance for the varied needs that only God can furnish for a completely contented and happy life of man in this world, and the world to come.

THE SPECIAL PURPOSE OF GOD'S NEW COVENANT

There is one more of the eight covenants previously mentioned that needs special consideration; that is, the *New Covenant*. This *New Covenant* is first mentioned in the writings of the Old Testament in an emphatic manner; namely, in the prophecy of Jeremiah 31, verses 31 to 33.

Not according to the covenant that I made with their fathers in the day that I took them by the hand to bring them out of the land of Egypt; which my covenant they brake, although I was an husband unto them, saith the Lord: but this shall be the covenant that I will make with the house of Israel; After those days, saith the Lord, I will put my law in their inward parts, and write it in their hearts; and will be their God, and they shall be my people (Jeremiah 31:32, 33).

Notice in the above verses that Jehovah declares that "I will make a new covenant" with the two divisions — the *house of Israel* and the *house of Judah.*

This covenant is to be far different than that made with "their fathers" in the wilderness at Mt. Sinai, where God spoke to the whole nation of Israel in the words given in the *Ten Commandments.* Mention is made by God that Israel, by their worship of the Golden Calf, had *broken* this covenant of God.

Instead of this New Covenant being written by God's hands on tables of stone, God declared through the prophet Jeremiah that "I will put my law in their *inward parts* and write it in *their hearts.*"

ISRAEL'S RETURN TO PALESTINE PARTIALLY FULFILLED

A repetition of this *New Covenant* given to Israel by the prophet Jeremiah is made in Jeremiah 32:37-44, at the time that Jerusalem was about to fall into the hands of Babylon. Notice in this repetition, that God will deliver them from "all countries" and "bring them again unto this place, and I will cause them to dwell safely: And they shall be my people, and I will be their God."

This promise has its partial, initial fulfillment in the return of exiles from Babylonian captivity by Ezra and Nehemiah to rebuild the temple and walls of Jerusalem. However, it cannot be said that Israel ever dwelt "safely" after their return to Palestine at that time, for they remained *under Gentile domination ever afterward* until the destruction of Jerusalem by the remnant under Titus in A.D. 70. This event brought about the dispersion of the Jews, reaching out into "all countries."

Furthermore, while nearly two million Jews have returned to their homeland, Palestine, to build it up, it cannot be said of Israel, under conditions of surrounding Arab nations, world tension, and constant danger of invasion by their enemies, that they are dwelling safely.

This can only become true when Israel's long-promised *Messiah* comes from Heaven in glory as "King of kings and Lord of lords" to sit upon the throne of David and to put an end to war, and thereby bring "peace upon the earth."

Messiah Made a New Covenant

Before taking up the teaching of the *New Covenant*, as set forth in the book of Hebrews of the New Testament, attention is called to the fact that our Lord Jesus Christ instituted the Lord's Supper on the night before His crucifixion and death. As He gave the "cup" to His disciples He said, "This cup is the new testament (covenant) in my blood" (Luke 22:20).

For this is my blood of the new testament [covenant], which is shed for many for the remission of sins (Matthew 26:28).

After the same manner also he took the cup, when he had supped, saying, This cup is the new testament [covenant] in my blood: this do ye, as oft as ye drink it, in remembrance of me (I Corinthians 11:25).

Jesus uses the same words as used by Jeremiah when speaking of the New Covenant given by God to Israel. What is the reason why Jesus did not make some reference to the New Covenant given by God to Israel? The reason is, that Jesus knew that the Jewish Fig Tree had borne no fruit — only leaves, and that the Jews would have to face the judgment of God in the destruction of Jerusalem and be led "captive into all nations."

And they shall fall by the edge of the sword, and shall be led away captive into all nations: and Jerusalem shall be trodden down of the Gentiles, until the times of the Gentiles be fulfilled (Luke 21:24).

Jesus knew that as long as the Jews would continue blinded with unbelief in their dispersion among "all nations," so long the fulfillment of the *New Covenant* promised to Israel by Jeremiah must be postponed.

Jesus ate of the Passover lamb on this occasion, but He, as the Lamb of God, "slain from the foundation of the world" (Revelation 13:8), now was about to die on the Cross, and sacrifice His precious blood for the redemption of the world.

And if ye call on the Father, who without respect of persons judgeth according to every man's work, pass the time of your sojourning here in fear: forasmuch as ye know that ye were not redeemed with corruptible things, as silver and gold, from your vain conversation received by tradition from your fathers; but with the precious blood of Christ, *as of a lamb* without blemish and without spot (I Peter 1:17, 18).

He definitely referred to the partaking of the cup as being *"My blood of the new testament* which is shed for many for the remission of sins."

This declaration of Jesus of making the Lord's Supper expressing the basis of His sacrificial offering for *"sins"* applies not only during the period of the Gospel Age, during which period the Church alone observes the Lord's Supper, but the sacrifice of Israel's Messiah on the cross of Calvary will also reach beyond the Church Age to the time when God will fulfill the New Covenant in *Israel's national conversion and complete restoration to their homeland in Palestine.*

Having called attention to the key of the New Covenant given by our Lord Jesus Christ (The Messiah) in His sacrificial offering upon the cross of Calvary by the shedding of His precious blood, one can understand why the writer of *Hebrews* makes frequent reference to the *New Covenant.* Let the reader take time to look up the references to the New Covenant in the following Scriptures: Hebrews 7:22; 8:6-13; 9:15, 16; 10:36.

THE RELATION BETWEEN THE OLD AND NEW COVENANT

In these references the fundamental thought is expressed of the *New Covenant's* being a *better testament (covenant).* This does not mean that the *Old Covenant* in itself was deficient, or that an error was made by God in the giving of the Ten Commandments, or in the service carried on in the sanctuary of the tabernacle, with its priesthood "daily offering sacrifices for the people." In the days of Moses, Israel as a nation was not yet ripe for the appearance of the Son of God as their national Messiah. The people were yet steeped in the idolatrous ways of Egypt. They had to be taught by symbols of various kinds how to be made to realize their waywardness, their rebellion against God, their *sinfulness* — thereby realizing their need of the *Messiah* promised by God.

The *New Covenant* was a *better Covenant,* "established upon better promises," because Jesus had offered Himself as the supreme sacrifice on Calvary's cross, and thereby, with His ascension to Heaven, He is given an unending priesthood, according to the order of Melchizedek, there in Heaven "to appear in the presence of God for us." By His own blood He entered in once into the Holy Place (Heaven), having obtained eternal redemption for us.

But Christ being come an high priest of good things to come, by a greater and more perfect tabernacle, not made with hands, that is to say, not of this building; neither by the blood of goats and calves, but by his own blood he entered in once into the holy place, having obtained eternal redemption for us. For if the blood of bulls and of goats, and the ashes of an heifer sprinkling the unclean, sanctifieth to the purifying of the flesh: how much more shall the blood of Christ, who through the eternal Spirit offered himself without spot to God, purge your conscience from dead works to serve the living God? (Hebrews 9: 11-14).

With the finished mediatorial work of Christ (Messiah), the Mosaic law, with its sacrifices and ordinances, was fulfilled. *It was abolished.*

For if that which is done away was glorious, much more that which remaineth is glorious. Seeing then that we have such hope, we use great plainness of speech: and not as Moses, which put a veil over his face, that the children of Israel could not stedfastly look to the end of that *which is abolished* (II Corinthians 3:11-13).

After Jesus had died on the cross, the great curtain separating the Holy Place from the Holy of Holies, "was rent in twain from the *top to the bottom*" (by the hand of God). "But this man (Jesus Christ, the Messiah) after he had offered one sacrifice for sins for ever, sat down on the right hand of God" (Hebrews 10:12).

This perfect sacrifice of Messiah, offered to God for man's sins, was acceptable to God the Father, who had sent His Son into this world of sin to provide redemption for mankind.

ISRAEL'S NATIONAL CONVERSION TO BE FULFILLMENT OF THE NEW COVENANT

This proof of God's acceptance of Christ's finished work on Calvary's cross is given positively by raising up His Son from the dead and, through His ascension, receiving Him in Heaven, to be seated at His right hand.

Paul, the writer of the Hebrew epistle, though he applies Christ's finished redemption for God's people in the Church, that make up the *body and bride of Christ,* does not do away with the application of this *better Covenant* to God's people, the Jews. The fact is that he repeats, nearly in full, the original New Covenant mentioned by Jeremiah (Jeremiah 31:31-34; Hebrews 8:7-12).

Long has been the time of waiting to have the New Covenant literally fulfilled in Israel, but sure as the promise is of the New Covenant referred to by Jeremiah, so sure will its realization be brought about when Israel accepts God's redemption provided for them through Messiah, when He comes in glory.

Considerest thou not what this people have spoken, saying, The two families which the Lord hath chosen, he hath even cast them off? thus they have despised my people, that they should be no more a nation before them. Thus saith the Lord; If my covenant be not with day and night, and if I have not appointed the ordinances of heaven and earth; then will I cast away the seed of Jacob, and David my servant, so that I will not take any of his seed to be rulers over the seed of Abraham, Isaac, and Jacob: for I will cause their captivity to return, and have mercy on them (Jeremiah 33:24-26).

✡ 8 ✡

THE EFFECT OF MESSIAH'S VISION UPON
THEODOR HERZL'S LIFE AND WORK

THE QUESTION ARISES — What effect did *Messiah's* vision and message have upon this gifted, ambitious lad? Did he understand what it meant for him to know what great things *Messiah* was about to do for the Jews? Did he consult with his parents? Or his teachers? Or any of the learned rabbis of his day? He, as well as all of these, was deeply steeped in Judaism, with little or no affiliation with the message entrusted to the Church, which has always claimed that Jesus is the one and only *Messiah*.

One thing is sure, this young lad had Messiah's message riveted and engraved upon his mind and heart, so that to his dying day he could not forget the solemn message given to him by *Messiah*.

In all of his training in educational institutions of Austria, in all of his vocation of Doctor of Laws, as a literary genius, as a commentator, as a playright, Herzl never attempted to confine himself to Jewish affiliation solely. He believed in Jews being *assimilated* into the life and service of the nation to which they belonged. How then, was this dream to become effective if he himself had no specific interest in the Jews as the "chosen people of God"?

A GREAT AWAKENING IN THEODOR HERZL'S LIFE

A tremendous awakening in his soul took place, when he was witnessing and reporting the farcical trial of Alfred Dreyfus, the Jew accused of being a traitor to his country, France. He became aware of the plight of the Jews in the outbreak of anti-Semitism all through Europe, which would bring disaster and perhaps extinction to the Jews.

A ray of divine light broke in upon his soul and stirred it with a mighty passion to work out some plan by which the Jewish problem could be solved. There were many small groups of the "Lovers of Zion" among the Jews in different countries of Europe, and there were some colonies already in Palestine, but there was no concerted effort of unity

96

among the Jews for a return to Palestine, the land of their fathers. After much toil and effort on his part, he had forged an effective plan for the emancipation of the Jews, in his book, entitled, *Der Juden Stadt (The Jewish State)*, published in the city of Vienna on February 15, 1896.

ONLY MESSIAH COULD UNRAVEL THE INTRICATE JEWISH PROBLEM

There can be no question that it was *Messiah* who gave Theodor Herzl to perceive how to unravel the intricate problems involved in founding a new nation. Moses was given a definite, complete revelation to organize and weld the millions of slaves of Israel into a free nation. Herzl was given divine wisdom in writing his book on *The Jewish State* to form of the Jews a live nation made up of people from many countries.

As Moses was obliged to deal with a rebellious people, often disgruntled with the conditions and trials they had to face, so Theodor Herzl, as leader for Jewish liberation, had to face many disheartening conditions with critics of many kinds. He was greatly disheartened because of the lack of support, which made his task difficult. Here again, the *Messiah,* who appeared to him in the night vision, manifested Himself in bringing him in contact with a specially gifted and qualified man to give counsel and needful assistance to solve the intricate problem of obtaining recognition on the part of government officials in Europe.

This man with appearance of a prophet, with a long gray beard, was Dr. William Heckler. Having studied the Bible from the standpoint of prophecy for many years, this man found that it gave a perfect solution to the Jewish problem, in declaring God's will and purpose for the return of the Jews to their homeland in Palestine, which would result in the re-establishing of *The State of Israel* in Palestine prior to *Messiah's* return in glory to establish His Messianic Kingdom for a thousand years.

Dr. Heckler had published the results of his study in a book that he gave to Herzl. These two men's hearts were knit and welded together, as was true with David and Jonathan, and henceforth they labored together for the solution of the Jewish problem, with one mind and heart.

Herzl now determined to forge the plan of the *Jewish State* into the hearts of millions of Jews.

And I will pour upon the house of David, and upon the inhabitants of Jerusalem, the spirit of grace and of supplications: and they shall look upon me whom they have pierced, and they shall mourn for him, as one mourneth for his only son, and shall be in bitterness for him, as one that is in bitterness for his firstborn (Zechariah 12:10).

Then it is brought to pass that "so all Israel shall be saved," when they behold the "Deliverer out of Zion," and then "He shall turn away ungodliness from Jacob" (all the Jews).

Is it any wonder that Paul is amazed at the "depth of the riches both of the wisdom and knowledge of God"? and the power to bring about the salvation of all Israel, and thus bring about a new era with God's redeemed people (the Jews), who will become God's messengers to the nations of the earth to bring God's blessing upon all the families of the earth (Romans 11:25, 26)?

THE VALUE OF WILLIAM E. BLACKSTONE'S DOCUMENT TO PRESIDENT HARRISON

One phase that has not been mentioned sufficiently in this treatise of the Jewish problem is the part the United States government had filled with regard to Theodor Herzl's project. It is not sufficient to state that upon the founding of *The State of Israel* in Jerusalem on May 15, 1948, the American government, through its President, was the first nation to salute the newborn State of Israel, but it can be stated, and should be recognized, that the United States government was given the opportunity to foster a plan for Israel's independence in Palestine five years before Theodor Herzl published his document of *Der Juden Stadt* in 1896.

This establishes the fact that the *Messiah* used the American government as the forerunner of the founding of the *State of Israel* in the land of Palestine. This is indeed a thrilling story, how God raised up an American citizen by the name of William E. Blackstone (October 6, 1841–November 7, 1936). He was not engaged in an active ministry, but he was a true patriarch of the Church, living to a ripe age of 95 years.

A business man of Chicago, engaged in the real estate business, which made him wealthy, he dedicated much of his time to God to carry on Christian work in public. He wrote and published many tracts and held evangelistic meetings in various parts of America and other lands. He wrote a best selling book entitled *Jesus Is Coming,* which had a circulation of several million and has been translated into more than forty languages. He was entrusted with funds running over eight million dollars, which was all used in supporting God's work in different mission fields.

He took a special interest in founding the *Chicago Hebrew Mission,* and through it began an effective work for Jewish evangelism.

The greatest achievement of this servant of God was that he wrote a document fostering the return of the Jews to Palestine. This document was a plea to the government of the United States to carry out a plan to encourage a speedy return of the Jews to Palestine, as foretold in the Word of God. Mr. Blackstone obtained the signature of 458 noted statesmen, clergymen, industrialists, editors, etc., and this document was sent to President Benjamin Harrison; and he dispatched it to all *sovereigns throughout Europe* and the nations of other continents in the world. This petition, pleading to make preparation for a speedy return of the Jews to Palestine, was sent to President Benjamin Harrison in 1891, which is *five years* before Theodor Herzl's document, *The Jewish State,* came from the press (1896).

JEWISH LEADERS CONSIDER BLACKSTONE THE FATHER OF ZIONISM

In 1918 a remarkable tribute was paid to William E. Blackstone, in connection with his petition, by a distinguished Jewish author, honoring him as the founder of Zionism. In recent years also he is being honored as such, as the following information attests:

After I completed the writing of this volume, being a subscriber to *The American Messianic Fellowship Magazine* of Chicago, Illinois, founded by William E. Blackstone in 1890, I found that in the issue of February, 1961, special attention is given to its founder in stating that the Jews of American Zionists are creating a special fund for the planting of two million trees, to make up a forest near Jerusalem to be known as "Blackstone Memorial Forest." This magazine is taking a vital interest in this great venture in contributing, through its subscribers and from other sources, all collected funds directly to Palestine. The price of the planting of a tree is two dollars, a certificate being forwarded to each contributor to this fund.

Among other items given in the January issue of 1961 of this magazine, calling attention to the fact that Mr. Blackstone took a vital interest in the Zionist movement, is one stating that he was given the opportunity of delivering an address to the Zionist mass meeting in Los Angeles. January 27, 1918, of which a vital portion gives expression to the great love and interest that this servant of God had for the Jews, and especially for the Zionist movement, which was founded by Theodor Herzl for the purpose of establishing *The Jewish State* in Palestine.

In his address Mr. Blackstone said:

Now this may lead you to ask of me, "Why are you an advocate of Zionism?"

In answer, I would say that for over thirty years I have been an ardent advocate of Zionism because I believe that true Zionism is founded on the plan, purpose, and fiat of the Everlasting and Omnipotent God, as prophetically recorded in His Holy Word, the Bible. In this blessed Book God has said:

If any of thine outcasts be in the uttermost parts of heaven, from thence will Jehovah thy God gather thee, and from thence will he fetch thee: and Jehovah thy God will bring thee into the land which thy fathers possessed, and thou shalt possess it; and he will do thee good, and multiply thee above thy fathers (Deuteronomy 30:4, 5, ASV).

And the streets of the city shall be full of boys and girls playing in the streets thereof (Zechariah 8:5, ASV).

And I will plant them upon their land, and they shall no more be plucked up out of their land which I have given them, saith Jehovah thy God (Amos 9:15, ASV).

Numerous other passages, all through the Word of God, confirm the Divine promise that Israel shall yet inherit their home in Palestine, in perfect peace and security. How then can I, as a true Christian, be anything else than a true "Zionist"?

But it is a fact that many Christians do not see this blessed truth, so plainly enunciated in the Scriptures. And it is more astonishing that many Jews do not see it.

Let me repeat what I said to a prominent Jew from Chicago during a pleasant conversation that we had on the train coming back from the West. After conversing about the awful War, I stated that there were only three courses open to every Jew, which practically divide them into three classes.

The *first* is, to become a true Christian, accepting Jesus as Lord and Saviour, which brings not only forgiveness and regeneration, but insures escape from the unequaled time of tribulation which is coming upon all the earth. We both agree that not many Jews will do this.

Second, become a true Zionist, and thus hold fast to the ancient hopes of the fathers — the assured deliverance of Israel through the coming of their Messiah, complete national restoration, and permanent settlement in the land which God has given them. . . .

My friend seemed to be intensely interested, but he asked: "What about the other, the third class?"

The third class are they who are *assimilationists*. They are the Jews who will be neither Christians nor Zionists. They wish to remain in the various nations, enjoying their social, political, and commercial advantages. . . .

God has put an overwhelming love in my heart for you all, and, therefore, I have spoken thus plain. But do not accept or reject anything that I have said simply on my word. No, no. Study the Word of God, this light that shineth in the darkness of the world's sorrows, and see how plainly God Himself has revealed Israel's pathway until the perfect day. God has spoken concerning Israel, as recorded in Psalm 68:13 (Newberry translation):

Though ye have lien among the sheepfolds, yet shall ye be as the wings of a dove covered with silver, and her feathers with yellow gold.

Elisha M. Friedman stated: "A well-known *Christian* layman, William E. Blackstone, antedated Theodor Herzl by five years in his advocating the re-establishment of a Jewish State." His memorial to President Harrison in 1891 was sent through the State Department to "all the principal sovereigns of the world."

In a Pan-Jewish Congress, Zion's Congress, held in Philadelphia, Blackstone was given the honor of being the *Father of Zionism*. This shows plainly that *the first* to call attention of the rulers of the world to the need of re-establishing a Jewish State in Palestine was a Christian man, William E. Blackstone, through a Christian (Messianic) government — that of the United States.

America has been a great haven for the Jews, giving them religious liberty as they never had since the dispersion. The Jews of America have furnished the largest amount of capital, reaching to nearly a billion dollars, to support the government in Israel, to develop its resources in Palestine. This all proves that *Messiah* fostered the cause of Israel through the channel of Christianity, embodied in the government of the United States of America.

✡ 9 ✡

THE TEACHING OF THE SCRIPTURES REGARDING THE RETURN OF THE JEWS TO PALESTINE

THE LAST AND MOST important proof of the Messianic origin of the *State of Israel* is the fact that the Scriptures of the Old Testament, as well as those of the New Testament, plainly teach that the Jews, at the close of the age, will return to Palestine in sufficient numbers to establish an independent government of their own.

It is remarkable that our Lord Jesus Christ, during the last week of His public ministry, after the cursing of the Fig Tree, symbolizing the unbelief of the Jewish nation during the period of their world dispersion, would not close his ministry without uttering a distinct *note of hope for the restoration of Israel* to their own land. This Jesus did in giving forth the parable of the *Rebudding of the Fig Tree,* as stated in His Olivet discourse, recorded in Luke 21:29-33.

JESUS' PROPHECY OF ISRAEL'S RETURN TO PALESTINE

Having spoken of the Jews' being "led away captive into *all nations,*" and of distress, with perplexity, coming upon the nations of earth (Luke 21:24-26), Jesus spoke of His coming in a cloud, "with power and great glory." And then He gave to His disciples another, the last, of the three parables regarding the Fig Tree.

Jesus then made mention not only of the Fig Tree but "all the trees" shooting forth, in proof that the "Kingdom of God is nigh at hand" (Luke 21:29-31). There never has been a time in man's history when nations asserted their individual rights to progress and expansion as today. Many nations have taken on new life, developing military skill to a fantastic degree, making universal annihilation of mankind possible through the use of missiles, nuclear weapons, and chemical warfare. Has there ever been a people that have suffered more than have the Jews during the period of their dispersion?

102

MESSIAH TO REBUILD THE TABERNACLE OF DAVID

Prior to His Second Coming, a large number of Jews will have returned to Palestine and founded the new *State of Israel* in partial fulfillment of the promise made by our Lord Jesus Christ, when He said, "I [Messiah] will build again the tabernacle [house] of David, which is fallen down" (Acts 15:16).

During the time of Jesus there were about 6,000,000 Jews in Palestine. This number in the Middle Ages was reduced to but *one million*. During the last century they have increased in great numbers. Over six million Jews were put to death by Hitler; millions were killed in Russia, Roumania, and other countries, yet they have increased to date to number twelve million. One of the greatest miracles of the ages is that of the Jews' preservation during their period of dispersion among the nations. Jesus – yes, it can be said that *Messiah* – made possible their preservation, for He said, "Verily I say unto you, This generation shall not pass away [the Jewish nation], till all be fulfilled. Heaven and earth shall pass away: but my words shall not pass away" (Luke 21:32, 33). Thus *Messiah* has kept the Jews from extinction.

Now, for what purpose did *Messiah* provide for their preservation? In this way many promises given in the Scriptures were being fulfilled pertaining to their restoration to God's favor to receive untold blessings at His merciful hand. Read the *triad* of chapters dealing with the past, present and future history of the Jews, each in his own way: that of Moses in Deuteronomy, chapters 28, 29 and 30; that of Isaiah in chapters 52, 53 and 54; that of Jeremiah in chapters 30, 32 and 33; and that of the Apostle Paul in Romans, chapters 9, 10 and 11. These and many other wonderful references foretell the glory awaiting restored Israel with the building of the Millennial Temple in the Land of Palestine.

Jehovah gave to David the pattern for the building of the temple so that David could provide vast resources for Solomon's temple; so also Christ (Messiah) has promised that He "will build again the tabernacle of David" (Acts 15:16).

It was at the council of the apostles held in Jerusalem to consider the relationship of the Jews to the Gentiles that Simeon (Peter) declared that first God would "visit the Gentiles to take out a people for his name." This refers distinctly to the building of the Church that must take place during this age of the grace of God. Before "the fulness of the Gentiles" will have been completed (the body and bride of Christ is the invisible Church, made up of regenerate, born-again believers), it is then that "I [Messiah] will return and *build again* the tabernacle of David, which is fallen down." Notice especially the closing words in Acts 15:16, where *Messiah* will "build again the ruins thereof, and I will set it up."

AN EVERLASTING KINGDOM PROMISED TO DAVID

In His first coming, Jesus, on account of the unbelief of His own nation, said, "I [the Messiah] will build my *church;* and the gates of hell shall not prevail against it" (Matthew 16:15-18).

This infers that Messiah had once built up the tabernacle of David. He had made a covenant with David of establishing, by the coming *Messiah,* an everlasting kingdom that "shall not be broken down, but endure forever."

When Jesus entered upon His ministry He gave forth the message, "Repent: for the kingdom of heaven *is at hand*" (Matthew 4:17). Did the Jews repent of their sinfulness and accept Jesus as their *Messiah* — as their Saviour and Redeemer? The Word says: "He came unto his own, and his own received him not" (John 1:11). How sad that "His own" said, "We will not have this man to reign over us." It was because of their rejection of their *Messiah* that the Jewish nation was doomed to a world-wide dispersion among the nations. The land of Palestine became a desolation, so that two centuries ago only 500 Jews remained in the land of Palestine. Thus was the tabernacle of David broken down, with the destruction of the temple and the loss of the priesthood (Hosea 3:4, 5). It needed rebuilding; but who was able to build again the tabernacle of David and make possible the rehabilitation of Palestine?

The same Messiah that said, "I will *build my church*," and has made it the greatest power for good to sound out the message of the Gospel says, "I will return, and will build again the ruins of the tabernacle of David."

No one but Jesus, the *Messiah,* the Son of God, could bring about conditions in the world to inaugurate the return and regathering of over two million Jews to their homeland in Palestine, to be welded into the *State of Israel.*

In the council of Jerusalem it was stated by Peter, the apostle, that the purpose of *Messiah's* building *again the tabernacle of David* was that the "residue of men might seek after the Lord, and all the *Gentiles.*" Abraham was told six thousand years ago that *"all* the families of the earth were to be blessed" through the promised Seed, the *Messiah,* including a redeemed Israel as the Seed produced through the *Messiah.*

In the vision of the valley of dry bones, Ezekiel was given to see a coming "together" of bone to bone and bringing flesh upon them, so that they could live. It has happened in the newborn State of Israel, but the prophet saw further that a mighty wind was *breathed* upon them, so that they would come to life by the regenerating power of the Holy Spirit at Christ's (Messiah's) coming in glory, so that *"all Israel"* will be saved (Ezekiel 37:9, 10 with Romans 11:25, 26).

A great transformation of Israel will take place, but it must first go through the time of *Jacob's trouble* (Jeremiah 30:17), set forth in the book of Revelation by the seven seal, seven trumpet, and seven vial judgments, coming to a climax (Revelation 6 to 16) in the Battle of Armageddon, at the close of Daniel's seventieth week.

ALL ISRAEL SAVED AT THE COMING OF CHRIST IN GLORY

The Jews in great distress will "cry to God" for a Deliverer; and then a Deliverer (the *Messiah*) will descend from Heaven on a white horse, with the armies of Heaven (angels and redeemed saints) accompanying Him. For then will be fulfilled what is stated in Romans 11: 25, 26 that "ungodliness" is taken away from Jacob and "all Israel shall be saved." Then will begin Messiah's reign in Jerusalem, sitting on the throne of David and ruling all nations for a warless period of a thousand years.

It is the mission of the Church to follow the example of Paul to preach the Gospel "first to the Jew and also to the Gentiles." Paul declared, "I have great heaviness and continual sorrow in my heart. For I could wish that myself were accursed from Christ [Messiah] for my brethren, my kinsmen according to the flesh" (Romans 9:2, 3), because his "heart's desire and prayer to God for Israel is, that they might be saved" (Romans 10:1). In chapter 11:25, 26 Paul declares that "blindness in part is happened to Israel, until the fulness of the Gentiles be come in. And so *all Israel shall be saved:* as it is written, There shall come out of Sion the Deliverer [the Messiah], and shall turn away ungodliness from Jacob."

An inspiring close to this chapter is to read a portion of Psalm 137, which inspired Theodor Herzl to carry on his great work entrusted to him by Messiah in his early youth. Read them and meditate upon them.

By the rivers of Babylon, there we sat down, yea, we wept, when we remembered Zion. We hanged our harps upon the willows in the midst thereof. For there they that carried us away captive required of us a song; and they that wasted us required of us mirth, saying, Sing us one of the songs of Zion. How shall we sing the Lord's song in a strange land? If I forget thee, O Jerusalem, let my right hand forget her cunning. If I do not remember thee, let my tongue cleave to the roof of my mouth; if I prefer not Jerusalem above my chief joy.
(Psalm 137:1-6)

THE PARABLE OF THE OLIVE TREE DECLARING ISRAEL'S RESTORATION

Attention has been given to the meaning and application of the Fig Tree. There still remains the task of making a brief study of the *Olive Tree* set forth in the eleventh chapter of Romans. The reader should prayerfully read the entire chapter to grasp the meaning.

This great chapter explains the relation that has taken place, and that also *will take place,* between the two great racial divisions of mankind — the Gentiles and the Jews. The word *Gentile* simply means *"nations."* Before the call of Abraham, there were only *nations,* all of which were steeped in idolatry and immorality.

Out of this idolatrous condition of humanity (Romans 1:25-32), God called Abraham and gave the promise to him that in his "seed" shall blessing come to all the families of the earth. From the beginning — from the time the nation of Israel came into existence — the sad comment is, that, with but few exceptions, they proved to be a disobedient and rebellious people against God. They heeded not the warnings of the prophets and messengers that God had sent. The Messiah devoted His entire mission to bring redemption to the "lost sheep of the house of Israel" (Matthew 10:6), the nation to whom He came. Instead of accepting Him as their Messiah, the rulers rejected Him and cried to Pontius Pilate to crucify Him, and thus Jesus was nailed to the cross.

Before His crucifixion, Jesus had wept over Jerusalem, saying,

If thou hadst known, even thou, at least in this thy day, the things which belong unto thy peace! but now they are hid from thine eyes. For the days shall come upon thee, that thine enemies shall cast a trench about thee, and compass thee round, and keep thee in on every side, and shall lay thee even with the ground, and thy children within thee; and they shall not leave in thee one stone upon another; because thou knewest not the time of thy visitation (Luke 19:42-44).

By their stumbling with regard to their Messiah, they have been set aside by God *for a season* in their being dispersed into all nations. In their place, the message of salvation has been entrusted to the Gentiles (to the Church, primarily made up of Gentile converts). Now notice what is stated at the close of Romans 11, verse 11, ". . . for to provoke them [the Jews] to jealousy." The Jews in their dispersion were given the opportunity to see the untold blessings and riches that God is giving through His faithful people in the Church, and became *jealous* of them. They should thereby be made willing to accept Jesus as their personal and national Messiah (Deuteronomy 32:21).

Have the Jews, as a nation, realized that the Church has brought to the world the "unsearchable riches of Christ" (Ephesians 2:7) in giving the Scriptures of the New Testament?

Have the Jews had any part in the task of translating the Bible into about 1500 languages, as the Church has done? Have the Jews sent out missionaries to the many lands of earth to bring the Gospel of salvation to the benighted heathen, steeped in idolatry?

The Apostle Paul, in this eleventh chapter of Romans, undertakes to illustrate, by use of the Olive Tree, what should be the right attitude of the Church to the Jews. They would then be prevented from practicing anti-Semitism. Instead of practicing anti-Semitism against the Jews, they would be bringing them the Gospel. The Gospel should be given to the Jew "first" (Romans 1:16). In his missionary journeys, Paul always preached to the Jews first, then to the Gentiles.

THE DISPERSED JEWISH NATION TO RETURN TO PALESTINE

The Apostle Paul declares to the Gentile Christian Church, that "some of the branches" of the Olive Tree have been "broken off" (the Jewish dispersion), and the Gentiles, "being a wild olive tree," were grafted into the Olive Tree (and thereby become the Church of Christ). The grafting into the Tree of Life, our Lord Jesus Christ, takes place in the supernatural power of the Holy Spirit to become the "sons of God" (John 1:12).

Then Paul sets forth the powerful argument, that ". . . if the casting away of them [the Jews in dispersion] be the reconciling of the world [believers among all nations], what shall the receiving of them [their national salvation] be, but life from the dead?" With Israel's national salvation, the promise given to Abraham will be fulfilled of bringing Messiah's redemption "to all the families of the earth."

Paul sends out a warning message to the Gentile Church in saying, that "if God spared not the natural branches, *take heed* lest he also spare not thee" (Romans 11:21). In many ways, not only in doctrine but in their living, the Church has departed from the teaching, the ideals, and principles of the New Testament, and for long periods the papacy and clergy persecuted and oppressed the Jews during the Middle Ages.

What wonderful declaration is given in verse 23, that "they [the Jews] also, if they abide not still in unbelief, shall be graffed in: for God is able to graff them *in again,*" since they are the "natural branches."

The two most important verses of this entire chapter are verses 25 and 26:

"For I would not, brethren, that ye should be ignorant of this mystery, lest ye should be wise in your own conceits; that blindness in part is happened to Israel, until the fulness of the Gentiles be come in. And so all Israel shall be saved: as it is written, There shall come out of Sion the Deliverer, and shall turn away ungodliness from Jacob.

By "the fulness" is to be understood *the full number of true believers* that make up the Body of Christ. The completion of the true

Church has taken place in the rapture of the saints, in taking them with their incorruptible bodies from their resurrection to meet with the Lord "in the air: and so shall we ever be with the Lord," in the heavenly home that He has gone to prepare (I Thessalonians 4:14-18; John 14: 1-3).

THE PROMISE OF ALL ISRAEL TO BE SAVED

Now comes the most important declaration made of Israel in the entire New Testament, in the words, "And so all Israel shall be saved" (Romans 11:26). After the rapture of the saints, God takes up His program with the Jews, and deals with them in judgment, by the seven seal, the seven trumpet, and the seven vial judgments set forth in Revelation, chapters 6 to 16. During this awful pouring out of God's wrath, God will have 144,000, with 12,000 from each of the twelve tribes of Israel, as His witnesses. Multitudes of God's people will be martyred under the Antichrist and False Prophet (Revelation 13:7, 8).

These plagues and judgments are sent upon mankind primarily to awaken the Jews out of their slumber of unbelief, so that they will cry to God to send them a Deliverer. Then will the Son of God come forth with armies of angels and redeemed following Him. "Out of His mouth goeth a sharp sword, that with it He should smite *the nations;* and rule them with a rod of iron."

Then it is that the sorely oppressed Jews will know Jesus by the nail-prints of His hands and feet. They will then realize that Jesus is their Messiah, their Saviour, their Redeemer, their Deliverer.

✡ *10* ✡

THE RISE OF ANTI-SEMITISM IN THE CHURCH

IT MAY SEEM OUT OF PLACE to inject a discussion of such a subject as anti-Semitism into the main theme of this book bearing on the subject of "The Messianic Origin of the State of Israel." Though it seems foreign to the subject of the State of Israel, the fact is that there is a definite relationship between the two since anti-Semitism, as was stated in previous chapters, was the fundamental cause for producing the great movement of Zionism, inaugurated by Theodor Herzl, to weld millions of scattered Jews into a vigorous, powerful nation in the land of Palestine.

THE MEANING OF ANTI-SEMITISM

To begin this investigation, some attention should be given to the understanding of the term *anti-Semitism*. How did it originate, and by whom? On the face of it, the name *anti-Semitism* embodies a very important character in Bible history. On the face of the word *Semitism* one can detect the name of Shem, one of three sons of Noah who survived the flood that devastated the earth and utterly destroyed the wicked generation of mankind.

After Noah was aroused from his drunkenness, he took occasion to pronounce a far-reaching prophecy, which has to this day divided the human race into three divisions, the three continents: that of Shem, primarily to the Oriental races of Asia; that of Japheth, to the races of Europe; and of Ham, to the black races of Africa.

The significant feature of this Noahic prophecy was that Shem was to be the channel to produce a nation (Israel) of which Messiah, the Redeemer of mankind, was to come in God's own time and way. The great contribution of this nation of Israel was not merely that it gave birth to our blessed Saviour and Redeemer, but also that it produced the thirty-nine books of the Old Testament, embodying the Ten Commandments, and all the ordinances of the sanctuary with its sacrifices, typifying the one great sacrifice made on Calvary's cross by the Son of God. The Jewish nation also produced the foundation of the Church on the day of Pentecost, to which was given the Great Commission to reach out to all nations with the Gospel of our Lord Jesus Christ. The New Testament Scriptures were given through the instrumentality of the Church.

Now, in this Noahic Covenant, the astonishing statement is made of "the Lord God of Shem," that God will "enlarge Japheth, and he shall dwell *in the tents of Shem*" (Genesis 9:26, 27). This signified that the nations of Europe were to be given the incentive for their astounding progress along many lines. The Greek and Roman nations had given stable governments, excellent contributions in agriculture, architecture, philosophy, and literature; and yet, with their beautiful temples, they were steeped in idolatry and pagan ways of living.

A great change came over Europe when Paul, on his second missionary journey, gave heed to the vision given to him of God, that "a man of Macedonia prayed him, saying, Come over into Macedonia, and help us. And after he had seen the vision, immediately we endeavoured to go into Macedonia, assuredly gathering that the Lord had called us for to preach the gospel unto them" (Acts 16:9, 10).

With this journey of Paul into Macedonia began the great transformation that took place with the establishment of the Church in Europe. It was the result of the influence of its church that did away with idolatry in the whole continent of Europe, and established governments that did away with slavery, and began to give liberty and freedom in a great measure to mankind.

WORLD LEADERSHIP TRANSFERRED FROM SEMITIC TO JAPHETIC NATIONS

Thus the leadership of the world, entrusted to Semitic nations in the Orient for many centuries, came eventually to be given to the Japhetic nations of Europe, and thereby the prophecy of Noah began the fulfillment that "Japheth was enlarged." But this was not all that Noah had declared that was to come to pass in future generations to Japheth.

Noah had declared that "Japheth shall *dwell* in the tents of Shem" by becoming the standard-bearer for the Bible, its preservation of ancient manuscripts, translation and publication by the invention of the printing press. The Japhetic nations of Europe became the standard-bearer for the Church which was founded by a Shemitic nation, that of the Jews. Jesus had declared that "salvation is of the Jews" (John 4:22). It was the church that sent forth missionaries to many nations of earth.

The main contribution for the progress of mankind made by

Japhetic nations was made possible by its continuing *to dwell* in the tents of Shem, to accept the Messiah and His teachings entrusted to Shem by God.

Now we arrive at last to the statement made in the New Testament: that mention is made of *Sem* in the genealogical table of Jesus, which goes back to Noah, and even back to Adam.

Now it is evident that the term *Sem* has a positive Messianic meaning, both in the Old and New Testaments. The Old Testament gives many incidents exhibiting anti-Semitism, such as Ishmael mocking at Isaac, the son of Sarah (Genesis 21). On a large scale, anti-Semitism was manifested in the oppression of the children of Israel by Pharaoh. Balak, the king of Moab, out of hatred for Israel, sought in vain for Balaam to curse Israel, three times. Still later by Sennacherib, in forcing the Ten Tribes of Israel to be taken into Assyrian captivity. Still later, Nebuchadnezzar taking Judah into captivity to Babylon; still later, the story of Haman's plot, under King Ahasuerus, of Persia, to destroy all the Jews in the realm. In the New Testament, at the birth of Christ, there raged the fierce wrath of Herod, manifested in destroying all the male children in Bethlehem under two years. All these and others were attempts to frustrate God's plan to have the Redeemer to be born of Israel, the descendant of Shem, in order to carry on God's plan of establishing His kingdom upon earth.

JEWISH LEADERS GUILTY OF ANTI-SEMITISM

Furthermore, as we search the Scriptures, notice that the anti-Semites proved to be the Jews themselves. One need only read the statement made in the beginning of the Gospel of John, where it is said of Jesus that "He came unto his own [Israel] and his own [Israel's leaders] received him not" (John 1:11). All through His ministry, Jesus was harassed, opposed, and at last rejected by Pharisees, Sadducees, Herodians, who led on by Annas, Caiaphas, Pilate and Herod brought about the crucifixion of the Son of God. The Messianic offspring of Sem (Luke 3:36), our Lord Jesus Christ, overcame all attacks made against Him, and finally gave indisputable, tangible proof of His divinity in His resurrection and ascension to Heaven.

It was because of this manifestation of anti-Semitism on the part of Jewish leaders, that Jesus announced a great change that was to take place in announcing the founding of the Church when He said, "I will build my church, and the gates of hell shall not prevail against it" (Matthew 16:16-19).

Now that the Church had begun its mission with the conversion of three thousand from among nineteen various nations gathered in Jerusalem, the instructions were to be carried out that the disciples of

Jesus were to proceed from "Jerusalem, Judea, Samaria, and unto the uttermost part of the earth" (Acts 1:8).

The book of Acts relates instances of anti-Semitism where Jewish leaders imprisoned the apostles and beat them, forbidding them to preach the Gospel or to utter the name of Jesus (Acts 5:18-29). Then followed the stoning of Stephen (Acts 7:58-60). Among those taking part in the stoning of Stephen was a zealous Pharisee, named Paul, who, at the time, was a disciple of Gamaliel who had taken a tolerant attitude to "refrain" from persecuting the disciples of Jesus. "And now I say unto you, Refrain from these men, and let them alone: for if this counsel or this work be of men, it will come to nought: but if it be of God, ye cannot overthrow it; lest haply ye be found even to fight against God" (Acts 5:38, 39).

Disregarding this wise counsel given by Gamaliel, "a doctor of the law, had in reputation among all the people," Saul of Tarsus, being exceeding "zealous of the law," breathing out threatenings and slaughter, obtained permission of the high priest to persecute the disciples of Jesus as far as Damascus (Acts 9:1, 2), when suddenly he was aware of the voice of the Messiah, the Lord, saying, "I am Jesus whom thou persecutest" (Acts 9:4-6). He yielded at once to give his whole heart and life to be a true follower of Jesus. Instead of continuing in his anti-Semitic (Messiah) attitude of opposition against the Son of God, he became the most valiant defender of the Messiah, and did more to contribute to the upbuilding of the Church through his four great missionary journeys and the writing of thirteen epistles of the New Testament than all others put together.

Throughout all his journeys, Paul found himself and his work harassed, not only by zealous leaders of the Jews, but also by Gentiles, as was the case at Corinth, Ephesus, and other places.

ANTI-SEMITISM CARRIED ON BY GENTILES

Nearing the close of the first century, anti-Semitism was carried on by Gentile opposition and persecution of the Church, as is seen in the banishment of the aged Apostle John to the Isle of Patmos. Then followed the ten great persecutions of the Roman emperors to destroy the work of the Church, but "the seed of the martyrs" proved the reverse; namely, to increase the number of Christian followers.

When the Church had increased to such an extent that it took possession of heathen temples, converting them into sanctuaries of the Church, a great change took place. This change resulted in the fact *the Church began persecuting the Jews on an ever-increasing scale,* so that the Church became the controlling anti-Semitic factor in Europe and other countries. How could such an astounding change take place to make the Church become the instrument of Satan to practice anti-Semitism on an ever-increasing scale? The nominal Church became a very enemy of the Jewish nation that had given birth to the Church and its Founder, our Lord Jesus Christ. This *radical change* came about because of a new spiritual interpreting of the Old Testament Scriptures regarding many of the promises given to Israel by God.

CHURCH FATHERS INTRODUCE ANTI-SEMITISM IN THE CHURCH

A number of the Church fathers taught that, because the Jews by their rejection of Christ were taken out of Palestine and scattered among many nations, that was definite proof that God had abandoned them and that they were no longer the "chosen people of God." They taught, furthermore, that because Christ Jesus had founded the Church to witness for Him to "all nations," the promises formerly given to the Jews were now transferred to the Church and henceforth belonged to the Church instead of to Israel, and were to be fulfilled in a *spiritual,* and not a literal manner. This spiritualizing of the promises given to Israel was unfair to the Jews. The Church appropriated the blessings, and left the curses to the Jews.

THE CURSE OF ANTI-SEMITISM

Origen, of the third century, is accredited in his allegorical interpretation of the Bible as being the originator of what is known as "Spiritual Israel." This method of spiritualizing the promises made to Israel and applying them to the Church is plainly seen in many of the headings of chapters relating to Israel of the Authorized Version of the Bible, where numerous psalms and writings of the prophets make use of such headings. A few samples are sufficient to show the utter folly of this theory of making the Church to inherit promises made to Israel. In Jeremiah the heading is, "The Stability and Amplitude of the Church." In Micah it is given, "The Glory and Victory of the Church."

Of the 35,000 promises said to be made to Israel in the Old and New Testaments, over 30,000 are distinctly given to Israel, and therefore, belong to Israel as a nation.

This false theory of spiritualizing the promises made to Israel is doing injustice to the Jewish nation in that it robs them of multitudes of promises made with that nation; but it works greater havoc in leaving the curses spoken against that nation to remain with them. This spiritualizing of the Scriptures has no logic in its claims, unless it applies both the curses as well as the blessings to the Church that were once given to Israel.

One needs only to study Deuteronomy 28 to see the falsity and the unfairness of this theory. In this chapter of 68 verses, 14 verses summarize the boundless blessings of God to Israel; whereas the remainder of the chapter of 54 verses are given to warn Israel of the curses that will come upon them for their rebellion against God. Among the curses pronounced by Moses was that of Israel's being *"scattered among all the nations of the earth,* from one end of the earth to the other." There will they find "no ease or rest," but will have a "trembling heart . . . and sorrow of mind" — "And thy life shall hang in doubt before thee; and thou shalt fear day and night, and shalt have none assurance of thy life" (Deuteronomy 28:66-68). This certainly is a plain announcement of anti-Semitism that will overwhelm Israel in their dispersion among all nations.

Jesus did not detract from the curses when He spoke of the "days of vengeance, that all things which are written may be fulfilled." Jesus definitely declared that the Jews "shall be led away captive into all nations." He said also that "Jerusalem shall be trodden down of the Gentiles, *until* the times of the Gentiles be fulfilled" (Luke 21:22-24). Notice that Jesus put a limitation to the Diaspora of Israel when He used the word *until.*

Now notice, with regard to the final address given to Israel by Moses, that He plainly stated that "the Lord thy God will bring thee into the land which thy fathers possessed, and thou shalt possess it; and He will do thee good, and multiply thee above thy fathers" (Deuteronomy 30:5). Jesus spoke of the restoration of Israel to their own homeland when He said, in connection with the rebudding of the Fig Tree, that "this generation [the Jews] shall not pass away till all be fulfilled" (Luke 21:32).

It is apparent, although Jesus had made preliminary announcement regarding the founding of the Church, that notwithstanding the fact that to the Church was given the Great Commission to "preach the Gospel to all nations" — yes, even to "every creature" — yet that was never to mean that the Jews were to be treated as aliens from the commonwealth of Israel and the household of faith and from the family of God.

HOW THE CHURCH BECAME THE ENEMY OF THE JEW

Before the Church was even born on the day of Pentecost, Jesus had commanded His disciples that after they had received the power of the Holy Spirit they were to "be witnesses unto me, both in Jerusalem, and in all Judea" (Acts 1:8). Throughout the entire book of Acts we find the Jews were to be given the first opportunity to hear the Gospel. Paul declared the Gospel first to the Jews and also to the Gentiles (Romans 3:9, 10). It was unfortunate, both for the interests of the Church as well as for the Jews, that as time went on friction entered between the two which grew into hatred, and eventually developed into anti-Semitism that resulted in the Church's becoming the enemy of the Jew instead of being his helper.

With the spiritualizing of the promises in God's Word given to the Jews and appropriating them to belong to the Church, came the claim that even Palestine itself must be conquered by the Church (during the Crusades).

The Papacy in Rome assumed the right to rule over kings and bring their countries into subjection to them. The Crusades of the Middle Ages proved a failure. They had reduced the Jewish population in Palestine to less that 500. The Papacy took upon itself to engage in fierce persecution of the Jews, so that the population of the Jews was reduced to less than a million in the countries of Europe. Some of the edicts against the Jews were given out by a number of Popes.

As a result of these terrible persecutions of the Jews by the Roman Catholic Church, the Jews became utterly opposed to receiving any message regarding the Deity of our Lord Jesus Christ as the Son of God.

THE ATTITUDE OF MARTIN LUTHER TO THE JEWS (1483-1546)

As one reads through the Bible, he comes in contact with many noble characters used of God in carrying out His plan of redemption. Not any of these were perfect in the sight of God; and yet there are those against whom no record is given which would reflect any imperfection in their walk with God, as was true of Enoch, Joseph, Daniel, and the three Hebrew children; also Mordecai and Esther belong to this category.

On the other hand there are others that were outstanding in their generation who committed grievous sins in the sight of God, as was true in Noah's being guilty of drunkenness; Abraham, guilty of lying to Pharaoh; Moses, guilty of an impetuous temper; David, guilty of murder and adultery; Solomon, guilty of polygamy on a large scale. The record of sons of the kings of Judah give evidence of this fact. We also have proof of this in the New Testament.

Failure to live a fully yielded life to God is seen in many instances of God's chosen men in Church history.

Attention is now called to one notable example of a man mightily used of God, one of the greatest, outstanding examples of Church history; namely, that of Martin Luther, who was bold in nailing the ninety-five theses on the door of the Catholic Church in Wittenburg, Germany. He stood boldly against the corruption of the Roman Catholic Church, and withstood the threats of excommunication by the papacy. He declared that salvation is not obtained by any works of man, but solely by the grace of God in his teaching that "the just shall live by faith" (Romans 1:17). Perhaps the greatest contribution to the cause of Christianity made by Martin Luther was his single-handed translation of the Bible into the German language, which is still recognized in nearly all — if not all — Lutheran churches as the standard version used in their services.

One of the most grievous events that occurred during the Reformation Period was one connected with the great career of John Calvin, who gave his consent to put to death in the city of Geneva, Switzerland, a noted theologian, Servetus, who would not accept the doctrine of the Divine Trinity, as set forth in the Word of God.

Attention is now called to a great mistake that was made by Martin Luther with regard to his attitude to the Jews.

Not only the Roman Catholic Church refused to acknowledge the Jews as "the chosen people of God," but, sad to state, the Protestant Church largely inherited this same false spiritualizing teaching from the Roman Catholic Church and also refused to consider the Jews as "the chosen people of God."

Strangely enough, the foremost champion of the German Reformation, Martin Luther, in his early ministry, was considered a crusader of gentleness on behalf of the Jews. But in later years he took the opposite stand, revealing his later bitter spirit of considering the Jews as "that miserable, wicked people."

MARTIN LUTHER'S ATTITUDE TOWARD THE JEWS CHANGED

That the reader might have a better understanding of the great change that took place in Martin Luther's life and career, a quotation is given with permission of the publisher, Alfred A. Knopf, New York, N.Y., from the book, entitled, *A History of the Jews,* by Abram Leon Sachar, Ph.D. (page 228):

At the beginning of Luther's career, this vigorous Protestant reformer was almost a liberal crusader, with a breadth of vision which was rare in the sixteenth century. He denounced the clergy for their brutal and senseless fulminations against the Jews and reminded them of their obligations which Christianity imposed upon them. "The Jews are the best blood on earth," he wrote. "Through them alone the Holy Ghost wished to give all Books of Scripture to the world." They are the children and we are the guests and the strangers; indeed, like the Canaanitish woman, we should be satisfied to be the dogs that "eat of the crumbs which fall from their master's table." In a fervent pamphlet, entitled, *Jesus Was Born a Jew,* which was republished seven times in one year, he sent a thrill of hope through Jewish hearts by saying, "If we would help, so must we exercise, not the law of the Pope, but that of Christian love — show them a friendly spirit, permit them to work so that they have cause and means to be with us and amongst us. . . . And if some of them remain obstinate, what of it? Not every one of us is a good Christian."

Luther's gentleness, however, seems to have been dictated by a desire to convert the Jews, who proved to be no more amenable to persuasion than they had been before. Meantime, Luther was beset on every side by virulent enemies, and as he grew older and his difficulties increased, he became harsher and less patient. It seemed impossible that the same man was speaking, when in 1543 appeared the stinging pamphlet, *Concerning the Jews and Their Lies.* Here the monk who had defied all the power of organized Christendom in his search for truth, joined with the worst bigots in accusing the Jews of poisoning wells, murdering Christian children, and remaining impossibly stubborn in the face of Christian revelation. He urged the Princes to destroy the Jewish synagogues, and to confiscate the wealth and devote it to maintain those who accepted Christianity. One of his best sermons denounced Jewish physicians for "understanding the art" of poisoning their patients, and concluded with the ominous admonition: "I say to you lastly, as a countryman, if the Jews refuse to be converted, we ought not to suffer them or bear with them any longer."

Inevitably, the Protestant communities took to heart the later utterances of Luther, rather than his early and more charitable ones. The tyranny which the Reformation had so often denounced, became part of the inheritance which he bequeathed to his devoted followers.

MARTIN LUTHER'S CONTEMPT FOR THE JEWS

To clarify this issue still further, a quotation is given from a booklet of 64 pages, entitled, *The Jews and Their Lies,* by Dr. Martin Luther. This quotation is taken from pages 49 and 50. Under the heading, "Jews Desiring the Death of the Christians" Martin Luther declared that

Whenever you see or think about a Jew, say to yourself as follows: Behold the mouth which I see there has every Saturday cursed, execrated, and spit upon my dear Lord Jesus Christ, who has redeemed me with His precious blood; and also prayed and cursed before God that I, my wife and children, and all Christians should be stabbed, and perish in the most miserable manner — would like to do so himself if he could, that he might come into possession of our goods.

Perhaps he has this very day often spit on the ground over the name of Jhesu (according to their custom), and the spittle is still clinging to his mouth, and beard where there is still room for it. Should I eat with, drink with, or speak to such a devilish mug (mouth)? I might devour many devils as, for a certainty, I would become partaker of all the devils who live in that Jew, and would spit upon the precious blood of Christ. God keep me from doing that.

This attitude of Martin Luther does not represent that of his followers today, but it does give an understanding of the bitter hatred against the Jews of that day, which has brought a great harvest of anti-Semitism from one century to another down to the present time.

THE ATTITUDE OF FRANCE'S VOLTAIRE TO THE JEWS (1694-1778)

Voltaire is numbered as one of the most prolific writers of all history, having composed seventy volumes. He was called the "Morning Star of the French Revolution." For his boldness to withstand the profligacy of French leaders and kings, he was imprisoned in the French Bastile, and yet he rose to great fame, being feted in Paris and many cities of France. He was called the "Father of French Journalism." He was one of the greatest leaders championing *Liberty* and *Equality* in all Europe. He attacked the ritualism, tradition, and beliefs of the Roman Catholic Church.

Although he was counted among the greatest of agnostics and free thinkers of the world, he uttered among his last words the following statement to the world: *"I die worshiping God,* loving my friends, not hating my enemies, but detesting superstition."

One of the most outstanding characters supporting anti-Semitism against the Jews was that of Francois Voltaire. He became especially well known by his work, *The Age of Reason,* which became very popular in America during the period of the Revolutionary War.

He had a bias that developed into fierce opposition and animosity against the Jews. Voltaire became an *open foe of religion,* declaring that *"Religion was a disease of the human race."* With regard to the Jews, he despised them because they gave rise to *Christianity,* for which he had no use whatsoever. One of his statements that showed his hatred for the Jews was his declaration, "Down with the Jews, wretched little Jews."

Voltaire's Contempt for the Bible and the Church

This great popular philosopher could not restrain himself from alluding to the Jews as "a greedy and selfish race, whose only ideals were *more money* and more children." He never had *one good word* to say on behalf of the Jews, but because of his fierce hatred of them became the most outspoken advocate of anti-Semitism, instilling prejudice and hatred into the minds and hearts of vast multitudes of people in many countries. He had *no use for the Bible and the Church* and yet it is a fact, that before his death at the ripe age of 84 years he became aware of his great folly of *antagonizing God, His Church, and God's chosen people, the Jews.*

Only a few years ago, in 1954, there was found in *Newsweek,* a statement of Voltaire's repentance, as taken from a document found in a Parisian archive. It reads as follows, under the caption,

Voltaire a Repentant Deist

I, the undersigned, having been *vomiting blood* for four days at the age of 84 years, and not having been able *to get to Church,* and the priest of Saint Sulpise having been willing to add to his good works, that of sending to me Pere Gaultier, priest, declaring that I die in the Holy Catholic religion in which I was born, hoping *the Divine Mercy will pardon all my sins,* and that *I have ever scandalized the Church, I ask for God's and her pardon.*

The signature on this Document dated March 2, 1778, is that of a man who had scandalized his Church very efficiently: Francois de Voltaire . . . .

It is true that his door was barred to the priest after March 2, but the document shows, that Voltaire wished to confess *again* the night he died, May 30. Unfortunately, Gaultier arrived too late. Voltaire was already in his last delirium. *Newsweek*, September 6, 1954, page 47.

Thus another celebrated exponent of doubt died asking God to forgive him for a lifetime of largely misdirected efforts. Let us take one more look at this man, as seen through the eye of his personal physician:

Look at this dying Voltaire — hear his dying confession, confided in the ear of his physician: "My friend," cried the sick man, "you are the *only one* who has given me *good advice.* Had I but followed it I should not have been *in the horrible position* in which I now am. I have listened to *flattery,* and have intoxicated myself with the incense that *turned my head.* I have swallowed nothing but smoke." And so in utter wretchedness he died.

Our God is a merciful God, who will pardon truly penitent sinners. The penitent malefactor on the cross was pardoned by Jesus and received up to be with Jesus in Paradise.

Anti-Semitism is not an unpardonable sin, but before God can pardon one for the folly of abusing and berating the Jews, he needs to cry to God for pardon, and thereafter have love for the Jews instead of hatred. Of one thing we may be sure, there is no anti-Semitism in heaven. Anti-Semitism belongs to the carnal nature that has not yet learned to keep the command of Jesus: "A new commandment I give unto you, that ye love one another; as I have loved you, that ye also love one another. By this shall all men know that ye are my disciples, if ye have love one to another" (John 13:34, 35).

THE DESTRUCTION OF SIX MILLION JEWS BY ADOLPH HITLER (1889-1945)

The book, entitled *Mein Kampf,* was written by Adolph Hitler during his imprisonment for revolutionary crimes. This writer has selected but one paragraph from page 18 to give Hitler's reason for seeking to exterminate the Jewish race from Europe:

Many Jews now become so arrogant that they proclaim themselves racially at last, and go so far as openly to admit, that they have no thought of actually carrying out Zionism, and that they really have no desire to build a Jewish National State in Palestine in order to inhabit it: they only want a central organization beyond control of other states, where villains can take refuge or future villains be schooled.

It is a sign of their increasing confidence and sense of security, that some Jews still fraudulently masquerade as Germans, Frenchmen, Englishmen; others openly admit that they are members of the Jewish race. . . . Religion is scoffed at, customs and morals are scorned as outmoded, until the last supports of national struggle for existence disappears.

In order for the reader to have some conception of how Adolph Hitler carried out his plan of mass murder of six million Jews, special attention is called to an article in *Look* magazine of August 2, 1960, in which the story of the special henchman is told, who was responsible for carrying out this horrible tragedy.

ADOLPH EICHMANN, HITLER'S TOOL IN JEWISH SLAUGHTER

The title of this story is, *The Untold Story of Adolph Eichman, NAZI BUTCHER, His Crimes, His Escape, His Fifteen Years of Hiding, His Capture.* If ever the warning, given in Numbers 32:23 by Moses, "Be sure your sin will find you out," has been literally fulfilled, it is in the life of this *mass butcher,* who was apprehended by the law after fifteen years of hiding. Eichmann was a professed atheist. The following excerpt is given with permission of the publishers:

He was constantly occupied with innovations in dealing with "the Jewish problem." When France fell in 1940, he thought he had found an ideal solution. He proposed that all the Jews in Europe be interned on the island of Madagascar, a French colony. Hitler approved the plan, but France's Vichy government refused to cooperate.

After the failure of the Madagascar plan, the policy of sending Jews into exile was abandoned, the Gestapo . . . armed with machine guns and machine pistols. These squads began to shoot down thousands of Jews in ghettos all over Europe, throwing the bodies into mass graves. But the commandos themselves began to break down, after wading through the blood of innocent people. Some committed suicide, others went mad, and even the most hardened had to rely on alcohol and drugs to deaden their senses.

Eichmann decided that a more efficient method of extermination was needed. He experimented first with death trucks, using exhaust fumes to kill Jews. But by 1941, he began to feel that this process also was too slow and inefficient . . . he proposed the establishment of death factories in various towns in Nazi-ruled Europe. He assigned professional engineers, chemists and mechanics to design the equipment. The gas chambers they devised soon began operating in towns that were to become everlastingly infamous . . . .

As the gas chambers went into operation, Eichmann was completely absorbed in working out the details. He would become angrily impatient when his schedule for the transport of Jews to the death camps was upset. In July, 1942, he telephoned his representative in France to ask, "Why haven't the Jewish shipments arrived?" The deputy answered hesitantly that the Vichy government was not cooperating. Eichmann complained that he had had many difficulties in getting the death-camp freight cars in which the Jews were to be shipped. "These freight cars have not been used yet!" he lamented. "This has never happened to me!"

While Eichmann was spreading terror across Europe, he continued to display . . . irrational fear . . . .

In Hungary in 1944, Eichmann reached the pinnacle of his bloody career. In a matter of weeks, he organized and carried out the deportation to Germany of half a million Hungarian Jews. Each day, 14,000 men, women and children were deported in packed freight trains. They were taken to Auschwitz, where four new gas chambers had been installed by Eichmann's order. The four chambers could kill only 10,000 people a day . . . . Of course, disease and starvation added to the toll.

. . . He dug graves in which he burned the bodies that could not be put into the ovens.

Hitler . . . expressed his pleasure by choosing a postwar title for Adolph Eichmann: "World Commissar for the Jews." . . . His Nazi superiors supplied him with poison and instructed him to use it if he fell into enemy hands.

A JEWISH REFUGEE'S THRILLING MESSAGE OF 'FISHERS OF MEN'

The reason the writer calls special attention to the horrors of Hitler's reign in putting 6,000,000 Jews to death is because this most fearful tragedy — the greatest in earth's history — is to prove this to be the judgment of God upon the Jews for opposing the opportunity given to them by Theodor Herzl to join in his crusade to weld the Jews together with a national consciousness with a desire to return to Palestine to establish there a Jewish state to be a center for culture and for prosperity to the world. It is a fact that Theodore Herzl offered to hold his First Zion Congress in the city of Munich, Germany, in 1896, but the Jews of Germany were so taken up with the idea of assimilation, to be a vital part of the German government, that they had no interest whatever in having any part in the Herzl Plan to establish a Jewish state. Now then, a half century after, when overwhelmed with cruelty and calamity, they could not escape Hitler's venomous rage.

This judgment of God is brought out in a most forceful manner in an article published in *Prophecy* magazine, published in Los Angeles, California, by a German refugee, whose name was not given in the startling message that he gives to his contemporaneous Jews of Germany:

We who bring into connection the Biblical prophecies with the present day and know Hitler's development, have no doubt that he is the forerunner of the Antichrist; and, with regard to Judaism, one of the great in the line of destroyers of "the temple" — like Nebuchadnezzar, Titus and others. So far as Hitler is concerned, he is for a punishment, a correction of "a wrong way" — and that wrong way was assimilation: *the desire of the Jews to be looked upon not as Jews but as Germans.* The *assimilationist* Jews have sacrificed everything for German patriotism, even truth and their honor. The assimilationist Jews were determined to forget Jerusalem — but "if I forget thee, O Jerusalem, let my right hand forget her cunning" (Psalm 137:5). And it forgot its cunning!

God has never allowed a misfortune to come over His people Israel without previously warning them through admonishers and prophets. Forty years ago God sent to the Jewish people a leader in the person of the Viennese author, Dr. Theodor Herzl. He wanted to call the first Zionist congress to Munich. But the Munich assimilant Jews protested: "We do not want to know anything about Zion. Germany is our Palestine and Munich our Jerusalem!"

Herzl went to Basle. There, in 1897, the first Zionist Congress took place. Herzl pointed to the dangers of anti-Semitism and entreated the Jews to acquire Palestine as a national home. The rich assimilant Jews all over the world answered with scorn and ridicule. In 1896 Herzl had begun his Zionist work. Eight years later, in 1904, he died in Vienna at the age of forty-four. He had sacrificed himself to the Jewish people and the Zionist idea. Hitler, the anti-Semite, would not have been possible if the German Jews had listened to the voice of Herzl and given up the fateful way of assimilation.

The road was now laid open; Satan was able to find it. The punishment of the Jews was upon them.

Jewry lost one position after the other. The rich Jews of Russia who would not give a copeke for the building-up of Palestine, lost in 1917 their rubles and their lives. Overnight they had become the victims of Bolshevism. The economic crisis after the Great War affected the right of Jews in other parts of Europe and in America, and drew them into the whirlpool. And after the position of world Jewry had thus been undermined, began the destructive blows against the Jews as such. Hitler came to the throne, anti-Semitism was raised to a state religion, and an anti-Semitic world center began its activities.

The German Jews had read Hitler's programmatical book, *My Struggle,* and heard the speeches of the Nazi agitators. They saw Hitler rise to power and use it. They ought to have known what was awaiting them, but they could not believe it. So much did they believe in Germany, so much did they love German civilization, so much were they connected with the Germans.

In February, 1933, the Jewish persecutions began. The storm troopers were given a free hand. Only a small fraction of the German Jews recognized the greatness of the danger and left Germany. *Within a short time Palestine began to flourish.* Hitler has done much for the building-up of Palestine. He forced the Jews to bring man-power and capital to Palestine.

That in which the requests of Herzl, the "enticing fisher" failed, Hitler, "the hunter who hunts" succeeded in, with the help of a few penstrokes. As it is written in the book of the Prophet Jeremiah: "Behold, I will send for many fishers, saith the Lord, and they shall fish them; and after will I send for many hunters, and they shall hunt them from every mountain, and from every hill, and out of the holes of the rocks. For mine eyes are upon all their ways: they are not hid from my face, neither is their iniquity hid from mine eyes" (Jeremiah 16:16, 17).

Theodor Herzl and the Zionists are the fishers. Adolf Hitler and the anti-Semites are the hunters.

This was a very important message which was given by a Jewish refugee with regard to the warning that God gave to the Jews of Europe, through the clarion call given by Theodor Herzl, of the increasing danger of annihilation awaiting the Jews of Europe.

✡ *11* ✡

THE MESSIANIC WARNING FOR ISRAEL'S REPENTANCE

THE MESSAGE GIVEN in this chapter deals with another section of Jewish life; namely, that of America, primarily that of the United States. This is a class of Jews that sought refuge and security under the flag of the Stars and Stripes, where they could enjoy unmolested liberty and freedom.

Notice that the population of the Jews in the first decades had increased to almost 16,000,000 Jews. Deducting at least 6,000,000 killed by Adolf Hitler's diabolical rage reduced Jewish world population to about 10,000,000. It is astounding that of this number nearly 6,000,000 have become a part of the American Republic. The Jews have been an integral part of our government since its inception. Both in the Revolutionary War, to George Washington, and in the Civil War, to Abraham Lincoln, they furnished large sums of money to the American government to bring the nation through its critical periods.

The Jewish people have prospered to such an extent that they have contributed over five hundred million dollars in support of the Zionist Movement, to help establish the State of Israel. The Jews of our government have maintained a high standard of education, culture, and morals. By instilling the Ten Commandments of God into the minds of their youth they have solved, to a large extent, the vexing problem of youth delinquency. They are to be commended for the large contribution they have made for good government and for the prosperity of America.

When one inquires as to the religious life of the Jews in our country, only a small percentage take any vital interest in the attendance of the synagogue. Engrossed in the material affairs of this world, the larger number of them are forgetful of the claims that God makes upon man's life. As for any vital interest in the teaching of the Word of God concerning the coming of the Messiah, there is manifest a great spirit of complacency among them, and there is need for a mighty awakening among them of sounding out a divinely empowered call for repentance and redemption.

Therefore, there is included in this chapter such a message, given especially to the Jews of America — not by a Protestant clergyman, but by a noted rabbi.

SOLEMN WARNING FROM RABBI JOSEPH ISAAC

There are many Jews crying to God in their synagogues and throughout this land for God to look down upon them in mercy. They are sending pleas to four hundred rabbis and are sending pleas to the churches of America to pray for them that God will deliver their race from the fiery trial through which they are passing. A most remarkable thing, to my mind, is that within the Jewish race itself has a voice recently been heard — a clarion call to repentance and to a new awakening. This call was first printed in a New York paper and was later printed in a magazine published in Chicago, entitled, "To the Jew First." The call is from a Jewish rabbi — Rabbi Joseph Isaac. It is as follows:

> They fail to see that God cares for His people. They think only of how to help the cause of democracy with money or even a Jewish army, but *do not think about repentance and prayer.* They reason falsely that if God did not save Jewry of Europe, which was more believing, then there is no use for American Jewry to try and become more pious, as their spiritual leaders ask them.
>
> Thus, those appealed to remain deaf. But this deafness is also a result of the failure of the spiritual leaders to resound the call of our sages: "When punishments come into the world, look for the approach of the Messiah." They have neglected to tell the Jewish masses about one of the foundations of Judaism which is: "I believe in the coming of the Messiah," and that before the Messiah comes we must expect just such tribulations as we are passing through now.

From the pulpit and through the literature of this church, we have heard this very thing proclaimed many times.

> To all appearances it may be that these are the birth throes of the Messiah before the salvation of Jewry comes.
>
> Indeed, this is no mere pious hope or vain consolation, but a fact. The Jewish people are suffering the "afflictions (travail) of the Messiah"; the perfect salvation is just behind our backs, and among our Jews in this country there is a confusion of thought, just as our sages have foretold: The Messiah, the Son of David, will come amidst confusion of thought, entirely unexpected.
>
> The Jewish people live in the period of tribulations preceding the coming of the Messiah. We have already overlooked the "beginning of the Messiah" period by a few decades; and now *we must repent for having failed to repent* and for having caused the tribulations of the Messiah's time to come upon us. They may become even worse if we fail to correct our blunder.
>
> The call must be a stirring awakening to welcome the Messiah — our Righteousness. We now need an awakening to have a clean heart, a clean thought, a clean house, clean schools of religious instruction, a clean family, and a seeking to bring our children to the Law and Faith.

Without the sincere "wash you, clean you" our weapons of repentance, prayer and fastings are useless.

Without the readiness of the community of Israel to be the Holy People, to go out to welcome the Messiah, we may appear in the eyes of the Angel of Destruction no better than all other nations.

"IMMEDIATE REDEMPTION!" Let this be our greeting when we meet each other, explaining to the uninitiated the meaning of these words.

"IMMEDIATE REDEMPTION!" This is the answer to the question, "Why is God silent?"

He is not silent. He keeps warning us, waking us. He wants to save us.

"Immediate Redemption!" This is not merely a way of comforting those who despair. This is our Good Tidings (Gospel) concerning a real "Salvation about to come."

"Immediate Redemption!" Be ready for instant salvation. It is approaching with hasty steps. The righteous Redeemer is just behind the wall and the time to get ready to welcome Him is extremely short!

Israel will soon, yea in our days, be blessed with perfect redemption.

This appeal is a warning to every Jewish individual to beware lest he, God forbid! be excluded from the community of Israel.

This is the call of a rabbi to Israel to repent and turn back to God. Notice he says: "In our days Israel will be blessed with perfect redemption." That looks forward to the coming of Christ in glory, when all Israel shall be saved.

It is interesting indeed that it required only one verse in the entire Old Testament to give the promise of the "Messiah" for the redemption of Israel. Judaism, from days immemorial, had seized upon this one promise for their national hope (Daniel 9:25), and that justly, for their nation to own Him as their divine Redeemer.

A RABBI'S CALL FOR JEWS TO REPENT

The above appeal, made to Israel by one of their rabbis, is a noteworthy example as to the use being made of the term "Messiah," whereby to awaken Israel out of its complacency and worldliness.

In examining this address as to the use made of "the Messiah," note the following instances of its use:

1. "The *approach* of the Messiah"
2. "The *birththroes* of the Messiah"
3. "The *travail* of the Messiah"
4. "The Messiah, the *Son of David,* will come"
5. "The beginning of the *Messiah period*"
6. "The Messiah, the *Righteous Redeemer*"
7. "The *afflictions* of the Messiah"
8. "The Messiah wants to *save us.*"
9. "I believe in the *Coming of the Messiah*"
10. "Messiah comes *before the salvation of Jewry.*"

It was stated in a previous chapter, that *Messiah* is the Hebrew word for *Christ,* and *Christ* is the Greek word for "The Anointed" (by the Holy Spirit) (Luke 4:18). Now let the reader insert *Jesus Christ* in the place of *Messiah* in reading over again those ten declarations of the aim and purpose given to *Messiah.* It can be seen that there is full agreement between Judaism and Christianity with regard to the Old Testament understanding of the *Messiah.* There is only one important factor lacking in these ten declarations of the Messiah. It leaves out other references of the Old Testament that explain in full the *earthly* ministry of Messiah. These references speak of the Immaculate Birth, His Divinely-inspired ministry of teaching, preaching, and healing; His vicarious suffering and sacrifice as the Lamb of God and of His glorious resurrection and triumphant ascension to heaven. All were plainly foretold of Messiah in the Old Testament and yet were totally ignored by Israel writers. These references were all perfectly fulfilled in the New Testament. The Messiah of the New Testament is as much for Israel as the Messiah of the Old Testament, for Jesus said, "I am not sent [from heaven] but unto the lost sheep of the house of Israel" (Matthew 15:24).

The first message that Christ (Messiah) preached was to utter the stern warning, "The time is fulfilled, and the kingdom of God is at hand: repent ye, and believe the gospel" (Mark 1:15).

It was to "His own" (Israel) that Jesus came, to give them God's salvation, but the leaders of Israel received Him not. "But as many as received him, to them gave he power to become the sons of God, even to them that believe on his name" (John 1:12). The leaders of Israel turned against Jesus as their Messiah, but the "common people [of the Jews] heard him gladly" (Mark 12:37).

Reverting back again to the noted appeal of the rabbi to his people Israel, the Jews, he sounded out the warning for his people to *repent* of their willful ways and give their hearts to Messiah.

Warnings given to beware of being *"excluded from the community of Israel":*

1. *Punishment* will come to the world.
2. *Salvation* is right behind our backs.
3. The Jewish people live in the period of tribulation *before Messiah comes.*
4. The tribulation may become worse if we do not *correct our blunder.*
5. Repent for *having caused* the tribulations of the Messiah.
6. *We must repent* for having failed to repent.

7. We need *an awakening* to have a clean heart.
8. Four times at the close of his plea, the rabbi calls for *"Immediate Redemption."*

As one examines these declarations, one can feel the vital yearning of the rabbi to bring his people to turn away from their evil ways and yield themselves to serve the living God.

That is what is needed today in the lives of all mankind, both Jew and Gentile. This message of repentance, of having contrition for sin, is needed not only in Judaism but in the Church of today. In giving His messages to the seven churches of Asia, as recorded in the second and third chapters of Revelation, Jesus took occasion to call the churches of Asia to repent of the evils that were existing in the churches with the exception of the Church of Philadelphia.

Israel from its very beginning was Messianic in essence, since it furnished the embryo from which Messiah received the virgin birth. In giving His whole time to reach the "house of Israel," He limited the sphere of His ministry to Palestine with but two exceptions, that of the centurion (Matthew 8:5-13) and the woman of Canaan (Matthew 15:21-28). Practically all of the disciples of Jesus were Jews. Jesus declared to the woman of Samaria, that "salvation is of the Jews" (John 4:22).

THE BARRIER BETWEEN JEW AND GENTILE REMOVED

After the birth of the Church on the day of Pentecost, for a time its work was confined to the Jews.

Ye men of Israel, hear these words; Jesus of Nazareth, a man approved of God among you by miracles and wonders and signs, which God did by him in the midst of you, as ye yourselves also know: Him, being delivered by the determinate counsel and foreknowledge of God, ye have taken and by wicked hands have crucified and slain: whom God hath raised up, having loosed the pains of death: because it was not possible that he should be holden of it (Acts 2:22-24).

The institution of the Church removed the barrier between Jew and Gentile, patterning them both on the basis of God's boundless grace in place of being under the bondage of the Law. Israel today needs to learn that the *grace of God* is far above the law of Moses. The latter produces only bondage of fear, while the former produces freedom and joy.

THE MESSIANIC CLIMAX OF THE STATE OF ISRAEL

The founder of Zionism, Theodor Herzl, derived his inspiration to undertake the herculean task of welding his countrymen together as a nation with the object of making Palestine their homeland from two distinct sources: first, from the Bible, from which he obtained the knowledge in his youth of *Messiah's* riding on a colt to enter Jerusalem; second, from *a personal experience of a living contact with the Messiah,* which was given to him in a dream when but a lad of twelve years.

The great attraction in Palestine was, for Theodor Herzl as with nearly all Jews scattered throughout the world, *that of Jerusalem,* designated in the book of Psalms as the "City of the great King," their promised Messiah.

The Psalm loved by Theodor Herzl above all others is the 137th. He made use of this Psalm in conducting one of the congresses of Zionists, to instill courage into the hearts of his listeners. This is indeed a notable Psalm, for it was composed at a time when Jewish captives, taken to Babylon, sat down by the rivers of Babylon, where they wept when "we remembered Zion."

Their enemies realized that the Jewish Zion, the City of Jerusalem, had something greater than was to be found in any part of the world. There stood the beautfiul, magnificent temple of Solomon, now in ruins, where the captives once assembled to sing praises unto the true and living God, who promised to send a Redeemer to bring blessing to mankind.

When asked to sing one of the songs of Zion, the captives, with their harps hanging "upon the willows," said, "How shall we sing the Lord's song *in a strange land?*" Then, in spite of their disheartened condition as slaves in far away Babylon, there burst out the refrain, heard in succeeding generations in every synagogue and in every Jewish home, the beautiful inspiring words: "If I forget thee, *O Jerusalem,* may my right hand forget her skill, let my tongue cleave to my palate; if I fail to remember you; if I fail to exalt Jerusalem above my chief joy" (Psalm 137:5-7, Berkeley version). Thus Jerusalem from ancient times has been the chief source of joy and inspiration to Jews scattered down the centuries in many lands.

JERUSALEM'S IDEAL THAT OF PEACE

The word *Jerusalem* means "founded peaceful." The main thought of this word is that of peace. Jerusalem dates back to the time of Abraham, who, returning from a battle to rescue Lot, came to meet with Melchizedek, who abode in Salem. Here we have the combination of "righteousness" set forth in the name of Melchizedek, with "peace" set forth in the meaning of Salem. No wonder that Melchizedek (King of Righteousness) is used in the Bible as a type of the Messiah, who alone can give peace based on righteousness.

The city of Jerusalem, held for centuries by the Jebusites, was finally conquered by David, who gave it a new name, that of Zion, meaning "Sunny," from its being the highest elevation of Jerusalem.

From Jerusalem was to go forth light — the light of a coming Messiah, who alone can bring peace to a world of sin and sorrow.

David made preparation for the building of a temple for the worship of God. After David's death, Solomon built the temple, said to be the costliest building ever constructed by man. At its dedication Solomon offered a most wonderful lengthy prayer, beseeching God's blessings upon every devout worshiper of God.

This temple was the wonder of the world, so that the Queen of Sheba was constrained to come with her retinue and costly gifts from far away Arabia to make inquiry with regard to the worship of God. At her departure, she testified that the half had not been told of what she had seen and heard during her stay in Jerusalem.

Sad to state that after the death of Solomon, who had reigned in peace during forty years of his kingship, Jerusalem became and remained henceforth a city of strife and warfare brought about by nearly all of its kings. Solomon's temple was profaned by shameful Baal worship, so that the wrath of God was executed in Jerusalem's being destroyed by Nebuchadnezzar in 587 B.C., and the people with its king being taken captive to Babylon. Jeremiah, the prophet, declared that this captivity was to last for a period of seventy years, after which God would make possible their return to Palestine.

THE DIVINE PURPOSE OF THE BABYLONIAN CAPTIVITY

This captivity served a useful purpose of forever delivering the Jews from any taint of idol worship down to the present time. The supreme character of this entire period, from beginning to end of this period of seventy years, was that of Daniel, the prophet of God, and with him the three Hebrew companions. Daniel interpreted a great dream of Nebuchadnezzar, that none of the magicians could interpret. The dream was that of a great image of gold, silver, brass, and iron that Daniel interpreted as designating the four great world empires — Babylon, Medo-Persia, Greece, and Rome, with the ten toes of clay and iron representing the Revived Roman Empire, to make its appearance in the last days. Then Daniel told of a "stone cut without hands" which fell from heaven upon the feet of the image and caused its complete destruction; but the "stone" (the coming Messiah) became a great mountain (Kingdom of God) that filled the whole earth. This dream, therefore, set forth the downfall of *all human governments* and the establishment of the Messianic Kingdom over all the earth, bringing peace upon earth for a thousand years.

The other great dream of Nebuchadnezzar was that of a great tree, that was to be cut down for a period of seven years. The remaining stump designated that it would take on new life after the seven years. Daniel interpreted this dream to imply that the King Nebuchadnezzar, because of his great pride, would become insane and make his abode with the beasts, eating grass, but at last after seven years, after his recognition of God, was delivered from his insanity and given back his kingdom. The designation of the seven times of divine judgment upon the pagan king had application not only to seven years of punishment for the king, but also setting forth the length of the time of Gentile rulership over the nation of Israel as being a period of 2,520 years from 604 B.C., destruction of Jerusalem, to A.D. 1917, the startling beginning of the time of the end. During this end-time, Messiah declared to Theodor Herzl, as a lad of twelve, in a dream, that He would "do great wonders and great things for My people, the Jews."

DANIEL'S VISION OF THE 'SEVENTY WEEKS'

There still remains one other matter that requires special attention with regard to this period of Babylonian captivity. It was while Daniel, at the close of the seventy years of captivity in Babylon, confessed the sins of Israel that had brought reproach upon Jerusalem, that the angel Gabriel appeared to him and gave him what he called a Messianic Timetable.

Gabriel informed Daniel there were to be seventy weeks determined by God to "make an end of sins, . . . and to bring in everlasting righteousness" in the Holy City. From the time of restoring of Jerusalem (under Nehemiah) unto *Messiah* shall be sixty-nine weeks or 483 years. This was fulfilled to an exact day in the ministry of Jesus on the day of His entrance into the city of Jerusalem. On this occasion the *"Messiah the Prince"* offered Himself to the nation as their rightful King. The leaders of the nation that same week brought about His crucifixion and death, but God raised up His Son from the dead, and after 40 days He ascended to heaven.

This vision of the "Seventy Weeks" clarifies the definite time of 483 years to the actual time when Jesus was about to close His ministry in Jerusalem. Between the end of the sixty-nine weeks to the beginning of the seventieth week takes place the Gospel Age, that lasts until the fullness (full number of believers) of the Gentiles comes in, which takes in about twenty centuries to the present time, when the rapture of the saints takes place.

At the beginning of the Seventieth Week, after the rapture, God takes up His program with Israel, dealing out the judgments of the seven seals, seven trumpets, and seven vials. These are recorded in the book of the Revelation, from chapter 6 to chapter 16, ending with the great Battle of Armageddon (Revelation 16:16).

It is as a result of these outpourings of God's wrath that Israel will be brought to repentance, and mourn greatly as they see Him whom they had pierced. "And I took my staff, even Beauty, and cut it asunder, that I might break my covenant which I had made with all the people. And it was broken in that day . . ." (Zechariah 11:10, 11a).

In a dream, Nebuchadnezzar saw a Stone from heaven (the Messiah) destroying all human governments, and in their place inaugurating Messiah's reign of justice and righteousness upon the earth.

'THE STATE OF ISRAEL' A PARTIAL FULFILLMENT OF PROPHECY

God already has done great things for His people in fulfillment of the promise given in the Word of God. Messiah also made specific promise to the young lad of twelve years, Theodor Herzl. The State of Israel is established, an independent, free nation in Palestine. The State of Israel is indeed a wonder and a miracle wrought by the mighty power of God in these last days. When the Jewish Fig Tree is budding, as it is in Palestine, we may know that the coming of the Lord is near at hand, and that the kingdom of God will soon be established upon the earth. God's covenants made with Israel are irrevocable. The prophet Jeremiah made the following statement of God's faithfulness to Israel:

> Thus saith the Lord, which giveth the sun for a light by day, and the ordinances of the moon and of the stars for a light by night, which divideth the sea when the waves thereof roar; The Lord of hosts is his name: If those ordinances depart from before me, saith the Lord, then the seed of Israel also shall cease from being a nation before me forever. Thus saith the Lord; If heaven above can be measured, and the foundations of the earth searched out beneath, I will also cast off all the seed of Israel for all that they have done, saith the Lord (Jeremiah 31:35-37).

The prophet Isaiah makes many sublime statements regarding the future glory of Israel under Messiah's reign. He tells that the government (of all nations) shall rest upon Messiah's shoulder, and He (His name) shall be called "Wonderful, Counsellor, The mighty God, The everlasting Father, The Prince of Peace" (Isaiah 9:7).

The one unfortunate feature of the State of Israel is that they are surrounded by enemies. They not only have to beware of the encircling Arabs, but also the hatred of Egypt and the peril of an invasion from the North by Russia. This condition makes it necessary to spend the largest amount of the government's taxes for military purposes, and they have to be on the alert continuously with the enlistment of a large army (Psalm 46:9).

When Israel's Messiah takes over His right to world dominion, sitting on that throne of David, Israel will need no army to defend its borders. Then will Messiah give command to "beat their swords into plowshares, and their spears into pruninghooks" (Isaiah 2:4); then shall the wild animals be tamed — the leopard and the lion shall be so tamed that a child can play with them (Isaiah 11:5-9); then shall the desert blossom as the rose; sinners shall be saved; the sick shall be healed; "the ransomed of the Lord shall return, and come to Zion with songs and everlasting joy upon their heads: they shall obtain joy and gladness, and sorrow and sighing shall flee away" (Isaiah 35). Then shall the law go forth from Zion, and then shall the earth "be full of the knowledge of the Lord, as the waters cover the sea" (Isaiah 11:9).

Israel indeed is the "chosen people" of God, and they are destined to enter into their rightful inheritance in the land promised to the patriarchs of old, reaching from "the river of Egypt to the Euphrates" (Genesis 15:18).

With all the blessings in store for all the Jewish people scattered abroad among the nations of earth, and especially for the State of Israel, for which Theodor Herzl sacrificed everything in pouring out his life blood for the solution of the Jewish problem, there should rise to God's throne in the heavens a mighty prayer from God's people in the Church, to join in the sublime request made by the Apostle Paul for the redemption and restoration of Israel, as expressed in the following words of Paul the Apostle: "Brethren, my heart's desire and prayer to God for Israel is, that they might be saved" (Romans 10:1).

Their enemies were to be conquered in battle and flee seven ways from them. God promised to restore the rains in their season, they shall lend to many nations and not borrow. The Lord will make them *the head and not the tail;* they shall be above only, and not be beneath — all these blessings are vouchsafed on condition of faithfully observing God's commands (Deuteronomy 28:1-14).

'THE STATE OF ISRAEL' NEEDS TO RECEIVE ITS MESSIAH

This is what the State of Israel needs today — to give wholehearted allegiance to Jesus as their Messiah. Jesus wept over Jerusalem (Luke 19:41, 42) as He foretold the destruction of the temple and the dispersion of the Jews into all the nations of the earth. The promise is plainly given in the Scriptures that *"all Israel* shall be saved," when they behold the Deliverer coming down from heaven to take away *"ungodliness from Jacob"* and "take away their sins" (Romans 11:26-28).

When *"all Israel shall be saved"* (have accepted Jesus as their national Messiah), then will begin the glorious reign of Israel's Messiah to prove Himself to be "King of kings, and Lord of lords" (Revelation 19:11-16).

✡ 12 ✡

THE TEACHING OF THE SCRIPTURES REGARDING ISRAEL

THE JEWS have rightly been called the miracle race of history. The nation of Israel alone can claim divine origin and divine preservation amidst the decay of the ages. When Frederick the Great asked his court preacher for a proof of the inspiration of the Bible, he answered in one word — the *Jew*. The glory of many nations of antiquity, such as that of Egypt, Babylon, Medo-Persia, Greece, and Rome has vanished, while the Jewish nation, which has been subjected to fierce persecution, and a number of times been brought near the brink of extinction, has survived to this day; and that nation has had a greater influence for the moral and spiritual uplift of mankind than any other.

THE MESSIANIC PROMISE ENTRUSTED TO ABRAM

God is directly responsible for bringing the Jewish race into existence and for sustaining and preserving it through the almost four thousand years of its history. When all the nations were steeped in idolatry, God called one man, Abram, out of Ur of Chaldea, to be the channel by which He would make Himself known to the world. The Messianic promise, given in the Garden of Eden, was entrusted to the descendants of Shem, one of the three sons of Noah; and of these, after many centuries, to only one man, Abram, who obeyed the call of God and became the progenitor of a new race. Here is the far-reaching promise which God gave to Abram: "I will bless them that bless thee, and curse them that curse thee; and in thee shall all the families of the earth be blessed." How true it has been that the nations lending their support to the Jews have been blessed of God; while those who have persecuted and oppressed the Jews have been cursed of God.

THE DIVINE ORIGIN OF THE JEWISH RACE

It was from the posterity of Abram that the long-promised Messiah was to come, by whom all the earth would be blessed with the knowledge of God. God also gave to Abram the promise of the land of Canaan and, later, all the land from the river of Egypt to the Euphrates. To Abram and Sarah, after a waiting period of twenty-five years, Isaac was born — the son of promise. Then, Isaac and Rebekah were the parents of two sons, Esau and Jacob. Although Isaac had planned to give the birthright blessing to Esau, his firstborn, it was bestowed upon Jacob. Twelve sons were born to Jacob, who became the patriarchs of the Twelve Tribes of Israel, which constituted the nation of Israel. (Genesis 12:1-3; 13:14-17; 15:1-7, 18; 18:19; Exodus 3:1-10; Psalms 105:6-15, 38-45; 106:34-48; Acts 7:2-4; Hebrews 11:8-12)

It was in Joseph's day of rulership in Egypt that Jacob's descendants were obliged to go down to Egypt to escape the seven-year famine. After some centuries a new Pharaoh greatly oppressed the children of Israel, until they cried to God for deliverance. Then it was that God appeared to Moses in a burning bush at Mount Horeb and gave to him the commission to deliver Israel from the opposition of Pharaoh. The burning bush has ever been the symbol of the Jewish nation, because although it has passed through many fiery ordeals, yet it has never been consumed.

THE DIVINE PLAN IN JEWISH HISTORY

Instead of Israel's at once entering the Promised Land, because they failed God at Kadesh Barnea, they were doomed to forty years of wilderness wanderings. When they reached Mount Sinai, God spoke audibly amidst thunders and lightnings, and gave them the Ten Commandments. Instead of seeking to serve God faithfully, Israel wanted to be like other nations and asked of Samuel a king. Israel became a theocratic monarchy, for God blessed the kings who served Him, but punished those who were wicked. The ten tribes of Israel were taken captive to Assyria and, later, Judah was carried away to Babylon. Under Nehemiah and Ezra a small remnant returned to build the temple and walls of Jerusalem: and thus preparation was made in Israel for the coming of the Messiah. (Exodus 20:1-17; Numbers 23:9; Joshua 1:1-9; 6:9-16; 10:6-14; I Samuel 8:1-9; II Samuel 7:1-11; II Kings 17:6-18; 24:10-16; Nehemiah 1:1-11; 2:12-20)

THE DIVINE PURPOSE OF THE JEWISH NATION

One of the greatest contributions made to mankind by Israel prior to the coming of the Messiah, was the large collection of sacred oracles contained in the Old Testament Scriptures. These plainly foretold the mission, the sufferings, the death, and the resurrection of the long-promised Messiah. Jesus came in the "fulness of time," and confined

His mission to the "lost sheep of the house of Israel." He said to the woman of Samaria, "Salvation is of the Jews." Jesus was born "King of the Jews" and Jesus died upon the cross as the "King of the Jews." Jesus came to His own, but His own received Him not. (Deuteronomy 6:3-15; I Chronicles 17:20-22; Isaiah 7:14; 9:6, 7; 43:10-12; 61:1-3; Jeremiah 31:35-37; John 4:22; 5:47; Romans 9:4, 5)

THE DISPERSION AND RESTORATION OF THE JEWS

God called the nation of Israel into existence to be His "peculiar treasure above all people." They were to be unto Him a "kingdom of priests, and an holy nation." This was to be true of them not only when they were in possession of the land of Palestine, but equally true of them during the period of their dispersion. Though the Jews today are still blinded with unbelief, and scattered throughout the world, they are, nevertheless, unwittingly witnessing to the veracity of the Bible, which portrays their history — past, present, and future. Israel is yet to become the head of all nations, taking its rightful leadership in proclaiming the Gospel of the Kingdom to the great Gentile world. The Church has the responsibility of reaching the Jews with the Gospel of Christ in order to prepare them for their world-wide mission.

The Cause of the Dispersion of the Jews

The cause for all the world's troubles can be summed up in one word — *disobedience*. Disobedience on the part of Adam and Eve plunged the entire human family into the maelstrom of evil. God promised to make of Abraham's seed a "great nation." God promised Israel that if they would "diligently hearken to the voice of the Lord their God, and do all His commandments," He would set them "above all the nations of the earth," that He would establish them "an holy people unto himself," and make them the "head, and not the tail." (Deuteronomy 28:1-25; Isaiah 5:1-5; 43:1-7; 62:1-7; Matthew 11:20-24; 23: 37-39; 27:11-25; Mark 12:1-27; Luke 13:6-9; 19:41-44; 21:20-32)

Why is it that the Jews are the *tail* and not the *head* today? Because of disobedience to God, Israel and Judah were uprooted from the land and taken captive to Assyria and Babylon. The greatest test of their obedience came with the appearance of their Messiah. Jesus confined His ministry to "the lost sheep of the house of Israel." How sad that "he came to his own and his own received him not"! The Jewish fig tree was barren of fruit, but Jesus patiently continued to seek for it to bear fruit. Because it did not bear fruit Jesus later cursed the "fig tree" and pronounced doom upon the Jewish nation. He wept over Jerusalem because they did not realize the hour of their "visitation."

Demanding of Pilate Christ's crucifixion, they said, "His blood be upon us and our children." Thus they crucified their King.

The Persecution of the Jews During Their World Dispersion

The judgment of God fell upon the Jewish nation in the destruction of Jerusalem by the Romans in A.D. 70. Over a million Jews perished during this national calamity. Many thousands of Jews were taken captive to Rome. In the course of the centuries, the Jews were scattered to all parts of the earth. They have held tenaciously to the doctrine of monotheism, that "God is one Lord," but have persisted in denying that this One Divine Being manifests Himself in Three Persons—Father, Son, and Holy Spirit. The prophet, Hosea, long before, had foretold that the "children of Israel shall abide many days without a king . . . and without a sacrifice." Moses had declared that they would be scattered among all people, "from one end of the earth even unto the other," and that among these nations they would find no ease, but "a trembling heart . . . and sorrow of mind . . . and shalt have none assurance of thy life." (Deuteronomy 28:45-68; 29:24-29; Psalm 102:8-18; Jeremiah 30:4-11; Ezekiel 20:34-38; 22:17-22; Hosea 3:4, 5; Matthew 24:21-35)

How terrible have been the persecutions of the Jews! The prophet Jeremiah also had declared God would make them to be a "reproach and a proverb, a taunt [sheninah] and a curse, in all places." The Jews have suffered great persecution in so-called Christian countries of Europe. Millions of Jews perished in Russia, and over six million in Germany and Poland during World War II.

The Promise of Their Salvation and Restoration

When God called Abraham, He gave him the promise that "in thy seed shall all the families of the earth be blessed." The word seed here applies not only to the coming Messiah, but looks forward to a saved and regenerated Israel. (Deuteronomy 30:1-10; Jeremiah 16:14-16; 31:35-40; Ezekiel 34:23-31; 36:16-37; 37:1-22; Amos 9:9-15; Zechariah 8:1-8, 20-23; 13:6-9; Romans 11:17-29)

It is made plain in the Word of God that the Jews will return to their homeland, Palestine, in unbelief for the purpose of building up Zion. The Zionist movement, started by Theodor Herzl in 1896, has put forth stupendous efforts in transforming Palestine into a blossoming garden. Over two million Jews have already returned to Palestine. Ezekiel's vision of the "dry bones" is being fulfilled. The Jews will yet need to go through "Jacob's trouble," in the period of tribulation which follows the rapture of the saints. The Church today needs to awaken to her solemn responsibility of giving the Gospel to the Jews.

NEBUCHADNEZZAR'S DREAM OF THE GREAT METALLIC IMAGE

In order to understand the vision of the Messiah which was given to Theodor Herzl in a dream, it is necessary to give attention to the study of the second chapter of Daniel.

To Daniel alone was given the opportunity to interpret the dream of the metallic image of gold, silver, brass and iron, given in a dream to Nebuchadnezzar, as set forth in this chapter.

In the Old Testament, there were only two classes in classifying the nations of earth, small and great; namely the Gentiles and the Jews.

There were nations on earth long before that of Babylon.

About 1900 B.C. Abraham was engaged in the "battle of the kings" for the rescue of Lot and his wife (Genesis 14:13-16). Abraham pursued the captors as far as Damascus with 318 armed men to engage in this battle (Genesis 14:1-16).

God waited to give His estimate of mankind which was seeking to create a kingdom on a large scale in order to conquer the world.

As far back as the Garden of Eden, we find that God entrusted Adam with universal dominion. Because Adam, called the son of God (Luke 3:38), yielded with Eve to the serpent's suggestion to eat of the forbidden "Tree" (of knowledge of good and evil), man forfeited the right to world dominion. Satan became the "prince of this world" (John 12:31). At no time did God forfeit His right to direct the affairs of mankind. God's plan of redemption reveals that world dominion will be entrusted to the "last Adam" (I Corinthians 15:45-48), who is the "second man," the perfect man that could not and did not fail God. He was born of a virgin who by a miracle of creation, brought forth a babe who was called the "Son of God." He is called the "Lord from heaven" (I Corinthians 15:45-47), the long-awaited Messiah, called the "King of kings, and Lord of lords" (Revelation 19:11-16).

The Theocracy Established in Israel by Moses

The beginning of preparing the Lord Jesus Christ to be given universal dominion is seen in the call of Abraham, to whom God gave the promise of making a great nation of him, in numbers, as the "stars of the heaven, and as the sand upon the seashore," to be ruled over by God Himself in an ordained new form of government, called a theocracy. Moses was entrusted to be the chosen leader of Israel at the burning bush (Exodus 3:1-10). He was to bring about the emancipation from the bondage and slavery that Israel had endured under Pharaoh in the land of Egypt. Moses led them on dry land, through the parting of the Red Sea, on their way to the promised land of Canaan.

On account of their revolt against God in listening to the report given by the ten spies instead of heeding the call of Joshua and Caleb to go up at once, and possess the land (Numbers 13:26-33), the whole nation was doomed to forty years of wilderness journey (Numbers 14: 26-34). God did not abandon or forsake Israel because of their disobedience, but gave them the *Ten Commandments* on Mt. Sinai. They constructed the tabernacle and Moses instituted the offerings and the priesthood to make of Israel a "holy nation." God promised to bestow all kinds of blessings, so that they would be the "head, and not the tail" of all nations (Deuteronomy 28:1-14). God also warned Israel of the curses that would come upon them, so that eventually they would become "an astonishment, a proverb, and a byword, among all nations whither the Lord shall lead thee" (Deuteronomy 28:15-65, especially verse 37).

NEBUCHADNEZZAR'S VISION OF THE "SEVEN TIMES"

Another chapter of great importance in understanding the meaning of the term, "the times of the Gentiles," that Jesus referred to in Luke 21:24, is that of Leviticus 26, in which God declared that He would punish Israel "seven times." *Four* times in this chapter God designates that their punishment would be "seven times" (Leviticus 26:18, 21, 24, 28).

Still another occasion where this expression, "seven times," is found is in Daniel 4:23, in connection with another dream given to Nebuchadnezzar, in which he saw a tree reaching to heaven that was cut down with only a stump being left of the majestic tree. The interpretation given to the king by Daniel explained that the growing tree reaching to heaven represented Nebuchadnezzar's being puffed up with great pride. He was to be punished by living among the beasts of the field until *"seven times"* pass over (Daniel 4:22-27), after which his mind and reason would be restored, and the king would be restored to his throne.

When this "seven times" expression is taken in terms of days, the "seven times" will equal 360x7, or 2520 days. This "seven times" can also be reckoned in years. And when so reckoned would make 2520 years that the Gentile rule is to be carried out over Israel.

The great image designates the nations which are to exercise rulership over Israel in one way or another, reaching from the head of gold (Babylon) to the toes, representing a ten-nation Roman confederacy of dictators. These ten kings are more fully described in Revelation, chapters 12-14.

Attention must now be given to a brief study of each part of this great image vision.

The Meaning of the Great Metallic Image

1. The first world power was that of Babylon, represented as the *head of gold*. The existence of the Babylonian kingdom as the first world power began with the otherthrow of Nineveh, its greatest rival Nabopolassar in 607 B.C. His son, Nebuchadnezzar, ruled after his father for a period of forty-five years, to 558 B.C. This kingdom was designated by Isaiah as a "golden cup," on account of its great wealth and vast territory. It lasted but a brief period, ending with the conquest of Babylon by Darius while the voluptuous feast of Belteshazzar took place in 538 B.C. (Isaiah 44:28; 48:1-4; Daniel 5:23-31).

2. *The silver breast,* the kingdom of the Medes and Persians, became the second great world power. The wonderful story of Daniel in the lions' den took place during the reign of Darius (Daniel 6:18-28). Isaiah made mention of Cyrus as the *deliverer of Israel one hundred seventy-six years before the birth of Cyrus* (Isaiah 45:1-5). The kingdom of the Medes and Persians lasted but a little over two hundred years. Xerxes, the great Persian ruler, attempted to invade Macedonia with a vast army of a million soldiers, but his project ended in utter defeat in the battles of Plataea, Marathon, and Salamis. Alexander the Great conquered the kingdom of the Medes and Persians. Alexander the Great died in Babylon, 323 B.C.

It was during this period that the exiles returned from captivity (Ezra 1:1-4; Nehemiah 2:1-8) to rebuild the temple of Jerusalem and that Nehemiah journeyed from the palace of Shushan to rebuild the walls of Jerusalem. The kingdom of the Medes and Persians came to an end in 333 B.C. The kingdom of the Medes was inferior to that of Babylon in that the king was controlled by one hundred twenty princes.

3. The *brass belly and thigh* represents the Grecian Empire. This empire began with the complete conquest of the Persians by Alexander the Great in 333 B.C. After Alexander's death the empire, in a modified form of two great rivals — the Selucidae and the Ptolemies — lasted to the conquest of Macedonia by the Romans in 145 B.C., thus having its existence over a period of one hundred eighty-seven years. Alexander the Great's career lasted for only a brief period of ten years. His life ended with a shameful drunken debauch. His kingdom was then divided among his four leading generals.

The Greeks were famous for their brass armors. The Greeks were also noted for their beautiful architecture and their great study of philosophy and science, as was evident in the work done by Socrates, Plato, Aristotle and many others.

4. The *iron legs* represent the Roman Empire. The city of Rome was founded in 753 B.C. by Romulus, ascribed in Roman mythology

to be the son of Mars (the god of war) by Vestal Rhea Silvia. As a babe, Romulus being left exposed to die was rescued by a she-wolf (mythology) which carried him to her den nearby and suckled him. According to this ancient legend a shepherd brought him home to his wife and reared him with his own children.

Rome became an empire under Julius Caesar and continued undivided until Constantine transferred the capital from Rome to Constantinople in A.D. 330, which divided the Roman Empire into two parts — the Eastern Roman Empire and the Western Roman Empire (the two legs of iron). The western division of the Roman Empire fell in A.D. 476 during the raid of the Vandals. The eastern leg of the Roman Empire continued to the fall of Constantinople in A.D. 1453, when it was conquered by the Turks.

This empire, symbolized by iron, was very strong, having greater solidity and cohesion because of its codes of law, which continue in use to this day.

All New Testament history, including the birth, life, and death of Jesus, falls into this period. The Roman spear was thrust into the side of the crucified Messiah, the despised King of the Jews.

5. *The ten toes* represent ten separate kingdoms of the revived Roman Empire during the Tribulation period of seven years.

Daniel's Vision of the Four Beast Kingdoms

In the seventh chapter of Daniel is given another vision, representing the four great world empires in the form of four beasts.

1. *The first beast,* representing the Babylonian Empire, is that of a lion with eagle's wings, setting forth strength combined with swiftness.

2. *The second beast* is that of a bear, representing the Medo-Persian kingdom. This bear is represented as having three ribs in its mouth, setting forth the conquest of Babylon, Lydia, and Egypt.

3. *The third beast* is that of a leopard with four wings, a revengeful ferocious beast, ready to devour its prey of other lands, representing the Empire of Greece under Alexander the Great.

4. *The fourth beast* is that of a terrible, hideous monster with ten horns, representing ten kingdoms arising out of the revived Roman Empire during the Tribulation period under the sway of the Antichrist, symbolized by a little horn (Daniel 7:24, 25).

The Falling Stone From Heaven Representing Messiah

Another matter of great importance in this vision of four metallic kingdoms is the final object in view: that of a stone falling from heaven upon the feet of this great image. The kingdom of God therefore is called the Stone Kingdom because Daniel interpreted that this stone from heaven "cut out . . . without hands," falling upon the feet of this image brought about the crash of the whole image, thus bringing about the close of the "times of the Gentiles" and the ushering in of the Mediatorial, Messianic Kingdom, which expands and covers the whole earth (Daniel 2:44, 45; Matthew 4:23, 24; 25:21-23).

Our Lord Jesus Christ came down from heaven to a revolted earth to establish a spiritual kingdom in the hearts of sinful people, as Jesus taught Nicodemus when He said to him, "Verily, verily, I say unto thee, Except a man be born again, he cannot see the kingdom of God" (John 3:3). Jesus was also concerned to bring about a visible, temporal, material kingdom of God as well as a spiritual kingdom. Our Lord Jesus Christ is represented in the Old and New Testaments as a rock upon which to build for time and eternity (Matthew 7:24, 25; 16:18). This stone became a stone of stumbling to the nation of Israel (Isaiah 28:16; Romans 9:32, 33).

God gave to the Gentile nations a long lease of "seven times" or 2520 years in which to prove whether man can rule himself without God.

Looking at this great image one finds that deterioration takes place from gold to silver, brass, iron, and at last clay. What are the nations doing today with all their military projects but preparing for earth's greatest and final slaughter, to be fought in the battle of Armageddon (Revelation 16:16)?

The final words of Daniel spoken to Nebuchadnezzar were to inform him that upon the total destruction of this great man-made image, God will have the *"stone"* (Messiah) come down from heaven, and God will "set up a kingdom [through Messiah], which shall never be destroyed . . . but . . . it shall *stand for ever"* (Daniel 2:44, 45).

Notice also the declaration made in the seventh chapter of Daniel, which represents these four kingdoms in the form of ravenous beasts, that the fourth beast is represented as having "ten horns," representing "ten kings" of the Tribulation period after the rapture. Then follows the declaration of a superior king (the Antichrist) uttering blasphemy against the Most High, and wearing out the "saints of the most High" (martyrs of the Tribulation period). Then will the "kingdom and dominion, and the greatness of the kingdom under the whole heaven" be established by the long promised Messiah (Daniel 7:28, 29).

THE IMPORTANCE OF THE TIMES OF THE GENTILES

The book of Daniel deals almost exclusively with the "times of the Gentiles," although that particular phrase is not mentioned therein. Our Lord Jesus Christ was the first and only one to use the term "times

142   *The Jew Returns to Israel*

of the Gentiles." This book sets forth not only a panoramic view of the four Gentile world governments which were to arise, but also furnishes the key determining the time during which the Gentiles are entrusted with world government. This is a period of 2520 years, reaching from the beginning of Nebuchadnezzar's reign to the "time of the end," when the "Son of man" will establish His Messianic Kingdom upon earth.

The Reason Why World Dominion Is Entrusted to the Gentiles

In the beginning of Israel's national existence, Moses taught that God's purpose was that His chosen people should be the "head and not the tail," that they should "be above only and not beneath." World dominion was entrusted to Israel on condition of full allegiance to God. Moses made perfectly plain that disobedience and unfaithfulness to God would put them in subjection to the Gentile nations. God delivered Israel many times from their enemies during the nine hundred years of their national existence. In Leviticus 26, Moses gives four warnings that God would chastise Israel "seven times" for their disobedience, and would bring upon them the sword, and make the land desolate. Both Israel and Judah were taken captive — the former to Assyria and the latter to Babylon. (Leviticus 26:14-18, 21, 27, 28; Deuteronomy 28:9-15, 36-50; 32:8; Hosea 3:4, 5; Jeremiah 27:19, 20; 24:1; Daniel 4:10-16, 28-37)

Israel in Subjection to the Gentiles

It is an historic fact that after the close of the Assyrian and Babylonian captivities, Israel never regained national independence as a sovereign nation. From that time, through succeeding centuries, Israel has been under Gentile rule. God gave Nebuchadnezzar the great vision of a tree having its branches broken off and only a stump with a band of brass and iron remaining, to teach him the needed lesson that pride comes before destruction. The proud king was to be humbled and was to make his dwelling with the beasts, and to eat grass as oxen, until "seven times" should pass over him. After living with the beasts of the field for a period of seven years, Nebuchadnezzar's reason was restored.

The Length of Gentile World Dominion — 'Seven Times'

Jesus, knowing the divine "plan of redemption," as set forth in the Old Testament oracles, knew that the "seven times" punishment pronounced upon Israel had a definite beginning and a definite ending. He knew also that the "seven times" of Gentile sovereignty over Jerusalem had reference to some definite, specific period of time. The Word of God gives various examples of applying a year for a day; as in the case of the children of Israel, who, because they rejected the report of Caleb and Joshua, two of the spies who spent forty days viewing the "Promised Land," were condemned to a forty-year wilderness journey. When this principle of applying a year for a day is applied to the "seven times" of Gentile sovereignty, it will give exactly 2520 years. (Numbers 14:26-34; II Chronicles 36:15-20; Daniel 4:16, 23-25; Luke 21:20-24; Revelation 12:6, 14; 13:1-5)

It is a historic fact that 2520 years have passed since the Davidic monarchy was overthrown. Judah lost her independence with the invasion of Nebuchadnezzar, which occurred in the year of 607 B.C. Counting exactly 2520 years from this invasion of Jerusalem by Nebuchadnezzar, brings us to the beginning of the first World War in A.D. 1914.

The Importance of the Balfour Declaration

The conquest of Jerusalem occurred just three years later in 604 B.C., which counting 2520 years reaches to the year A.D. 1917. This year had a most epochal event in the noted Balfour Declaration, wherein the British government promised the Jews upon their conquest of Palestine, that they would be guaranteed the right to have Palestine as their national homeland. Jerusalem was delivered from the despotic yoke of the Turks by General Allenby on December 9th, 1917, just 2520 years after the destruction of the temple by Nebuchadnezzar. This fact is a definite indication that the times of the Gentiles are drawing to a close.

The Ending of Gentile World Dominion at Christ's Coming

As the "times of the Gentiles" began with a ruler holding sovereign power over the nation of Israel, so the "times of the Gentiles" will close with a great ruler known as the Antichrist. He will continue for a period of seven years. This will be known as the "time of Jacob's trouble" (Jeremiah 30:7). At the close of that period, the Battle of Armageddon will take place and Christ Jesus will appear in glory to rule as King of kings and Lord of lords, and thus fulfill all the promises of the coming Messiah set forth in the Word of God. (Daniel 7:19-26; Isaiah 62:1-7; Luke 17:26-30; John 5:43; Romans 11:25, 26; Revelation 13:1-8; 17:8-14)

DANIEL'S VISION OF THE SEVENTY WEEKS

The study of prophecy is one of the most important aspects of the Bible, though it is the most neglected. Many look upon prophecies of the Bible as a sealed book, but God wants His people to unseal and disclose these mysteries that relate to individuals, cities, and nations.

The second chapter of Daniel is rightly called the pivotal prophetic chapter of the Bible. This panoramic chapter may be designated as unfolding the "times of the Gentiles," extending through a period of "seven times," or 2520 years, from the reign of Nebuchadnezzar, and pointing forward to the time when our Lord Jesus Christ shall reign supreme over all nations for the duration of one thousand years, and that without having one single war.

One astonishing feature in this long panorama of history is that no reference is made in any way to Israel or the Jewish nation. The reason for this omission is that Israel was not to be restored as a nation (Numbers 23:9) during this long period because of her unfaithfulness to God. This unfaithfulness made it necessary for God to punish the people by uprooting them from their land of Palestine and dispersing them among the Gentile nations.

Instead of God's unfolding this dream to Daniel, He imparted it to Nebuchadnezzar, who was a worshiper of pagan gods. This dream of the metallic image greatly troubled Nebuchadnezzar, so that he called the wise men to tell the dream and give the interpretation, or else be slain. When Daniel heard of this matter, he begged for a brief time to seek God for wisdom to unravel the dream and give its interpretation.

Daniel, with his three captive companions, gathered for prayer to entreat God for the needed wisdom to solve this most perplexing dream. Daniel was brought into the king's presence and declared that no human being was able to solve this dream, but God only.

This dream deals with the subject of world dominion, and reveals the futility of kings, emperors, and tyrants to bring all the earth under their subjection. It is true that in the beginning of the creation story, God entrusted to Adam "world dominion."

The Vision of the Four Great World Powers

To Nebuchadnezzar was given this vision of four kingdoms — four great world powers, that would have rulership over a period of 2520 years. No mention is made of the nation of Israel in this dream given to Nebuchadnezzar. The reason for this startling omission is that God had an altogether different plan for Israel than He had for any of the other nations of earth. All the nations of earth were steeped in idolatry and immorality. It was for this reason that God called Abraham (Genesis 12:1-5; 15:7) out of Chaldea to make of him a great nation, bequeathing to him all the land of Palestine and all the land from the river of Egypt to the river Euphrates (Genesis 15:18). When the revelation and knowledge of God was given to them on Mount Sinai in the Ten Commandments and all the various details of sacrifice and priesthood in connection with the tabernacle worship, Israel was called to be "an holy people unto the Lord thy God: the Lord thy God hath chosen thee to be a *special people* unto himself, above all people that are upon the face of the earth" (Deuteronomy 7:6). Notice the command that is given to Israel in the following words, "Thou shalt therefore keep the commandments, and the statutes, and the judgments, which I command thee this day, to do them" (Deuteronomy 7:11).

Israel was called to be a "special people" (Deuteronomy 7:6). Its purpose was to bring God's blessing "to all the families of earth." It was as the "chosen people of God" that Israel was entrusted with the message of redemption and salvation (Romans 9:1-6) to earth's remotest bounds. In this ninth chapter of Daniel is made known for the first time the name by which the Redeemer is to be known; namely, by the name of "the Messiah." This name means *"the Anointed One,"* who is to be Prophet, Priest, and King. The word Messiah has become a household word within both Jewish and Christian homes.

The High Water Mark of the Old Testament

The ninth chapter of Daniel may be called the "high-water mark of the Old Testament." Not only does this prophecy point definitely to the coming Messiah, as many other prophecies do, but the distinguishing feature, belonging only to this prophecy, is the definite, accurate, chronological fixing of Messiah's triumphal entry into Jerusalem and of His atoning death (Daniel 9:24-27; Matthew 21:1-11).

Not to Noah, not to Abraham, not to Moses, not even to David or Solomon was any indication given as to *when* the long-awaited Messiah would accomplish full redemption for fallen man. To Daniel, and to him alone, belongs this honor of fixing *the exact time to the very day* when "Messiah the Prince" would enter Jerusalem acclaimed as king, and in but a few days "be cut off" and have nothing "for Himself" (Daniel 9:26, margin). He was despised and rejected of His own nation. Only by such a Messiah, set forth by Isaiah the prophet, as the "Man of Sorrows," could the Messianic Kingdom be established upon earth (Isaiah 53:1-5, 12).

In the dark period of Israel's history, when the people had been in captivity in Babylon for seventy years, Daniel was given this wondrous "Morning Star" of prophecy pointing, not to Messiah's birth in Bethlehem (yet including it), but to *the accurate time* of His agonizing death on Calvary. Next to His birth, His death was of greatest importance for Israel's redemption.

Jesus' Triumphal Entry into Jerusalem

Jesus alone had *this accurate timepiece* of prophecy in mind when He beheld Jerusalem from Mount Olivet on the day of His Triumphal

Entry into that city and, weeping over it, said: "If thou hadst known, even thou, at least in this thy day, the things which belong unto thy peace! but now they are hid from thine eyes" (Luke 19:42).

Jesus knew, when the multitude were crying, "Hosanna! Blessed be the King that cometh in the name of the Lord," that in but a few days others would cry out, "Crucify him, crucify him. We will not have this man to rule over us; we have no king but Caesar."

In recording this vision of the "Seventy Weeks," Daniel tells the circumstances which brought about this most wonderful revelation of the coming Messiah. Upon the completion of the seventy years of exile, foretold by Jeremiah the prophet (Jeremiah 25:9-13), Daniel was looking expectantly for the next event following the many years in captivity; namely, the restoration of the captives to God's favor, so that the walls of Jerusalem could again be rebuilt (Jeremiah 29:10, 11).

Although it was necessary for God to mete out judgment upon Israel, yet He had not disowned nor forsaken them. In the years of their exile God made it known through Jeremiah the prophet, that He would punish and overthrow Babylon at the termination of the seventy years of exile.

Then would follow the restoration of the captive exiles to their own land, according to Jeremiah's declaration, "I will bring them again to this land [Palestine]" (Jeremiah 24:6). God had promised to extend this mercy to His chosen people, and this was a definite reason for Daniel to pray for it. Daniel had been in the habit of praying to God with his windows open toward Jerusalem (Daniel 6:1-10).

Because of their rebellion against God, the curse came upon the ten tribes of Israel in the Assyrian captivity, and upon the two tribes of Judah in the Babylonian captivity. Daniel prayed for *all* Israel in this intercessory prayer, for he acknowledged that *all* Israel had sinned (Daniel 9:1-8).

Daniel's Prayer of Intercession for Israel

In pleading God's mercy, Daniel called to mind the great deliverance of Jehovah in bringing forth "Thy people out of the land of Egypt with a mighty hand." Only by a like miraculous deliverance could Israel now return from captivity. He prayed, "Let thine anger and thy fury be turned away from thy city Jerusalem" (Daniel 9:8-19).

God has given His Word as a lamp, a light, a chart, a compass, and a guidebook, so that the pilgrim travelers may be given definite knowledge in understanding the past, the present, and the future. Prophecy always looks to the future for fulfillment (II Peter 1:19-21).

This prophecy of the "Seventy Weeks" centers around the Jews, to bring about their complete national regeneration and reconciliation to God through Messiah's atoning work on the cross.

While this prophecy *specifically* declares the time of Christ's *First* Advent, when He was "cut off" (Daniel 9:26a) at the cross, without having established His Messianic Kingdom, it also looks forward most definitely to Messiah's *Second* Advent, when it will effect Israel's national reconciliation to God, making Jerusalem the seat of His world-wide Messianic Kingdom (Daniel 9:24).

The wide scope of this Messianic prophecy covers the work of Messiah in deepest humiliation and especially of His Second Coming as triumphant king, removing transgression from Israel, putting to an end the desolation which has been upon Jerusalem, and meting out judgment upon the Antichrist, who is referred to as the "prince that shall come" and the "man of sin" (Daniel 9:26b, 27).

Daniel was given this most wonderful revelation of the "Seventy Weeks" because he had been pleading for God's mercy upon rebellious undeserving Israel. In the vision of the "Seventy Weeks" the first and the second Advent of Messiah are blended into one. In the Old Testament, prophecy deals primarily with Israel. No notice is taken of the entire period of the Church in this vision. Notice in reading Luke 4:10-19, that Jesus, in quoting the prophecy of Isaiah 61:1, 2, only referred to its application to his First Advent, making no mention of the "day of vengeance," because that event was yet far away, belonging only to His Second Advent. Because Israel, for many centuries, had been in a world-wide dispersion during this entire gospel dispensation, no cognizance of this period is made in this prophecy of the "Seventy Weeks."

The Explanation of 'The Seventy Weeks'

The "Seventy Weeks" represents a period of (7x70) 490 years of Israel's history. From Daniel 9:25 it can be seen that 69 weeks, or 483 years, reach to Messiah's death. It is very important to realize that the declaration made in verse 24 belongs to the *very close* of the seventieth week.

However, between the close of the sixty-ninth week and the beginning of the seventieth week lies the long period of the Church Age. The six declarations of verse 24 are fully realized at Messiah's second Advent. Then and not till then, will Messiah bring in the righteousness of the ages, seal the vision and prophecy (in their complete fulfillment), and anoint the "Holy of Holies" by His Presence in the millennial temple (Ezekiel, chapters 40-48).

The period of "Seventy Weeks" is divided into three sections: the *first,* "seven weeks," or 49 years; the *second,* 62 weeks, or 434 years; the *third,* one week of seven years.

The beginning of the "Seventy Weeks" takes place with the decree of Artaxerxes, given to Nehemiah in 445 B.C. to rebuild the walls of Jerusalem, which were broken down (Nehemiah 1:1-11). The returned exiles, responding to the decree of Cyrus in 536 B.C., had restored the temple and temple worship (Ezra 1:1-11). In the first period of seven weeks, or 49 years, the "street and wall" were built "in troublous times" (Daniel 9:25b).

Adding 62 weeks to the 7 weeks, making a period of 69 weeks, or 483 years, leads up directly, to the very day, to the greatest of all events in Messiah's ministry, to the very close of His *entire ministry* (John 12:12-15), to His crucifixion and death.

It has been demonstrated that although there are only 476 solar years between March 14, 445 B.C. and A.D. 32, yet allowing for leap years and *other special days,* when the 173,740 days from March 14, 445 B.C. (verse 25) to the day of Christ's entrance into Jerusalem April 6, A.D. 32 (Matthew 21:1-6) are counted, including *116 leap year days* and *24 special days,* it makes exactly 483 calendar years or the 69 full weeks. The rejection and crucifixion of Messiah was proof that Israel did not receive Jesus as her Messianic King. Messiah's work was "cut off" at the cross, leaving Him without the mediatorial Davidic kingdom. However, His ascension to heaven and His Second Coming make possible the national salvation of Israel and the establishment of His kingdom upon earth (Isaiah 53:1-11; 61:1-6; Luke 19:11-15).

The Roman Prince the Antichrist

The word *prince* in verse 26 has no application to "Messiah the Prince" of verse 25. The "prince," or leader, of verse 26 refers only to the Antichrist, who will come out of the Fourth World Empire—Rome. It was the Roman people who fulfilled Jesus prophecy (Luke 21:6, 20-24) in destroying Jerusalem and the temple in A.D. 70. Since the dispersion of the Jews, Jerusalem has been exposed to a "flood" of enemies, and throughout the entire Gospel Age Jerusalem has been kept "desolate" by war, especially by the Saracenic conquerors, who raised the Crescent on the temple site.

At the end of the Gospel Age, Daniel's *seventieth week* of seven years takes place, during which time the Antichrist is revealed when he "confirms" a (not *the*) covenant with many for seven years, breaking it in the middle of the period. God is not a covenant-breaking God, but a covenant-keeping God.

The Antichrist as the superman, "the man of sin," will reign as a "Beast," spreading "desolation" over all the nations, devouring the "whole earth" with his fury. This "desolation" will be consumed and destroyed "with the brightness" of Messiah's coming in His glorious second advent (John 5:43; Matthew 24:22-31; II Thessalonians 2:3-8).

THE COMPARISON OF THE 'SEVEN TIMES' WITH 'THE SEVENTY WEEKS'

These are two visions: one, that of a great metallic image of gold, silver, brass, and iron; the other gives expression of a timetable of "Seventy Weeks." These two visions have a much deeper meaning than is apparent on the surface.

The first was given to a pagan king, the other to a devoted prophet of God.

The first covers a long span of history, involving the four greatest world powers; the other, a limited period of history, covering only 490 years, with but one nation in view — that of Israel. The first gives an impressive representation of the Messiah as a *stone* falling from heaven on the feet of the metallic image; the other gives Messiah in person as the *Prince* entering Jerusalem, acclaimed as a prophet by some (Matthew 21:11), by others acclaimed as king (John 12:13).

The first portrays a great meaning of the futility of mere earthly possessions and glory; the other, of a far greater blessing in one's being interested in seeking first the kingdom of God, to obtain spiritual blessings for time and eternity.

Bearing these observations in mind of the distinction between these visions — one of a king interested in earthly possessions and glory and the other of a prophet of God, concerned only in the redemption of a despised, downtrodden people known as the Jews, or Israel — can anyone find some feature wherein both visions are in full agreement? The answer to this inquiry is, that there is great element of agreement between the two totally different visions.

Both visions were given, inspired of God, to reveal the work committed to the *Son of God* in His capacity as a Saviour and also as a *ruler* of mankind.

The Person to whom is committed this great task of solving the material as well as the spiritual problems that have vexed mankind from time immemorial — that Person is given the name of the *Messiah,* one qualified as *prophet* to declare the will and purpose of God for mankind; qualified as *priest* to provide atonement and redemption for mankind by this substitutionary self-sacrifice upon the cross of Calvary; and also qualified as *king,* having conquered that dread monster, death, by His glorious resurrection and ascension to heaven to be man's advocate, seated at the right hand of God the Father, awaiting the day and time when He will return to earth to exercise world-rulership over all nations as *King of kings* and *Lord of lords.*

The Glory and Honor of Messiah

A careful study of these visions will reveal that both of them are in accord to display the glory and power given to this Divine Person, the "Messiah."

In the first vision, given to Nebuchadnezzar, that of a *stone,* cut out without hands, coming down from heaven to earth to demolish what emperors, rulers, and kings have sought to build up in ages gone by — perishable treasures of earth that are blown away as dust to the four winds, and in their places establishing the kingdom of God, founded on justice and peace for the whole world.

In the other vision, given to Daniel the prophet, that of the "Messiah" to bring redemption to an obstinate people that brought untold sorrow and trouble upon themselves for their rejection of the Son of God, who made Himself known as the Son of man, who "came not to be ministered unto, but to minister, and to give his life a ransom for many."

Both of these visions have a distinct time element — the first, a period of *"seven times";* the second, a period of *"Seventy Weeks";* the first represents "seven times," or 2520 years, of punishment meted out by the Gentiles upon Israel; the second, a period of "Seventy Weeks," or 490 years, to designate the time of the Messiah's entry into Jerusalem, followed by His crucifixion and death.

Our Lord Jesus in His Olivet discourse, spoken but a few days after His triumphal entry, in which He foretold the destruction of the temple and also of Jerusalem itself, stated definitely that the Jews would be "led away captive into all nations: and Jerusalem shall be trodden down of the Gentiles, until the times of the Gentiles be fulfilled" (Luke 21:24). Jesus is the only one who ever used the term, *"the times of the Gentiles."*

It is not difficult to know what kingdoms were used of God to bring punishment upon Israel, or the Jewish nation. They were Babylon, Medo-Persia, Greece, and Rome. It is not difficult to know how long the "times of the Gentiles" would be. It was Moses who designated the time of Israel's punishment for her sins as a period of "seven times." Moses specifically uses the term, "seven times." He uses it *four times* in Leviticus 26:18, 21, 24, 28. There is no record anywhere in Israel's national history where she was punished for only *seven years.* It is true there were periods of punishment upon Israel during the time of the Judges and of the Kings. The great national punishment causing the destruction of the temple and also that of Jerusalem, when large numbers of Jews were taken captive to Babylon, was about 606 B.C.

Distinction Between 'Seven Times' and 'Seventy Weeks'

Both of these visions have a distinct time element. The first vision was given to Nebuchadnezzar, designating the four greatest world powers, covering a long period of history. In a still later dream, given to Nebuchadnezzar, a large tree reaching to heaven was cut down for a period of "seven times," at the end of which it was to be restored. This prefigured that King Nebuchadnezzar was to lose his reason for a period of "seven times" (seven years). Then after seven years he was to be restored to his kingdom (Daniel 4:23). In this vision the "seven times" meant *seven years,* that the king would lose his reason.

When a year is reckoned for *one time* of 360 prophetic days, then *"seven times"* 360 days equals 2520 days; and when each day is reckoned for a year the period represents a total of 2520 years. In the event of Israel's failing (when they came out of Egypt) to obey Joshua and Caleb in their plea, given at Kadesh-barnea, to "go up at once, and possess the land," God decreed the punishment. He decreed that for every one of the forty days that the twelve spics had been going through the land of Canaan, the nation of Israel were doomed to spend a whole year wandering in the wilderness, so that they had to endure forty years of punishment (Numbers 13:25-33; 14:30-37).

With this great disaster which came upon Jerusalem in 606 B.C., began the "times of the Gentiles," to which Jesus had referred in His Olivet discourse. Since, from this event on through the kingdoms of Babylon, Medo-Persia, Greece and Rome, the Jews have been subject to the Gentiles, as represented by these four kingdoms.

Now, when one takes the *"seven times"* of punishment referred to by Moses, as a period of seven-year days, 7x360 calendar years equals a total of 2520 years as covering the period of the *"times of the Gentiles,"* referred to by Jesus. When 2520 years are to follow the destruction of Jerusalem by Nebuchadnezzar in 606 B.C., the 2520 years reach down to the year A.D. 1914 – 606 B.C. plus A.D. 1914 equals 2520 years. The year 1914 is the beginning of the First World War.

The Balfour Declaration

With the beginning of the First World War in A.D. 1914, God made the beginning of world events to bring about the giving forth of the *Balfour Declaration.* It was this *Balfour Declaration* that made it possible for more than two million Jews to return to Palestine from their exile, to finally establish the State of Israel in A.D. 1948.

The object of Daniel's vision of the "Seventy Weeks" is to identify three important events in the history of Israel, as stated in the ninth chapter of Daniel. The first event, mentioned in verse 25, is that of the "going forth of the commandment to restore and to build Jerusalem."

This commandment to build Jerusalem was given forth in 445 B.C. by Nehemiah, who was given permission by King Artaxerxes (Nehemiah 13:6) of Medo-Persia to leave Babylon and travel to Palestine in order to rebuild the broken-down walls of Jerusalem. To accomplish this took Nehemiah and his helpers one year week of 49 years in "troublous times."

The second event mentioned is to ascertain the meaning of the words *"The Messiah the Prince,"* in verse 25. The statement is made that from the going forth of the commandment to rebuild Jerusalem to Messiah the Prince would be 7 weeks and 62 weeks; the 7 weeks of 49 years followed by 62 weeks of 434 years, both being added, making a total of 483 years — from the time that Nehemiah began to rebuild Jerusalem to *Messiah the Prince* would be 483 years, dating from 451 B.C. plus A.D. 32 to specify the time of month and day when Jesus had made His triumphal entry into Jerusalem.

There were various names given to the Son of God before His incarnation, symbolizing His character: "seed," "rock," the "sun of righteousness," the "rose of Sharon," the "lily of the valley," and others, but the greatest name given to Him was that of Messiah, made known only in the ninth chapter of Daniel, verses 25 and 26.

The word Messiah means the *"Anointed One."* The custom in Israel was to anoint with oil anyone becoming a prophet, priest, or king. Jesus was anointed by the Holy Spirit during His baptism by John the Baptist at the River Jordan (Matthew 3:16; Luke 3:22; Acts 10:38).

Reason for Messiah Called "The Prince"

The reason Jesus is referred to in Daniel 9:25 as *"Messiah the Prince,"* is to single out the greatest event of His ministry of three years and one-half, which was that of His triumphal entry into Jerusalem. It was on this occasion that Jesus offered Himself as King who had come to found and establish the "kingdom of heaven upon earth."

All other events in the life of Jesus, including His virgin birth, His baptism, and even His transfiguration, were passed by in order to emphasize more strongly that Jesus offered Himself as *Messiah the Prince,* the promised son of David, who was to establish a greater kingdom than any referred to in Nebuchadnezzar's vision of the great metallic image. These all had been smitten by the stone from heaven and at last became as the "chaff of the summer threshingfloor; and the wind carried them away, that no place was found for them" (Daniel 2:35).

But Messiah the Prince was to be given a kingdom which should *"never be destroyed: . . .* it shall break in pieces and consume all these kingdoms, and it shall stand for ever" (Daniel 2:44).

Definite mention is made of the crucifixion of the "Messiah" (Daniel 9:26a). After threescore and two weeks Messiah was to be "cut off" (crucified) and have nothing for Himself (no kingdom established on earth).

Notice should be given to the fact that in the last — the seventieth — week of Daniel's vision mention is made of another prince who will arise of the people that had destroyed Jerusalem in A.D. 70, the Roman people. From this Roman people will one arise known as the "Antichrist," the "man of sin," the "Son of perdition," during Daniel's seventieth week, in the period known, after the rapture, as the period of *Tribulation.*

During the Tribulation period, this "prince," the "Antichrist," will confirm a covenant with the Jews for a period of seven years to restore the temple worship, but will break the covenant in the middle of the week, after three years and a half, and bring desolation to Jerusalem (Daniel 9:26, 27).

It is under these terrible conditions that the Jews will cry to God for a Deliverer, and Jesus Christ, the Son of God, will come with all His holy angels to smite, with the sword going out of His mouth, the nations and rule them with a rod of iron as King of kings and Lord of lords (Revelation 19:11-16).

Then will He, with restored and redeemed Israel, by finishing the transgression and making an end of sins, and making reconciliation for iniquity, bring, during this millennial reign, everlasting righteousness, and anoint the majestic millennial temple that is specified in every detail in Ezekiel, from chapter 40 to chapter 48.

One important matter needs attention with regard to the relation of Daniel's "Seventy Weeks" to that of Nebuchadnezzar's vision of the majestic metallic image exercising its power over a period of "seven times," or 2520 years.

Comparison Between 'Seven Times' and 'Seventy Weeks'

In the vision of Daniel's "Seventy Weeks," Messiah is not referred to at His birth, although the angel had announced to the shepherds, watching over their flocks by night in Bethlehem fields, that they were bringing "good tidings of great joy, which shall be to all people. For unto you is born this day in the city of David a Saviour, which is Christ [the Messiah] the Lord" (Luke 2:10, 11).

Jesus was born "King of the Jews" (Matthew 2:2), but He was also born "Christ the Lord."

Notice, now, if the sixty-nine weeks, or 483 years, are laid *along* side of the period of "seven times," or 2520 years, Daniel's "Seventy Weeks" do not begin with 606 B.C., the time of the destruction of Jerusalem by Nebuchadnezzar.

The *"Seventy Weeks"* do not begin with the beginning of the *"seven times,"* or 2520 years, which was 606 B.C., nor do the "Seventy Weeks" begin with the time this vision was given to Daniel, at the close of the Babylonian captivity of seven years, which would be about the year 536 B.C.

The "Seventy Weeks" were to begin with *Nehemiah's* undertaking to *build Jerusalem,* which was about the year 445 B.C.

Now, notice that the sixty-two weeks or 483 years reach 32 years beyond the birth of Christ, so that the entire life of Jesus must be accepted as being a *part of Messiah's life work.*

It is wrong, therefore, for Judaism to pass over the whole life story of Jesus in their conception of Messiah. Messiah does not refer to the coming of Christ in glory as distinctly as it refers *to the whole, the entire life of Jesus on earth, finding its climax in His crucifixion, death, and resurrection.*

World Dominion Given to Messiah

In the dream given to Daniel, in Daniel 7, the climax is reached in the coming of Messiah in great glory and power, when the kingdoms under the whole heaven "shall be given to the people of the saints of the most High, whose kingdom is an everlasting kingdom, and all dominions shall serve and obey him" (Daniel 7:27).

When Messiah shall come in His glory, as stated in Revelation 19: 11-16, then Israel will "look upon me whom they have pierced" (Zechariah 12:10); they will "mourn over their unbelief and rebellion against God; and then will be fulfilled the dream given to Theodor Herzl, in which he heard Messiah declare that He will do "great and glorious things for my people," which will mean the fulfillment of the words of Paul the Apostle, when he declared that "all Israel shall be saved: as it is written, there shall come out of Sion the Deliverer, and shall turn away ungodliness from Jacob" (Romans 11:26).

Then Messiah will occupy the throne of David in the city of Jerusalem and rule the world in justice and righteousness; then will the prayer be answered that Jesus taught His disciples, "Thy kingdom come. Thy will be done, as in heaven, so in earth" (Luke 11:1-4).

The Divine Effect of the 'Seven Times' and the 'Seventy Weeks'

These two chapters in Daniel by their chronological arrangement prove positively by the inspiration of the Holy Scriptures that God sits on His throne in the heaven, from which He directs and overrules the events of human history.

How does it come that the *"seven times"* of 2520 years of Gentile world dominion begin with Babylon, ruled over by Nebuchadnezzar? The statement has been made that there were many nations before that of Babylon. Great battles were fought in many lands. The word *Gentile* is used in the days after the Flood, when God divided the isles of the Gentiles "in their lands; every one after his tongue" (Genesis 10:5).

When Jesus used the expression, "the times of the Gentiles," He did not use this reference in Genesis. He wanted the "times of the Gentiles" to begin with a great world power — great enough to move a mighty army more than 700 miles over the vast Syrian desert to attack and conquer the city of Jerusalem and then take vast numbers of the Jews into captivity over this same great distance to Babylon.

Among the captives were Daniel and the three Hebrew children, who lived an uncompromising, godly life in the midst of an ungodly environment. To Daniel was given, for the first time, opportunity to prove the greatness of the God of despised Israel above all the gods of the heathen so that King Nebuchadnezzar, after Daniel had interpreted the meaning of the great metallic image, now had to declare, *"Of a truth it is, that your God is a God of gods"* (Daniel 2:47).

The setting of the beginning of the "times of the Gentiles," therefore, had to begin with the recognition of the superiority of Israel's God over all pagan gods. The God of Israel was recognized as such by the greatest military man of the whole world in that day — Nebuchadnezzar, the King of Babylon.

The "times of the Gentiles," covering a period of 2520 years, was permeated with the grossest element of idolatry and immorality. Their altars had for their symbols the male organs on one side and the female organs on the other side. (Read Romans 1:21-32.)

The Divine Torch Shining in Pagan Darkness

What darkness, yes, gross darkness, covered the most enlightened, progressive world powers of ancient times!

Was there no light at all amidst this gross darkness? Yes; a young man Daniel, about eighteen years of age, and the three Hebrew youths brought light with them before the seventy years of captivity. They kept the torch of the true worship of God with them. Daniel did not close his windows but kept them open so that his enemies could hear him pray for the forsaken city of Jerusalem.

What matters that the three Hebrew children were cast into a fiery furnace — *Messiah was there* and brought them out unsinged.

What matters that Daniel was cast into the lions' den — *Messiah was there* to deliver.

The flaming torch of divine truth that was lit at the burning bush by God Himself was carried into Egypt to bring terror to Pharaoh, so that he had to release the children of Israel from their bondage and set them free.

This flaming torch was used by Gideon and his 300 valiant soldiers to overcome the hosts of the Midianites. This torch was carried by David in his writing the Psalms, by Solomon in the book of Proverbs, and by the prophets' proclaiming the coming of the "Messiah." This torch was carried to Babylon by Daniel and the three Hebrew youths. This torch was carried by Esther, the Queen, to Medo-Persia to save a whole nation of Jews from extermination. This torch was carried by the noble Maccabees, when Antiochus Epiphanes offered a swine on the altar of the restored city of Jerusalem.

This torch with its flaming light became the sun of righteousness when the Messiah at last had come and declared, "I am the light of the world: he that followeth me shall not walk in darkness, but shall have the light of life" (John 8:12).

The Revelation of the Messiah Given in the Gentile World

Take notice now of the Messianic element that God planted to become a part of the "times of the Gentiles." God alone knew how to plant the startling message of the *Messiah* — not in Israel or Jerusalem, no; it was in Babylon that Daniel received the revelation of the vision of the "Seventy Weeks." What wonder that God took a strong hand to combat paganism at its headquarters in Babylon.

Now see what God has done to accomplish this. He did not need 2520 years, He only needed "Seventy Weeks" or 490 years. Put these 70 weeks or 490 years side by side with the pagan 2520 years. Only twice did God need to declare that the coming of the long-awaited Messiah would take place 69 weeks from the time Nehemiah was given permission by a pagan king of Medo-Persia, Artaxerxes, and provision made for him to be the leader for the rebuilding of Jerusalem, where *Messiah* was to bring His mission to a tragic end by having His hands and feet pierced by Roman nails and crowned with a crown of piercing thorns upon His head.

Yes, 69 weeks of 483 years go absolutely parallel with the *"times of the Gentiles";* in fact, they contain God's painting of redemption encased in the framework of the "times of the Gentiles."

What effect did this great message of the *Messiah* have upon the Gentile world? The "times of the Gentiles" began with 606 B.C., 1914 years were left for Nebuchadnezzar's image to be fulfilled. It would bring the image down to the legs of iron. Is there any trace of actual idolatry left in the area of the ancient Rome world power? What has made the change to smite idol worship and bring its many temples to ruin — yes, in Rome, in Greece, in Egypt, in Arabia, and even in far-away Nineveh and Babylon?

How is all time made to be reckoned? Its center is the manger of Bethlehem, where a sweet baby, sent from heaven, was born. It was "Messiah"; it was "Christ the Lord" (Luke 2:10, 11). All time before this event is counted B.C. (before Christ). All time since that event is called A.D., *Anno Domini* (in the year of the Lord [Messiah]). To Messiah belongs all time upon earth.

What effect would *Messiah* have upon the world?

The Jews' unbelief had witnessed for the God that gave the Ten Commandments, the Torah, at Mt. Sinai. Yes, the *Torah* was given to Israel as a schoolmaster to lead to the *Messiah* (Galatians 3:24). The Word of God declares that at the close of the "times of the Gentiles," during the Tribulation Period, *"all Israel shall be saved"* (Romans 11:26).

The Word of God declares that God will gather dispersed Israel back to Palestine, as is shown in another chapter.

Jesus made it plain that the beginning of Israel's return to the Holy Land would take place when the Gentiles will lend their influence and give their support in order to bring God's plan for Israel's return.

Only one question is left to consider: When did the latter Roman part of Nebuchadnezzar's image bring it to pass that Israel could obtain Palestine for their homeland?

The answer is easy. The *"times of the Gentiles"* began in 606 B.C. Then, 1914 more years must follow A.D. to bring them to the close of the 2520 years of the Gentile rule over Jerusalem.

The Result of British Conquest of Palestine

Do we know what happened in 1914 to make possible the return of Jews, flocking back in vast numbers, to their homeland? The year 1914 has one great epochal event — the *beginning of World War I.* This event led to the conquest of Turkey by the British army. It brought about the complete conquest of Jerusalem by a Christian general of the British army, who prayed to God to solve the problem of taking Jerusalem. And in a most marvelous way he took Jerusalem without a single shot being needed.

Is anything more necessary to prove God's overruling power of the times of Daniel's *"Seventy Weeks"* to overpower the great image of gold, silver, brass, and iron? Instead of an image God planted the Fig Tree, which is taking root in the soil of the city that had been destroyed by the pagan world. Today, the State of Israel envisioned by Theodor Herzl in 1896 by the document of *The Jewish State,* has become a reality at the close of the 2520 years of the "times of the Gentiles," which fixed the time for the preparation for the State of Israel to become a living reality.

Ah, what wonder, what wisdom, what power, yes, what love of God Almighty was manifested in all these moves of history, represented by the long period of the "times of the Gentiles," beginning with the pride of an austere king, Nebuchadnezzar, destroying Jerusalem, and reaching into the distant future until in 1914 it reaches its climax in having the British army in charge of a general with a higher regard for Jerusalem than had the first king ruling over Babylon.

Jerusalem Conquered by a Christian General

This General Allenby was a true follower of Jesus the Messiah. He could not ravish the city made holy by the Son of God. He remembered the whole tragedy of the mock trial before Annas, Caiaphas, Herod and Pilate. The general could not destroy this sacred city, where Solomon built the majestic temple, and where the Son of God will return from heaven to sit upon the throne of David, not bearing a crown of thorns, but crowned with many jewels of the redeemed. The general was acquainted with the Bible that tells the sweet story of Jesus and His love in sacrificing His life, for a wicked world, on the cross. Jerusalem was saved this time from any blast of cannon.

Jerusalem had a sacred origin in the days of Abraham, when he returned from the battle of the kings to pay tithes to Melchizedek, the priest of Salem, the city ruled over in peace by this servant of the Most High (Genesis 14:10-24).

This Jerusalem was spared because it has a destiny reaching far beyond the "times of the Gentiles." It belongs to Israel by a perpetual covenant made with David, that his Seed (the Messiah) shall here sit upon the throne of David to rule for the first time over a saved nation — that of Israel, but His rule shall reach to the ends of the earth, to have all nations acknowledge the crucified Saviour and Redeemer of men as King of kings and Lord of lords (Revelation 19:11-16).

In the "times of the Gentiles" of 2520 years are embodied 20 centuries of Christianity, by which power great transformations have taken place in the history of mankind.

The man of Macedonia, representing a continent steeped in idolatry, had one altar only, and only one, "to the Unknown God" (Acts 17:23). All the gods of idol worship brought only brutality and degradation to the masses of humanity (Romans 1:21-32). Help must come from some source, but from where will come help to lift the "times of the Gentiles" to a higher level of living?

The man of Macedonia was directed by the living God to call for a servant of His, Paul, called to be the Apostle to the Gentiles (Acts 16:9, 10). His cry reverberated across the Aegean Sea until it entered the heart of Paul, the great Apostle, to drop all of his plans at once to bring to them the message of God's saving grace. And thus was impregnated, infused into the "times of the Gentiles" the message of Divine Redemption, entrusted to the Church founded by our Lord Jesus Christ.

This is the factor that ripened into the possibility of taking possession of the Holy City of Jerusalem in 1914, and of returning it to God's chosen people, Israel, for them to found the State of Israel.

It takes God to do the impossible. When planning the creation of the universe, He needed but two elements — *space and time.* All history is bound up in these two elements.

With the "times of the Gentiles," God controlled or overruled from the beginning its time and space, until *Jerusalem was delivered from its enemies.*

With the "Seventy Weeks" of Daniel's vision, God also controls its time and space to bring to fulfillment its promise of the "Messiah" in His incarnation, ministry, crucifixion, resurrection, and ascension, to be fulfilled in the glory and splendor revealed at His Second Coming, when Messiah will govern the nations for a thousand years without war and turn "their swords into plowshares, and their spears into pruninghooks" (Isaiah 2:4; Micah 4:3).

THE MESSIANIC ORIGIN OF THE STATE OF ISRAEL

The Jew has been called "the wonder of the age" because of his survival while great kingdoms such as Babylon, Medo-Persia, Greece and Rome have decayed. This section shows that when the Jews return in large numbers to their own land, Palestine (as set forth in the parable of the Fig Tree), Christ's millennial reign is near at hand.

The Jewish nation has had a marvelous history: it was miraculous in its beginning as the birth of Isaac took place when Abraham and Sarah were in their old age, when normally the birth of a child was out of the question.

The development of the nation, their deliverance from Egyptian bondage, their entrance into the Promised Land, the judgments visited upon them in the Assyrian and Babylonian captivities, their return from exile to rebuild the temple and the walls of Jerusalem in preparation for the coming Messiah were all miraculous manifestations of God's dealings with Israel. The Jewish nation has also been preserved since their rejection of their Messianic King. Moses definitely foretold of their dispersion and also of their conversion and restoration to their own land. (Read the thirtieth chapter of Deuteronomy.)

Although Jesus wept as He foretold the doom awaiting Jerusalem, which was to be "trodden down of the Gentiles, until the times of the Gentiles be fulfilled," He also spoke words of hope to the nation of which He Himself was a member. On a previous occasion, Jesus had spoken the parable of the Barren Fig Tree which had encumbered the ground for three years but was spared for another year because of the plea of the dresser of the vineyard. The Jewish Fig Tree was spared after the crucifixion of Christ until the year A.D. 70, when the Roman legions cut down the walls of Jerusalem. They destroyed the temple and the city and inaugurated the dispersion of the Jews. In speaking this parable of the Fig Tree during the Passion Week, Jesus looked down to the close of the Gospel Age. He saw the trees of the Gentile nation taking on new life preparatory to Armageddon; likewise the Jewish Fig Tree taking on new life, which has been evidenced in the Zionist movement and the return of vast numbers of Jews to Palestine. (Luke 21:29, 30; Deuteronomy 28:63-68; 30:1-10; Isaiah 11:10-16; Ezekiel 37:1-13; Luke 13:6-9; Romans 11:23-29)

The Word of God not only speaks of the regathering of Israel but also of their conversion and acceptance of Jesus. In his teaching of the "olive tree," Paul spoke of its natural branches being cut off, and wild branches (Gentile believers) grafted in. He also said that because of their unbelief, the Gentiles at the end of the age would be cut off, and the natural branches (Israel) grafted into their own olive tree. Israel will accept Jesus as their Messianic King when He comes in glory and "all Israel will be saved." James declared in the Council at Jerusalem, that after the completion of the Church, Christ "will return, and will build again the tabernacle of David, which is fallen down." The Messianic Kingdom will not be established apart from the salvation of Israel as a nation. (Luke 21:31; Isaiah 43:1-6; 60:1-5; Jeremiah 22:1-9; Ezekiel 34:11-16; 36:16-27; Joel 3:9-17; Acts 15:13-18)

From the time that God called Abraham, Satan has sought to prevent his seed from becoming as "the sand of the sea" and as "the stars of the heaven for multitude." In the time of David, Israel had increased to over six million. At the time of Christ there were only four million Jews. During the Middle Ages, as the result of fierce persecution, the

Jews were reduced to one million. Today they have increased to about twelve million. Only God could have preserved them from utter extinction. A century ago there were only 500 Jews in Palestine. Today there are two and a half million. (Luke 21:32, 33; Deuteronomy 33: 1-12; Psalms 102:16-22; 105:37, 38; Zechariah 2:8-13; II Peter 3:7-13)

The Budding of the Fig Tree is seen in the Zionist movement organized by Theodor Herzl in 1896. Shortly after Theodor Herzl had reached the age of twelve, he was visited by a dream.

The King Messiah came, a glorious and majestic old man, took me in his arms and swept off with me on the wings of the wind. On one of the iridescent clouds, we encountered the figure of Moses. The features were those familiar to me of my childhood in the statue of Michelangelo. The Messiah called to Moses: It is for this child that I have prayed. But to me he said: Go, and declare to the Jews that I shall come soon and perform great wonders and great deeds for my people and for the whole world.*

Since then the "dead bones" of Ezekiel 37 have come together. The people are learning to speak the Hebrew language and are rebuilding the cities and villages of Palestine. Jesus said, "This generation shall not pass away, till all be fulfilled. Heaven and earth shall pass away: but my words shall not pass away" (Luke 21:32, 33).

* The above statement of Dr. Herzl's vision of the Messiah is taken by permission of the publishers of the Jewish Publication of America, Philadelphia, from the book entitled, *Theodor Herzl,* pages 12 and 13, written by Alex Bein.

✡ *13* ✡

THE PHENOMENAL VALUE OF THE CHURCH

THE MOST OUTSTANDING EVENT in the ministry is without question the fact that Jesus made a clear announcement of the founding of the Church. From the very beginning of His Messianic ministry, when Jesus announced His program (taken from the prophet Isaiah, chapter 61), it was stated that the opposition against Him was so strong, that they sought to thrust Him down from the precipice.

Jesus devoted His entire time of His three years of ministry to "the lost sheep of the house of Israel," yet it was stated that He came to His own, but they received Him not. On many occasions this opposition on the part of the leaders of the Jewish nation, sought to bring about His death. Jesus knew that the forces of Satan were arrayed against Him. He declared in the announcement of the founding of the Church that "the gates of hell" would be arrayed against the Church, but that it would be founded and become the most important factor with reference to God's plan of establishing His Messianic Kingdom over the whole earth.

This opposition and persecution began soon after the actual founding of the Church on the Day of Pentecost, and became more violent during the first three centuries, and yet notwithstanding the martyrdom of a large number of martyrs, the Church survived.

In order to understand more fully the development that took place in the early history of the Church, attention is herewith called to a chapter in a most valuable book by Dr. Arthur W. Kac. These excerpts show a profound understanding of the periods through which the Church had to pass:

THE CHURCH DIVIDED INTO THREE PERIODS

(1) *The first period.* "And after they had held their peace, James answered, saying, Brethren, hearken unto me: Simeon hath rehearsed how first God visited the Gentiles, to take out of them a people for His name" (Acts 15:13, 14). The

162

first period of the Christian Era is often referred to as the Church Age. Church in the Greek language is "Ecclesia," which literally means an assembly of people called out from among the Gentiles. Only a partial ingathering of the Gentiles is to take place in the first period. The Gentile world as a whole, James informs us, is to be converted to God in the third period.

(2) *The second period.* "After these things I will return, and I will build again the tabernacle of David, which is fallen: and I will build again the ruins thereof, and I will set it up" (Acts 15:16). The second period of the Christian Era begins with the return of Jesus Christ. The Church Age is terminated. God resumes His dealings with Israel. Jesus Christ causes the full and permanent national restoration, and spiritual regeneration of the Jewish people. The declaration of James is in full agreement with Paul's teaching on this subject: "For, brethren, I would not have you ignorant . . ." Paul writes of this mystery, "lest ye be wise in your own conceits; that a hardening of heart hath befallen Israel." The spiritual regeneration of all Israel will take place only after the process of the partial ingathering of the Gentiles will have been completed. And so all Israel will be saved . . ." (Romans 11:26). James emphasizes the national period of the Christian Era, while Paul emphasizes the spiritual regeneration aspect of the redemption of Israel. Both these phenomena will take place in the second period of the Christian Era.

(3) *The third period.* "That the residue of men may seek after the Lord, and all the Gentiles, upon whom my name is called . . ." (Acts 15:17). This passage tells us what is the purpose of the full national restoration and spiritual regeneration of Israel, which will take place in the second period with the return of Jesus Christ. When He comes back, He will complete what they began. The Jewish people will then enter upon their God-given mission, and the effect of this upon the world will, according to Paul, be equivalent to a resurrection from the dead (Romans 11:15)

. . . But while Israel is taking, as it were, a back seat in the Church Age period, God nevertheless wants Israel to learn certain needful lessons. And the Church Age will last long enough, until it is certain that Israel has learned these lessons. And not only this. The nations of the world that are bent on working out their salvation apart from, or in opposition to, God are to be given full opportunity to have their way, and to find out where this will lead them. And the Church Age is to last at least long enough for the cup of national willfulness to reach its brim.

It is when all these historical processes will have attained the end of their development that the Church Age — the first period of the Christian Era — will be terminated. Jesus Christ will return. Israel will be fully and permanently restored, and the nations of earth will be converted to God. Israel's first mission, in the centuries before the Church Age, was to receive, write, and preserve God's Word. Israel's second mission, after the Church Age, the conversion of nations to God.

One of the most convincing proofs that the first period of the Christian Era is fast drawing to a close, is the culmination of the process of intellectual, moral, and spiritual ripening taking place today in the whole world. Western civilization is transforming all parts of the world into one way of life, while modern means of communication make it possible to present the Christian message to the whole human race. Thus, for the first time in the world's history, each nation is in a position to choose for or against the God of the Bible. This development, together with the extraordinary phenomenon of the re-establishment of the State of Israel, shows that the goals of the first period of the Christian Era are rapidly being achieved.

In his closing message of this notable book on the subject, *The Rebirth of the State of Israel,* the author, Dr. Arthur W. Kac, states:

God's punishment was to leave man to his own devices, and allow him to follow his own inclinations to their logical conclusion. History has been a continued conflict between God-centered and man-centered way of life. The Bible teaches that human history, as we know it, will terminate in the complete breakdown of man-centered world order. It is at this point that the kingdom of the earth will pass under the rule of God.

The current world crises affecting all areas of human life — religious, moral, political, economic, and social, is the cumulative effect of the unspiritual, man-centered trend in human history. The steadily deteriorating world situation since the First World War, the growing frequency and destructiveness of wars in modern times, the advent of the atomic bomb era, with its threat of world annihilation, these and many other events, all point to man's decreasing ability to cope with the situation. The re-emergence of "The State of Israel" at this critical juncture of world history indicates that God is moving to prepare a way to save man from himself. In the day of the First Commonwealth, Israel wrote most of the Old Testament. After the exiles had returned from Babylon and established the Second Commonwealth, the Israelites completed the Old Testament and gave to the world Jesus Christ.

What will this present coming together between Israel and the land of Israel produce? If this present restoration is preparatory to Israel's final and complete redemption — and all signs point in that direction — it will issue forth in the transformation of the kingdom of this earth into the Kingdom of God. This is the teaching of the whole Bible — Old and New Testaments. In the New Testament this event is associated with the return of our Lord Jesus Christ. "Even so, come, Lord Jesus" (Revelation 22:20).

NOTE: The above excerpts taken from the book, entitled, *The Rebirth of the State of Israel,* pages 366, 367, 369, 374, 375, by permission of its author, Arthur W. Kac, M.D., and his publishers, Marshall, Morgan & Scott, London and Edinburgh.

Notice the following conclusions that are made by Dr. Kac in the above excerpts taken from his book:

(1) Israel's restoration to Palestine means its resulting in their regeneration to accept Jesus as their national Messiah.

(2) Israel's regeneration in accepting Jesus as their national Messiah means the completion of the call given to Abraham in which He promised to make of them a great nation.

(3) This will enable Israel to become God's greatest channel to bring the message of the Gospel to "all the families of the earth."

(4) Israel's experience of a true spiritual regeneration will enable God to establish the long promised Davidic Theocracy in the land of Israel.

(5) History has been a repeated conflict between the God-centered and man-centered way of living.

(6) World dominion of the kingdoms of this world to become the Kingdom of The King of kings and Lord of lords.

(7) All signs of the times point to the soon coming of Messiah, uniting the Church with Israel in Messiah's millennial reign.

This remarkable evaluation of the Church and of Israel gives a true insight into an understanding of God's purpose in replacing the founding of the Church for that of Israel.

Israel was given a long probation of nearly twenty centuries from the call of Abraham to the ministry of Jesus. Israel had failed to carry out its calling to bring God's blessing of salvation to "all the families of the earth" (Genesis 12:1-3).

It proved its unfitness to continue its unique place given to it by God to Abraham, Moses, David, and the prophets. Israel proved its unfitness because when Messiah declared that He was sent solely to "the house of Israel," when He came to His own, His own (the Jews), the leaders of Israel "received him not" (John 1:11). This was the fundamental reason for Jesus announcing the building of the Church (Matthew 16:16-18), to be followed and consummated at His Second Coming with "the building again of the house of David" (Acts 15:16).

✡ 14 ✡

THE DESTINY OF MESSIAH'S ISRAEL

THE CONFIRMATION OF ISRAEL

IN THE WORD OF GOD the human race is divided into three distinct divisions — Jews, Gentiles, and the Church of God. In God's plan and purpose priority of these three divisions belongs to the Jews. Their existence dates back before the Christian era nineteen centuries to the call of Abraham, by whom "all the families of the earth" were to be blessed.

The Unbroken History of Israel

The Jewish people, also designated in the New Testament as Israel, have had an unbroken existence for forty centuries and have survived the fierce Satanic persecutions which were to cause their utter destruction. This is sufficient proof that there is a definite divine purpose at work in their history. It is clearly revealed in the Scriptures that they are the principal factor in connection with the establishment of the Messianic Kingdom, "to whom pertaineth the adoption, and the glory, and the covenants . . . and the promises" made to Israel (Romans 9:4).

The term *Zion* is frequently used in the Word of God in connection with the past and future history of the Jewish people. It is of more than passing interest that the most dominant factor in the Jewish race today — Zionism — is distinctly set forth in the declaration in Psalm 102 that Jehovah "shalt arise, and have mercy upon Zion: for the time to favour her, yea, the set time is come. . . . When the Lord shall build up Zion, he shall appear in his glory" (verses 13, 16 and 21).

Theodor Herzl, Founder of Zionism

Zionism was founded by Theodor Herzl in 1896, and was to revitalize Jewish energies and give birth to Jewish nationalism that they might regain their God-given heritage in Palestine which has been lost for twenty centuries. The Zionist movement in but one generation wrought marvels in the spiritual transformation of Palestine, which has been barren and desolate for nearly twenty centuries. Thus again it is "a land flowing with milk and honey" because of the vast agricultural and horticultural projects which have been carried on through immigration of sturdy Jewish farmers and workers.

There is no question but that the Jews in almost every country (Russia excepted because forbidden by the government) have been deeply stirred by Zionism. Since the issuance of the Balfour mandate in 1917 over 2,500,000 Jews have contributed the astounding sum of nearly one-half billion dollars in donations and investments, which sum has been most conscientiously used in buying vast tracts of land in Palestine. Over 300 colonies have been founded. The great Jewish city of Tel Aviv has been built and has a population of over 150,000. It has up-to-date modern improvements in architecture and city planning.

Under the awakening of Zionism, many Jews have established their homes in and about Jerusalem. This has extended its area far beyond its former borders. There many large buildings, including the new Hebrew University, have been erected. Jerusalem again has become the cultural and spiritual center of the entire Jewish world, and has taken on a new meaning to the Christian and Moslem world. The heart of every tourist in Palestine (as was that of this writer) is deeply touched as he witnesses the marvelous changes taking place in all parts of Palestine as a result of the enterprising work of the Jewish movement.

Your attention is called to some of the results of the Zionist movement in order to prove that the Jewish nation has been awakened out of its age-long slumber to a new life. Its people have been seized by a new vision, and the whole world knows that they have been stirred with a new enthusiasm.

Zionism Confirmed by Prophecy

This is a definite confirmation of prophecy given by Ezekiel, that the "dry bones of the house of Israel" would come together. The sinews of Jewish capitalism are united with Jewish genius in science and industry for the rehabilitation of Palestine. It is no exaggeration that the enthusiasm aroused by the Zionist movement far exceeds that of the returning exiles under Ezra, when on completion of the foundation of the temple of the Lord "the people sang together in praising and giving thanks unto the Lord."

It is remarkable to see the Word of God confirmed by the Zionist movement. It describes the first divine work wrought within the Jewish nation as that of the *"dry* bones." This is interpreted as people without any spiritual life, thus showing that the return of the Jews in the latter days will be in unbelief. It should inspire the Christian Church to a deeper sense of responsibility to send the message of the Gospel to the Jew everywhere, so that he may be delivered from his state of unbelief and be confirmed in the many specific promises given in the Old and New Testaments.

The Jews are returning to their own land in unbelief, with little regard to God Almighty but merely aiming to restore Judaism to its pristine glory as in the days of Solomon. This should arouse the Christian Church to greater activity in teaching the Jews the meaning of their own Scriptures. These Scriptures have the principal theme of *the coming of Messiah* and the establishment of His Messianic Kingdom upon the earth, with Israel as the leading national head.

It is this Jewish unbelief that is responsible for the postponement of the Messianic Kingdom, and it will remain postponed as long as this unbelief continues.

When Jesus was born in Bethlehem He was acclaimed by the Wise Men of the East as the "King of the Jews." When He engaged in the conversation with the woman of Samaria regarding God's plan of redemption, He said, "Salvation is of the Jews." When He entered upon His public ministry He confined most of His attention and energy to giving the Gospel to the "lost sheep of the house of Israel." When at last He was arraigned before Caiaphas and Pontius Pilate, He was condemned to death and nailed to the cross and the superscription was written over the cross: "Jesus of Nazareth, the King of the Jews."

Christ's Crucifixion Postponed the Kingdom

Why did the Jews reject the claim Jesus had made for Himself as the "light of the world," the "bread sent down from heaven to give life unto the world," the "good shepherd that giveth his life for the sheep"? They had the Scriptures of the Old Testament which portrayed Messiah in such a manner. Jesus said it was because they did not search the Scriptures with an open, unprejudiced mind and heart, for had they done this they would have become aware that the Scriptures testified to His Deity which was being literally fulfilled in many details of His life and ministry. The Apostle Paul declared that the Jews were blinded by the veil of unbelief which was resting not only upon their minds, but also "upon their hearts."

After giving the Great Commission to the disciples, Jesus told them to abide in Jerusalem until they be endued with power from on high. Jesus told these humble fishermen-disciples that they should be His witnesses "both in Jerusalem, and in all Judea, and in Samaria, and unto the uttermost part of the earth." The Gospel was to be proclaimed to "every creature" of earth, yet it must never be forgotten that the Jews were to be given first attention, as Paul had distinctly declared: "To the Jew first, and also to the Greek" (Romans 1:16).

It is sad that within the first three centuries the Christian Church already had taken the position that God had forever set aside the Jews, and transferred to the Church the promises made to Israel in a spiritual way, yet leaving the curses pronounced upon Israel to the Jews in a literal way. Not only did the Church cease to give the Gospel to the Jews, but during the Middle Ages it actually became participant with ungodly nations in the persecution and slaughter of the Jews. The Jewish population, which numbered about six million during the time of Christ, was reduced to but one million in the Dark Ages.

The Great Awakening in the Church

Today there are twelve million Jews in the world — more than five million in our own country. God has signally blessed Great Britain and the United States for giving to the Jews economic, social, and religious freedom. There has been a great awakening in the Church during the last century in the giving of the Gospel to the Jews. However, only a beginning has been made, and only a short time remains for the Church to engage in this most important work. Soon the Lord will take His saints from the earth in the rapture, and who will be on earth to witness for God to the nations of earth during the time of Tribulation?

After the Church has been taken from the earth, God will use a Jewish remnant made up of 144,000 from all the twelve tribes of Israel, and these will give forth a world-wide proclamation of the Gospel.

This obligation to preach the Gospel will fall upon the Jewish remnant, that is the 144,000 of the twelve tribes of Israel, after the rapture of the saints, and therefore it is important for the Church to put forth the greatest effort in its history to reach the Jews with the gospel message, that they may be prepared and trained to witness for God.

Future candidates for church membership should be given specific attention and instruction that they may be enlightened in their minds and hearts with the knowledge of God's Word. They must be prepared for the day of their confirmation when they make public confession of Christ in the church.

Special attention should be given by the Church of Christ to Jewish Missions in preparation for the confirmation of the Jewish believers. The 144,000 Israelites will be sealed in their foreheads with the "seal of the living God," thereby authenticating that they are God's special witnesses to the nations of earth during the time of Tribulation, when the great day of God's wrath comes upon the nations of earth.

THE CONSOLATION OF ISRAEL

Israel's place among the nations of earth has indeed been a unique one in that it is rightly called *"the miracle race"* of history. Not only is this designation true with reference to its miraculous beginning forty centuries ago, reaching back to the time of Abraham, but also its miraculous preservation and sustenance during this long period amidst the many vicissitudes and fiery persecutions and trials through which it has had to pass.

Now that the world has entered into the period designated in the Scriptures as the "time of the end," it is important to consider another phase of this miracle race of history; namely, the miraculous spiritual transformation still awaiting this people in connection with Christ's coming in glory, by which it will become the "head" and not the "tail" of all nations (Deuteronomy 28:13).

The great nations of history — Egypt, Assyria, Babylon, Medo-Persia, Greece, and ancient Rome, with their culture and civilization and great military prowess, have sunk into oblivion, and thus passed completely from the stage of history. But Israel, though "scattered and peeled" through the centuries of the past, has survived all the onslaughts of her enemies and is yet destined to take her place as a "kingdom of priests and an holy nation," accomplishing the world's full evangelization during the thousand years of Christ's reign upon the earth.

Let it be understood that Israel has a separate and distinct place in the plan and purpose of God, different from that given to the Church. The Church constitutes a heavenly-called people, with the New Jerusalem in heaven as her goal; whereas Israel constitutes the earthly people of Jehovah, with an earthly Jerusalem having the "throne of Jehovah" in the midst, as her goal. Both the heavenly-called people and the earthly-called people sustain a vital relationship to Abraham — the latter being the natural seed, while the former constitutes the spiritual seed of Abraham; the latter is symbolized by the sand upon the seashore, while the former is likened to the stars of heaven for multitude (Genesis 22:17).

It was to Paul, "an Hebrew of the Hebrews; as touching the law, a Pharisee," to whom was entrusted the unfolding of the mystery of the Church — that in the Church "there is neither Greek nor Jew . . . . but Christ is all, and in all" (Colossians 3:11). However, even though Paul considered the Church the great masterpiece of God Almighty, he never ceased to pray to God for Israel, "that they might be saved" (Romans 10:1). Yes, he had "great heaviness and continual sorrow" in his heart, wishing himself to be "accursed from Christ for . . . my kinsmen according to the flesh" (Romans 9:2, 3), the Jews, to whom had been committed the "covenants . . . and the service of God, and the promises . . .

of whom as concerning the flesh Christ came . . . God blessed for ever" (Romans 9:4, 5).

The three most important chapters of the entire New Testament bearing on the intimate relationship between the Church and Israel, are the ninth, tenth, and eleventh chapters of the Roman epistle. This dissertation of Paul depicts the Church as the olive branch "wild by nature graffed contrary to nature into the good olive tree" (Romans 11:15-21). The olive tree in the Old Testament represents Israel as a nation. Then, to prove that God has not yet finished with Israel — though they are cast aside because of their unbelief — he says that the "natural branches" shall "be graffed into their own olive tree . . . that blindness in part is happened to Israel, until the fulness of the Gentiles be come in. And *so all Israel shall be saved"* (Romans 11:24-26).

Read these chapters over and over again and your heart will throb with divine love for Israel, which still has the veil of unbelief over its eyes (II Corinthians 3:13-18). You will also be made to realize that "as touching the election" the Jews still "are beloved for the fathers' sakes. For the gifts and calling of God are without repentance" (Romans 11:28, 29).

By giving attention to the study of these chapters, the Church never, in the least degree, can be guilty of the Satanic spirit of anti-Semitism, for why should there be hatred and opposition between the heavenly-redeemed seed of Abraham and the earthly seed of Abraham, to whom the promises are given by God? By studying these chapters the Church is made to realize that these promises still hold good. Rather than being engaged in hating, opposing, and persecuting the Jew, every child of God should have a vital interest in helping him to obtain the knowledge of God's salvation through the New Testament gospel message.

The Church to Be the Consoler of Israel

The Church in the first place should be the consoler of Israel, extending comfort, help, and mercy in the distress and trouble through which multitudes of them are passing. Not only in Isaiah's time, but today the command is: "Comfort ye, comfort ye my people, saith your God" (Isaiah 40:1). The Jew needs above all else the message of the Gospel in order for him to find Him of whom Moses and the prophets have written. In order for the Jews to have this salvation of God, they must be given the writings of the New Testament, which show how Jesus was born according to the Scriptures, of a Virgin; how He was imbued with the Holy Spirit for His ministry to give forth the teaching and work the miracles. They must be given the writings of the New

Testament in order to know how Jesus was rejected, reviled, and re-buffed by His enemies according to the Scriptures; how He was the "man of sorrows . . . wounded for our transgressions and . . . bruised for our iniquities" (Isaiah 53:3-5); how He suffered, bled, and died and rose again, after which He ascended to heaven according to the Scriptures; and how He will come again in glory to establish His media-torial kingdom according to the Scriptures (Revelation 19:11-16).

Israel can have no *consolation* and no redemption apart from God's salvation through His Son, our Lord and Saviour Jesus Christ. Notice the two examples that will be given in support of this statement, one from the Old Testament, the other from the New Testament, and both of aged, devoted servants of God.

The first instance is that of a patriarch on his dying bed surrounded by his twelve sons, upon whom he is bestowing a special parting bless-ing. Singled out among the twelve brethren is Judah, upon whom he bestows the *Messianic blessing,* saying, "The sceptre shall not depart from Judah, nor a lawgiver from between his feet, until Shiloh come; and unto him shall the gathering of the people be" (Genesis 49:10). So profoundly was Jacob, the dying patriarch, stirred in his inmost soul by the thought of the coming Messiah, that he soon burst out with the exclamation, "I have waited for thy salvation, O Lord" (Genesis 49:18). Over two thousand years had come and gone since God had given the first promise of the coming Messiah in the Garden of Eden (Genesis 3:15). Still the Saviour of men had not come. Would the faith of the antediluvian and postdiluvian patriarch falter because of this long de-lay? No, a thousand times No. Through this long delay Enoch, Noah, and Abraham had waited and Jacob also, on his dying bed, declares, "I have waited for thy salvation" (Genesis 49:18).

Another long delay of seventeen hundred years takes place. What does this long delay mean? Does it mean that God had forgotten His promises and that He was indifferent to the dying needs of humanity to provide redemption? No; during all this long delay God was making the necessary preparation for the coming Messiah. And "when the ful-ness of the time was come, God sent forth his Son, made of a woman, made under the law, to redeem them that were under the law, that we might receive the adoption of sons" (Galatians 4:4, 5). At last, after a four-thousand-year delay, the Saviour was born in the little town of Bethlehem, and was in that very night worshiped by the shepherds (Luke 2:17, 18).

Now we come to the second example, giving expression to the same longing Jacob had had regarding his waiting for the "salvation of God." In Jerusalem, the aged Simeon had been waiting for the "consolation of Israel," the coming of Israel's Redeemer, who alone could bring *consolation* to the human heart in removing the burden of sin and bringing pardon and peace to the longing soul of man.

It was revealed to Simeon by the Holy Spirit that he was not to see death before he had seen the Lord's Christ, and when he came into the temple for worship the "parents brought in the child Jesus, to do for him after the custom of the law"; and Simeon, overwhelmed with joy and praise to God, took up the child "in his arms, and blessed God, and said, Lord, now lettest thou thy servant depart in peace, according to thy word: for mine eyes have seen thy salvation" (Luke 2:27-30).

Consolation for Israel Provided Through Christ's Salvation

Was this *consolation* through Christ's salvation only for Simeon? only for Jacob? only for Abraham? No; it was for all the seed of Abraham, so that through his seed "all the families of the earth" would be blessed (Genesis 12:1-3). Today the world has a greater number of Abraham's racial descendants than ever in any preceding generation, numbering over eighteen million Jews, twelve without counting the six million slaughtered by Hitler, but Israel is still in blindness as it was when Jesus was rejected by them as their Messianic King in nailing Him to the cross.

Let the Church with the full light of a finished redemption wrought by the Son of God on Calvary's cross and forever sealed by His resurrection from the dead, be mindful of the fact taught by Paul, the apostle, that in giving forth the gospel message to the world, it should remember that it should be "to the Jew first" (Romans 2:7-11).

How can this present generation of Jews be reached with the Gospel in order to obtain the *"consolation of Israel"?* There are many ways in which it can be done: by the preaching of the Gospel, by distribution of tracts, by means of the radio and television. However useful all these means may be to reach the Jew with the gospel message, the one way set forth in the story of the Eunuch returning from Jerusalem to Egypt cannot be improved upon; namely, by personal contact and conversation with Jews in their homes and elsewhere. The Jews today need to be taught (as Philip taught the eunuch, Acts 8:26-40) how to understand the meaning of Abraham's offering up his son Isaac on Mount Moriah; how to understand the meaning of the Passover Feast, with its message of blood redemption; how to understand the meaning of the *Day of Atonement,* when the high priest went into the holy of holies to make reconciliation for the sins of *all Israel:* how to understand the message of the uplifted brazen serpent in the wilderness; of how the Messianic Psalms, especially the twenty-second Psalm, and the fifty-third chapter of Isaiah, have had their actual fulfillment in the life and ministry of Jesus, who on various occasions attested to the fact that He was the Messiah which should come into the world to bring consolation to Israel and to Gentile believers.

THE CONSUMMATION OF ISRAEL

The message of the Gospel has a far greater and more profound message for Israel than only to bring them the "consolation of Israel," telling them of pardon, of forgiveness, of regeneration, and justification of redeemed sinners. This glorious gospel message deals also with Israel's *consummation,* with her destiny as a nation to inherit the Messianic Kingdom. It deals with the fact of Israel's being *saved as a nation,* thus being restored to Jehovah's favor when "the Redeemer shall come to Zion, and unto them that turn from transgression in Jacob." Then will again Jerusalem be made "a praise in the earth," and God will be glorified.

While the consolation of Israel looks to the past, to the finished work of Jesus upon Calvary's cross, the *consummation of Israel* looks to the future, to the time when this same Jesus will sit upon David's throne in Jerusalem, exercising world-wide dominion (Isaiah 9:6, 7; Matthew 25:31, 32). The Old Testament Scriptures literally abound with this theme of Israel's *consummation.* Beginning with the writings of Moses, and continuing in the Psalms and last of all in the Prophets, we find this theme recurring again and again of a redeemed people, a restored land, with God's chosen people reunited with the Promised Land after age-long separation. Attention will now be given to each of these three divisions with regard to Israel's *consummation.*

Moses Wrote of Israel's Consummation

Attention must first be called to the covenant which God had made with Abraham, in which God gave not only the land of Canaan, but all the land reaching from the river of Egypt to the river Euphrates as an everlasting possession (Genesis 12:1-4; 13:14-17; 15:1-7, 17, 18; 17:1-8). Israel as yet has never entered upon its inheritance set forth in the covenant made with Abraham. For twenty-five hundred years and over, the Gentiles have been in possession and control of this land, and they will remain in control as long as Israel remains in a state of unbelief. But when they as a nation accept Jesus as their Messianic King as He comes in glory, then will Israel enter a fuller possession and control of all the Promised Land than when Joshua divided it among the twelve tribes after their crossing the Jordan River following the death of Moses.

Further attention is called to the chapters in Deuteronomy, twenty-nine and thirty, which deal with the Palestinian covenant. These chapters show how the curse pronounced upon Israel in the twenty-eighth chapter will finally be removed when Israel returns to the Lord with their whole heart. Not only a partial remnant of Israel, as has been the case after the Babylonian captivity and, more recently, since the Balfour Declaration, but God will turn the captivity of all Israel, so that they will return from "all the nations" whither the Lord had "scattered them."

The Book of Psalms Teaches Israel's Consummation

Many of the Psalms are Messianic in character, and cannot be understood except in the light of fulfilled prophecy in the life and ministry of Jesus, the Son of God. One of the most important phases of these Messianic Psalms is that of their direct bearing upon Messiah's Second Coming in glory to establish a kingdom of righteousness upon the earth.

The second Psalm represents Jehovah, rejected by the rulers of earth, seated as King upon the "Holy Hill of Zion," receiving the nations for His inheritance and the "uttermost parts of the earth" for His possession. To accomplish this, however, He must use the "rod of iron" to "dash" the ungodly nations "in pieces like a potter's vessel." Before Israel can come forth conqueror over her enemies, she must first go through great tribulation and suffering. Seeking God in her trouble, she will indeed find Him to be her refuge and strength, and a "very present help in trouble" (Psalm 46:1). Psalm 47 speaks of Jehovah's triumph as a "great King over all the earth," subduing Israel's enemies under her feet. Psalm 48 brings Zion into view as the "city of the great King," as the "city of the Lord of hosts" and "of our God . . . for ever."

Psalm 72 declares that there will be "abundance of peace" in the earth when Jehovah "shall break in pieces the oppressor" and when He exercises "dominion . . . from sea to sea, and from the river unto the ends of the earth." Then it is that "all nations shall call him blessed." Too numerous to refer to are the references to Israel's consummation and greatness in the book of Psalms, but special mention must yet be made of Psalm 89, which is devoted to the covenant which God made with David concerning the establishment of the Messianic Kingdom. In this Psalm are found three references, verses 4, 29, and 36, to *Messiah,* as David's seed, being given an enduring throne that shall last forever "as the sun before me. . . . and be established for ever as the moon." What a blessed privilege it is for the Church today, in her mission of giving the gospel message "first to the Jews," to call attention to God's faithfulness to keep the covenant which He had made with Abraham, with Moses, and with David, which are all to have their literal fulfillment in the near future in connection with Messiah's coming as King of Israel to redeem and bless Israel as His chosen people.

The Prophets Teach Regarding Israel's Consummation

It would take many pages to enumerate the many references to be found in the four major and twelve minor prophets regarding Israel's glorious consummation. Of outstanding importance in the survey of this subject is the book of Isaiah, in which many chapters are found to bear on the glorious future still awaiting Israel as a nation. Passing hastily through this book, we find that chapter two gives the picture of the "last days," when the "mountain of the Lord's house shall be established in the top of the mountains . . . and all nations shall flow unto it." Then "out of Zion shall go forth the law, and the word of the Lord from Jerusalem." Then by Messiah's command "they shall beat their swords into plowshares, and their spears into pruninghooks: nation shall not lift up sword against nation, neither shall they learn war any more."

Chapter 11 describes the great social and political transformation that will take place as the result of Messiah's reign of righteousness, and with it takes place the transformation of the animal creation. Then comes chapter 35, telling of the great Syrian desert and wilderness which "shall rejoice, and blossom as the rose." This wonderful psalm of praise ends with the declaration that the "ransomed of the Lord," having been saved, healed, and made to walk in the "way of holiness," will then "return, and come to Zion with songs and everlasting joy upon their heads."

Chapter 52 speaks of Messiah's redeeming Jerusalem, thus giving Jehovah occasion to make "bare his holy arm in the eyes of all the nations," when "all the ends of the earth shall see the salvation of our God." Chapter 54 refers definitely to the Redeemer as the "Holy One of Israel; the God of the whole earth shall he be called." Chapter 60 speaks of the Deliverer coming "out of Zion," making His people "all righteous," and giving them the land promised to Abraham to "inherit for ever," so that Israel will no longer be the tail but the head as "a strong nation." A good place to close, but by no means the end of this study in Isaiah, is the prayer found in chapter 62, which is appropriate for God's people in the Church today, never to "hold their peace day nor night," and to give God no rest "till he establish, and till he make Jerusalem a praise in the earth."

Then passing over so many references to be found in the prophecy of Jeremiah and that of Ezekiel bearing on Israel's glorious future, attention in closing is called to the book of Daniel, which is the only book of the Bible showing the rise, development, and overthrow of the four great Gentile monarchies dominating Israel for a period of 2500 years.

God's Covenant With Abraham and David Upheld in the New Testament

Passing from the Old Testament to the New Testament one is at once confronted by the first verse of the Gospel of Matthew, that "Jesus Christ," the promised *Messiah* of the Old Testament, was not only to inaugurate but also to consummate the kingdom of God upon earth that was promised to Abraham ("in thee shall all families of the earth be blessed" — Genesis 12:2) and to David ("His seed shall endure for ever, and his throne as the sun before me. It shall be established for ever as the moon and as a faithful witness in heaven" — Psalm 89:36, 37). The first declaration of the New Testament, therefore, was to give assurance that God's covenant with Abraham and David was to be carried out in the ministry of Jesus Christ, and thereby bring God's plan of redemption for Israel and for the world to its consummation.

Jesus' Ministry to the Lost Sheep of the House of Israel

In the brief time of three and a half years allotted to His ministry, it was impossible for Jesus to reach out to all the nations on earth. This brief period was to be given to the "lost sheep of the house of Israel." Jesus therefore directed His Twelve Apostles not to go "into the way of the Gentiles," nor "into any city of the Samaritans . . . But go rather to the lost sheep of the house of Israel," and "preach, saying, The kingdom of heaven is at hand" (Matthew 10:5-7).

Instead of His own, the Jews, receiving this great message of having God's Kingdom established, they "received him not" (John 1:11). Jesus had to pronounce judgment upon the nation of Israel, declaring that the temple would be destroyed and the walls of Jerusalem leveled to earth, and that the people of Israel were to "fall by the edge of the sword, and shall be led away captive into all *nations:* and Jerusalem shall be trodden down of the Gentiles, until the times of the Gentiles be fulfilled" (Luke 21:24).

Jesus declared that the long rule of the Gentiles of "seven times," of 2520 years, over Jerusalem was to come to an end, and Jerusalem was to fulfill its destiny of becoming the "glory of the earth," *by Messiah's* reign of justice and righteousness. The beginning of this liberation can already be seen in the State of Israel, that was born in 1948. This liberation of Israel took place in their unbelief and, therefore, is not able to display the full glory of God's redemption to Israel.

The Barren Fig Tree to Rebud

In the closing days of Jesus' ministry, He declared in the sermon on Mount Olivet, but a few days before His crucifixion and death, that the barren fig tree would rebud, and that "this generation shall not pass

away, till all be fulfilled" (Luke 21:29-33). Before the consummation
of Israel can take place, Israel must repent; they will mourn and weep
over their sins. It is stated by the prophet Zechariah that there shall
be a "great mourning in Jerusalem . . . and the land [of Palestine] shall
mourn." They shall look upon Him "whom they have pierced," and
they shall "be in bitterness for him" (Zechariah 12:10-12).

All Israel Saved at Christ's Coming

With this initial step of Israel's national repentance, Israel's salvation can and will take place, so that "all Israel shall be saved: as it
is written, There shall come out of Sion the Deliverer, and shall turn
away ungodliness from Jacob: for this is my covenant unto them, when
I shall take away their sins" (Romans 11:26, 27).

When this has taken place, Israel's national redemption will come
to its consummation. Israel will then become the first truly saved nation and will then be used during the millennium in giving forth the
message of salvation to the whole Gentile world, so that at the end the
Disciples' prayer will be fulfilled: "Thy will be done in earth, as it is
in heaven" (Matthew 6:10).

✡ *15* ✡

THE MATERIAL STANDARD OF MESSIAH'S ISRAEL

THE BIBLE is the most important of all books ever written by man. It gives the solution to the great problems pertaining to the material, spiritual and eternal interests of mankind. The Bible presents the sublime story of the creation of the universe. The most important problem that the Bible deals with is that of the human race. Notwithstanding all the evils that have brought disaster and ruin to mankind in many different ways, the Bible is the only book that gives a satisfactory solution at the close of its divine revelation in presenting a new heaven and earth wherein dwells righteousness.

The Bible is not only the most important of all books, but it is likewise the most fascinating of all books in dealing with the plan God has revealed in His Word to bring His blessing to mankind.

In previous chapters, two outlines have been presented. First, that of the seven dispensations of testing mankind that always ended in failure; and the seven covenants that always ended with perfect fulfillments of the promise therein contained. Special attention was given to that of the New Covenant, dealing primarily with God's particular plan for Israel's redemption, made possible through the redemption wrought by the redeeming blood of Jesus, the Son of God, and also the Son of man.

In the closing chapter of this volume, another approach is presented to cover the entire scope of Israel's history. The first section deals with the material standard of Messiah's Israel. The following section deals with the spiritual standard of Messiah's Israel; and the closing section, with the eternal standard of Messiah's Israel.

The material standard of Messiah's Israel covers a span of 4,000 years, from the call of Abraham in 1900 B.C. to the Battle of Armageddon.

179

Adam's Stewardship of the Material Earth

Let it be understood that the writer sees nothing wrong in man at his creation, living on a strictly material basis. He was given full dominion over all the earth. But notice that Adam was given this dominion as a stewardship by God Almighty. The human race from the time of Adam to Abraham, a period of about 2,000 years, had with but few exceptions, miserably failed in this stewardship. This stewardship from the beginning involved the distinct recognition of the Messiah which God had promised to Adam in the Garden of Eden.

The failure of heeding this promise had already begun to decline with Abraham's marriage to Hagar. This marriage made possible many vexing problems that Israel had to face in the future through the birth of Ishmael. The polygamy begun by Abraham, and more extensively with Jacob, with his four wives, laid the foundation of the many vexing problems of Israel's future.

Living as an enslaved nation in bondage to Pharaoh, Israel had almost forgotten their divine call given to the patriarchs.

A New Era With Moses Begins for Mankind and Israel

With the call of Moses a new era began to bring about the deliverance from this bondage, and brought the Israelites across the Red Sea on their pilgrimage to the Promised Land. Because of Israel's unbelief, they were made to wander in the wilderness for forty years. Here God gave the Ten Commandments audibly to the entire nation of Israel. Moses gave to Israel the full form of their worship in the building of the Tabernacle with its priesthood and sacrifice.

Before entering the Promised Land, Moses taught Israel how to be faithful in serving God, which would bring blessing on their material standard, as set forth in Deuteronomy 28. Moses made it perfectly plain in this great chapter that if Israel failed to serve God, nothing but calamity would come to them.

No sooner had Joshua conquered the Land of Canaan and divided it among the Twelve Tribes than they became enslaved by the nations of Canaan. God raised up the Judges to bring deliverance from their bondage, but there was no real turning to God by Israel. Instead of following the counsel of Samuel, the prophet, the people demanded of him to produce a king. Israel wanted to be like other nations. Because Saul disobeyed God, David was chosen to become Israel's king, and to restore the worship of God to Jerusalem. David provided one half of the book of Psalms. Solomon was given the task of building the temple and writing the sublime books of Proverbs, Ecclesiastes and the Song of Solomon. These books set forth a standard based on a Messianic foundation for Israel to live by.

Soon after Solomon's death, decay set in the nation of Israel. Of all the forty kings who ruled a divided Israel, only about six gave any real attention to the worship of God in Jerusalem. The nation of Israel ended with Assyria for Israel and Babylon for Judah.

Israel's Subjection to Gentile Nations

The one great benefit that came to Israel during the captivity was the total abolishment of idolatry. Ezra and Nehemiah restored the Temple for Israel to worship God. The synagogue was conceived as a gathering place of worship. Henceforth Israel became subjected to the great nations of Babylon, Medo-Persia, Greece and Rome. Because of their failures in their stewardship, the Old Testament had to close its long record of unfaithfulness with the word "curse," instead of blessing.

When one enters the period of Messiah's activity of going about "doing good" in preaching the Gospel of the Kingdom, which would bring deliverance from the bondage of sin and Satan, one would expect that the whole nation would be ready to accept Him as their long promised King. In this they miserably defaulted as a nation. Jesus had to begin His ministry with the cleansing of the Temple from its merchandise, and strange as it may seem, after His triumphal entry into Jerusalem, Jesus had to close His ministry by again cleansing the Temple of its merchandise. The leaders of the nation brought about His trial before Caiaphas and Pontius Pilate which resulted in His crucifixion and death.

Israel's Rejection of the Messiah

Instead of remaining in the tomb, as the leaders had arranged for, God had made Jesus of Nazareth the King of the Jews as designated on the Cross of Calvary. God raised Him from the dead. Though comparatively few Jews became believers on the Day of Pentecost, which constituted the forming of the Church, God did not cast off His chosen people, the Jews. The summons went forth through the Church to give the Gospel *first* to the Jews and then to the Gentiles. A few thousand believers constituted the apostolic Church in Jerusalem and surrounding towns and cities.

In almost every city that Paul entered in, he was opposed by the Jews. Jesus, Himself, had wept over Jerusalem for not accepting Him as the Redeemer, and definitely foretold the destruction of the Temple as well as the dispersion of the Jews to all the nations of the world. It is perhaps one of the saddest pages in church history that the ministry of Jesus and His apostles fell on the deaf ears and hardened hearts of the Jews. Had they accepted Christ as their Redeemer and King, it might well have prevented their dispersion of two thousand years in foreign lands.

The State of Israel — The World Dispersion of the Jews

The only bright spot of hope for the future of Israel is the founding of the State of Israel. This is only a partial solution of the so-called Jewish problem. It is surely the positive guidance of their Messiah which brought about the founding of the State of Israel.

More than twelve million Jews preferred assimilation in foreign lands to accepting God's provision for them to claim Palestine and the great desert between the Nile and the Euphrates Rivers. They could not believe that this material part of the earth was to be cultivated by millions of Jews and to be made to "blossom as a rose."

There must be more than a material success in store for Israel. God wanted Israel to make the true worship of God, by accepting Jesus as their Messiah, to be the true and abiding superstructure of Messiah's Israel as given in the following chapter. There can be no failure with God's working out His own plan for Messiah's Israel.

THE SPIRITUAL STANDARD OF MESSIAH'S ISRAEL

There is continual disagreement among Bible teachers as to whether the Church or a part of the Church must go through the Tribulation period set forth in the book of Revelation between chapters six to nineteen. There can be no disagreement as to the fact that this period of Tribulation is called "the time of Jacob's trouble." A large number of the plagues and catastrophes are poured out on all the earth. The Antichrist, the man of sin and son of perdition will rule as Satan's agent over all nations.

Down through the ages there has been nothing but trouble in this world of ours. There has been war, famine, pestilence, the outbreak of idolatry, immorality and wickedness of all kinds. The Tribulation Period will bring chaos to human society. It can be traced back to Jacob, who after being taught the way to serve God by accepting the promise of the coming Messiah, gave himself to intrigue, lying and deceit in obtaining the Messianic promise from his blinded father and in his taking of four wives.

The Old Testament gives far more detail regarding God's plan to punish a rebellious and disobedient Israel. The pleadings of the prophets of old, the warnings of Jesus and of the apostles to have Israel accept Jesus Christ as the promised Messiah, for whose coming Judaism has been praying for nearly two thousand years of the entire Gospel Age were in vain. What can be done to break this wall of stubborn resistance that has the Jews bound in unbelief to this day? Something can and will be done which will result in the ultimate conversion of the Jewish nation. Just one word holds the complete story of the disaster facing an unbelieving Israel. That one word is the word *"trouble."* The prophet Jeremiah was outspoken when he declared that *Jacob's trouble* would be a time of great sadness and punishment for the Jews.

The 144,000 of Israel Sealed

It was trouble that came to Jacob on his return to his homeland in Palestine when he discovered that Esau was coming with 400 armed men to destroy him and his entire family. This trouble caused him to spend the whole night wrestling with the Angel of the Lord. Jacob said to the Angel of the Lord, "I will not leave thee except thou bless me." The whole problem of Jacob's security was solved. He had a change of heart and a change of name from Jacob to Israel.

The Jews have had much trouble down through the centuries and have sought out their existence, whenever it might be, on a mere material basis. Yes, the day of Jacob's trouble will arrive, when God's saints will be removed from the earth at Christ's coming. When the Church has completed its mission in the rapture of the saints, God will take up His program with His Chosen People, the Jews, and unleash the fearful era of trouble for the whole world as set forth in the book of Revelation in the seven seal, trumpet and vial judgments. Yes, the Book deals specifically with the fearful troubles to come upon Jacob and it tells specifically of the astounding conversion of the 144,000 of Israel.

The world today is populated with a vast throng of people and nations reaching into several billions. Of this vast population, the majority is steeped in idolatry and its accompanying evils. Of this vast multitude, only about 800,000,000 are nominally affiliated with the Church and about 12,000,000 Jews are scattered among the nations. When the Lord takes out the true believers of Christ, there will not be one saint left upon earth. Then will come war, pestilence, famine and plagues of all kind upon the whole world as punishment during the rule of the Antichrist.

The book of Revelation records the fact that a vast multitude, which no man can number, will repent of their evil ways. They will accept Jesus as their Saviour and Redeemer. There are no details given about this except to state that many will be martyrs.

It surely is a wonder what effect Jacob's trouble will have upon Israel as a whole. In Revelation the seventh chapter, the statement is made that an angel had sealed 144,000 of Israel as a nation and the astounding detail that 12,000 will be sealed of each of the twelve tribes of Israel. On the day of Pentecost, the astounding result will be the conversion of over 3,000 Jews from among the 19 different nations represented.

In the Tribulation of Jacob's trouble, a vast throng of 144,000 Jews, divided equally among the twelve tribes of Israel, will be converted. As wonderful as this result is, 144,000 is a negligible number when considering a Jewish nation of 12,000,000. Many of them will perish in the plagues, and multitudes of Jews will persist in their unbelief. But this sealing of 144,000 of Israel will definitely take place and it is then that they will enter upon a spiritual plane of living rather than the mere material plane. Then will follow God's sending forth of the *two witnesses,* generally taken as being Moses and Elijah, to give forth more trouble of plagues of a fearful kind. No definite details are given regarding Israel in the succeeding chapters in the book of Revelation, except in the fourteenth chapter where Israel is again mentioned specifically. Whether this throng of 144,000 is identified with that of the seventh chapter is of secondary importance and cannot be definitely established.

This much is stated: this 144,000 of redeemed Israel will be clothed in white raiment and will assemble in the presence of the *Lamb of God* on Mount Zion singing with harps in their hand the praises of the Lord, who made possible their redemption. Surely this is proof enough to show that God will have begun to bring the nation of Israel on to a high spiritual standard.

All Israel Is Saved

Is this all that God can do for the redemption of Israel? No, this is not all. The Apostle Paul definitely bears this out when he writes that *"All Israel* shall be saved" (Romans 11:26, 27). The twentieth century has had two mammoth world wars that have taken the toll of many millions of people. But these two great world wars, even including a third World War, with its satanic horrors, are nothing to be compared with the great Battle of Armageddon, which will be fought by all nations in the Valley of Megiddo.

All Israel in a Spiritual Standard

Here, at the world's greatest battle being fought against God, we read in the prophecy of Zechariah that Israel laments and calls upon God for deliverance and then they will behold the Son of God come riding upon a white horse with the armies of heaven following Him. The Jews, facing extermination, beholding Jesus' pierced hands and feet, recognize Him as their Saviour, Deliverer and Redeemer and then will take place the astounding miracle of the nation, Israel, God's chosen people, accepting Jesus as their Messiah, their Saviour and their King; so that the whole nation of Israel is lifted out of its age-long material standard of life, to live henceforth on a high spiritual standard.

The reader needs to read a large portion of the book of the Revelation, from chapters 6 to 19, which deal with the punishment of God's wrath upon all nations, especially that which will come upon the Jews by means of the seven seals, the seven trumpet judgments and the seven vial judgments which will cause millions to be killed and large numbers of martyrs to suffer for their refusal to worship the Antichrist.

God will send two special messengers (Revelation 11) from heaven to witness for God during this critical period. These two witnesses, generally taken as being Moses and Elijah, are put to death, but after three days are raised from the dead and ascend to heaven.

There can be no doubt that mention is made in chapters 7 and 14 of a company of 144,000 believers out of the twelve tribes of Israel. They are the first-fruits from among the nation of Israel.

Israel's national salvation will take place after the battle of Armageddon, when the remnant of Jews will behold Jesus sitting on a white horse with all of the armies of heaven following. This acceptance of the Messiah will bring the entire nation of Israel upon a spiritual level. The millennial reign of Christ for a thousand years will be known as the Golden Era of mankind.

Messiah Judging All Nations

The closing words of Christ's ministry were spoken to His disciples when He gave the Great Commission to His disciples at the time of His ascension, commanding them to go to all nations and preach the Gospel to every creature. Almost twenty centuries have come and gone and the task is far from having been accomplished. On numerous occasions, Jesus had spoken of His return in glory. In the nineteenth chapter of the book of Revelation it is stated that the first great act of His return will be to gather all nations of earth before Him in judgment. The sheep, or those who had followed Him truly, will be accepted to inherit the Kingdom which Christ Jesus will establish. The goats, or those who had refused the divine call, will be rejected. The greatest event pertaining to "Messiah's Israel," will be that of their conversion. Thus Paul's promise that all Israel be saved will be fulfilled. The twelve apostles will sit upon twelve thrones judging the twelve tribes of Israel.

Messiah to Rule All Nations

At this second coming in glory, Jesus will not merely rule over twelve restored tribes of Israel, but will rule over all nations of earth as "King of kings and Lord of lords." Before Jesus can establish His theocratic government He will cast the Antichrist and the false prophet into the lake of fire (Revelation 19:20) and an angel sent from heaven with a long chain in his hands will bind Satan and curse him into the bottomless pit. After Satan is sealed in this pit he will be a prisoner there for a thousand years, so that he cannot deceive mankind during that period (Revelation 20:1-3).

One more event foretold, prior to the reign of Christ Jesus, will be the resurrection of the martyred souls, after which they will be given part in the reign of Christ.

Ezekiel's Temple for Messiah's Worship

The great event which will take place in carrying out the reign of Christ will give fulfillment of Ezekiel's prophecy of the building of a temple for worship with all the specifications of detail as set forth in Ezekiel, chapters 40-48. A specific form of worship is set forth with a priesthood offering sacrifices and the Levitical order restored for giving instruction to the people on how to carry on the worship of God. The Lord Jesus Christ will sit upon the throne of David and govern the nations of earth (Isaiah 9:6, 7). This will not be an easy task for the Son of God must rule with a rod of iron to preserve peace during the thousand years (Psalms 2; 4:6). God has promised to give abounding prosperity, especially for the redeemed nation of Israel, that will have returned to the land promised to Abraham, Moses and Joshua, reaching from the River Nile to the Euphrates, a distance of nearly 800 miles. The prophet Isaiah has given many details of this rulership of Jesus over the nations of earth as seen in chapters 11; 55; 60 and 62. He devoted an entire chapter to envisioning the glory of the desolate land that will blossom as a rose (Isaiah 35). The wild animals are to be tamed.

Before Israel ever entered the Promised Land, God had given the promise through Moses of a boundless prosperity that will come to Israel when they obey God (Deuteronomy 28:1-14). In the closing words of this great promise of prosperity and success, God declared that Israel would be "the head and not the tail" of nations. Strange to state, that never in all their existence have they attained to this standard of perfect and abiding independence.

Messiah's Glorious Reign for a Thousand Years

No one can question the prospect for training the youth during the millennium by making the Bible the main textbook (not only the Old Testament, as is the case today in the State of Israel, but the entire Bible). Then will there be little or no juvenile delinquency, for all will know the Lord, from the least unto the greatest. They will all be taught not only about God's creation of the universe which was entrusted to the Son of God "who made all things and by whom all things consist" (John 1:1-3); all the world will have been taught that Jesus is the ruler and is sovereign. He is the One who died upon the Cross of Calvary to prove His love for and to save the sinful and provide a complete and perfect redemption for mankind. Then can the angels of heaven repeat their songs that they gave to the shepherds of Bethlehem at the birth of Jesus, "Glory to God in the highest, peace on earth and good will to men." Then will not only the angels sing the "Hallelujah Chorus" but all the saints of heaven and all of saved Israel upon earth will give praise and glory unto Jesus Christ as King of kings and Lord of lords — the Messiah!

THE PERIOD OF ISRAEL'S SPLENDOR IN THE HEAVENLY JERUSALEM

This period, covering the last two chapters of the book of Revelation presents the most spectacular manifestation of God's wisdom and love and power recorded in the whole Bible, for it represents God creating a new heaven and a new earth, void of every semblance of sin and evil.

John, banished on the Isle of Patmos, was given the vision of the New Jerusalem descending from heaven upon a renewed earth.

The Eternal Splendor of Messiah's Israel

The splendor of this heavenly city surpasses any imagined splendor in the whole universe. This city is to be 1500 miles in breadth and length and height (Berkeley translation), all equal to 1500 cubic miles (Revelation 21:16). On each of the twelve gates of pearl will be written, by divine hand, the names of one of the twelve tribes of Israel. On the twelve foundations, made of all manner of precious stones, will be engraved the names of each of the twelve apostles of the Lamb.

All the inhabitants of the heavenly city are redeemed by the blood of the Lamb. This city is the crowning work of God the Almighty; the crowning work of God in redemption as well as creation. Israel, united with the Church of the Lord, will have Christ in common as Saviour and Redeemer, thus attaining the highest perfection of eternal life in this city of pure gold.

The Names of the Twelve Tribes of Israel on the Pearly Gates

One cannot be surprised that it is said of our Lord Jesus Christ, the Founder of the Church, that He loved the Church and because of that love looked forward to the time of His having a glorious Church without spot or wrinkle, to be holy and without blemish (Ephesians 5:26, 27). One would expect that Messiah, the Lamb of God, would engrave the names of the twelve apostles on the jasper walls of the city of God, the New Jerusalem. However, what great surprise when our Lord had to weep over Jerusalem, foretelling the world-wide dispersion which covers nearly twenty centuries down to the Battle of Armageddon, when Israel's national salvation has its beginning.

Can any man or angel ever imagine such divine love, such amazing grace as that which will exist with Israel combined with the Church in a co-existence of eternal harmony and peace and love through all ages to come? The seed of Abraham, in the person of a returned fugitive became Messiah's Israel when at the end of a night spent wrestling the Angel of God, Jacob's name was changed to Israel. Messiah gave Himself on that occasion to the redeemed nations that can be trusted in the heavenly city of Jerusalem to remain through all eternity. Jesus thus proved Himself to be the Messiah promised to Israel in the Old Testament and fulfilled in the New Testament. Yes, this Messiah is truly "the Lamb of God that taketh away the sins of the world" (John 1:29).

What God Hath Wrought

Can any reason be given for God having the eternal city located for thousands and thousands of years in heaven above and then changing its location to earth? This city of God had been in heaven above in the days of Abraham, for he was motivated by seeing in a vision "a city of God; which hath foundations, whose builder and maker is God" (Hebrews 11:10).

This city of God, the New Jerusalem, had its location in heaven above for four thousand years, since the time of Abraham, and to this four thousand years must be added one thousand years of the millennium, making it at least five thousand years. It is folly for one to think that God would create such a majestic edifice on an earth cursed with sin, crime and iniquity. Furthermore, there is no location anywhere on this earth, with its oceans, seas, mountains and hills that would provide security for this city of God.

Therefore, it became necessary for God to create a new heaven and also a new earth, without any oceans, seas, mountains or hills. Furthermore, God never intended that this city of God should remain in heaven, for He will provide a proper location. This will be done by God when He creates a new heaven and a new earth. The Word of God gives no reason for this super gigantic move, made by the hand of God in bringing this heavenly city to its permanent and everlasting location on the new earth.

The promises of the coming Messiah had already been given to Adam and Eve in Paradise and this promise was followed by many others in the history of mankind. Many failures can be pointed out in the career of the Church as well as in Israel's history.

Has God failed because of the twenty centuries of Israel's dispersion among the nations of earth? No, Israel had to go through the period of Jacob's trouble, but behold, at Christ's coming in glory, it will in reality be that all "Israel shall be saved" (Romans 11:26, 27).

Has God failed with the Church because Messiah had to spew the last of the seven churches of Asia, the Laodicean Church, out of His mouth?

The four words, "What God hath wrought," used in the first message tapped out by Samuel Morse, on his invention which would one day be one of the means of intercontinental communication, are also fitting in considering God's majestic creation in the beginning, to be consummated with a new heaven and a new earth. There are no words adequate to express the supreme splendor that Messiah will have wrought upon Israel and the Church.

No, the Church will not perish because Messiah "loved the church and gave himself for it" (Ephesians 5:25-32). Vast multitudes of the seed of the natural as well as the spiritual seed of Abraham will inherit this city of God (Galatians 6:15; 3:17). The vast multitude which will become inhabitants of the holy city of God, the New Jerusalem, depends not only on the election of God, of being "saved by grace," but this election of Israel, as well as of the Church, includes every fallen son of Abraham, "whosoever shall believe" on the *Messiah* shall be saved (John 3:16), and "whosoever will, let him take the water of life freely" (Revelation 22:17).

Not only will Messiah's Israel, with its uncountable multitude of saints become partakers of the eternal splendor of the New Jerusalem, as vouchsafed by the divine hand writing the names of the twelve tribes of Israel on the beautiful gates of pearl, but also the saints which make up the body of Christ with their multitudes.

The words referred to above, "What God hath wrought," are fitting to be used at the conclusion of this volume. That which was only a dream with Theodor Herzl will become a stupendous accomplishment by God's Almighty power manifested in the atoning work of Christ Jesus the Redeemer of the Church and His people — Israel.